Emilio Uranga's *Analysis of Mexican Being*

Also available from Bloomsbury

African American Philosophers and Philosophy, John H. McClendon III and Stephen C. Ferguson II
A Practical Guide to World Philosophies, Monika Kirloskar-Steinbach and Leah Kalmanson
Doing Philosophy Comparatively, Tim Connolly
How to Talk to a Fascist, Marcia Tiburi
Philosophy of the Bhagavad Gita, Keya Maitra
The Philosophies of America Reader, edited by Kim Díaz and Mathew A. Foust

Emilio Uranga's *Analysis of Mexican Being*

A Translation and Critical Introduction

Emilio Uranga

Translated and Introduced by
Carlos Alberto Sánchez

BLOOMSBURY ACADEMIC
LONDON • NEW YORK • OXFORD • NEW DELHI • SYDNEY

BLOOMSBURY ACADEMIC
Bloomsbury Publishing Plc
50 Bedford Square, London, WC1B 3DP, UK
1385 Broadway, New York, NY 10018, USA
29 Earlsfort Terrace, Dublin 2, Ireland

BLOOMSBURY, BLOOMSBURY ACADEMIC and the Diana logo are
trademarks of Bloomsbury Publishing Plc

First published in 1952 in Mexico as *Análisis del ser del mexicano*

First published in Great Britain 2021

English Language Translation © Carlos Alberto Sánchez, 2021

Carlos Alberto Sánchez has asserted his right under the Copyright, Designs and
Patents Act, 1988, to be identified as Translator of this work.

For legal purposes the Acknowledgments on p. ix constitute an extension
of this copyright page.

Cover design by www.ironicitalics.com
Cover image courtesy of the Fondo Emilio Uranga,
Departamento de Filosofía, Universidad de Guanajuato

All rights reserved. No part of this publication may be reproduced or
transmitted in any form or by any means, electronic or mechanical,
including photocopying, recording, or any information storage or retrieval
system, without prior permission in writing from the publishers.

Bloomsbury Publishing Plc does not have any control over, or responsibility for,
any third-party websites referred to or in this book. All internet addresses given
in this book were correct at the time of going to press. The author and publisher
regret any inconvenience caused if addresses have changed or sites have ceased
to exist, but can accept no responsibility for any such changes.

A catalogue record for this book is available from the British Library.

A catalog record for this book is available from the Library of Congress.

ISBN: HB: 978-1-3501-4527-6
PB: 978-1-3501-4528-3
ePDF: 978-1-3501-4529-0
eBook: 978-1-3501-4526-9

Typeset by Newgen KnowledgeWorks Pvt. Ltd., Chennai, India

To find out more about our authors and books visit www.bloomsbury.com
and sign up for our newsletters.

For
Tricia, Julián, Ethan, and Pascual

Contents

Acknowledgments	ix
Note on Translation	x
Part One Critical Introduction	1
1 Prolegomena to *Analysis of Mexican Being*	3
Mid-20th-Century Mexican Philosophy	4
Context and Method: From Ramos to Existential Phenomenology	6
2 *Analysis of Mexican Being*: A Reading	21
Reading "Part I: Introduction"	24
Reading "Part II: Philosophy"	30
Reading "Part III: History"	44
Reading "Part IV: Poetry"	53
3 Key Concepts	71
Accidentality	71
Auscultation	75
Autognosis	75
Corazonadas (Intimations)	76
Insufficiency	78
Nepantla	79
Substance	83
Zozobra	85
Part Two Translation: *Analysis of Mexican Being*	91
4 I. Introduction	93
1. *Lo mexicano* as Our Culture's Central Theme	93
5 II. Philosophy	103
2. The Accident and the Mexican Person	103

	3. The Radical Sense of the Investigation into Mexicanness (*lo mexicano*)	120
	4. Humanism and the Mexican Person	125
6	III. History	133
	5. Insufficiency and Inferiority	133
7	IV. Poetry	161
	6. The Meaning of the Mexican Revolution	161
	7. Character and Being of the Mexican in the Poetry of López Velarde	166
	8. Note on the Original and the Originary	180

Notes	187
Annotated Bibliography	205
Index	213

Acknowledgments

This book seeks to introduce Emilio Uranga's *Análisis del ser del mexicano* to a new audience. The soul of this book is thus the translation of Uranga's text, the publication of which would not have been possible without the generosity of Ms. Cecilia Uranga, who graciously allowed me to translate and publish, for the first time, her father's groundbreaking contribution to the history of Mexican philosophy. Although translation is by its very nature a solitary activity, the present translation would not have been possible without a few selfless and patient readers. I will especially like to thank Clinton Tolley, John Herman, and Amy Oliver for their valuable feedback, corrections, and suggestions on earlier drafts. The Critical Introduction, included here as Part One, which discusses historical and historiographical context, as well as my interpretive reading of *Análisis*, was developed and enriched by conversations with a number of colleagues in the United States and abroad. I'm forever indebted to Guillermo Hurtado, Clinton Tolley, Manuel Vargas, Robert E. Sanchez, José Manuel Cuellar, Carlos Pereda, Aurelia Valero, and Francisco Gallegos for engaging with me in indispensable conversations. Finally, I could not have written this without the loving support of my family, Tricia, Julián, Ethan, and Pascual, and my colleagues at the Department of Philosophy at San José State University.

Note on Translation

The translation included here is from the first edition of *Análisis del ser del mexicano* published in 1952 by Porrua y Obregon, Sociedad Anónima, Mexico City, as Volume 4 of the series *Mexico y Lo Mexicano*. All rights reserved by the author's estate.

Translations of epigraphs and poetry extracts included in this work are my own.

Part One

Critical Introduction

1

Prolegomena to *Analysis of Mexican Being*

In the fall of 1952, the celebrated Spanish philosopher José Gaos wrote in his personal journal: "With Emilio Uranga, Mexico possesses the greatest *opportunity* to have its own great philosopher."[1] Gaos's remark follows the publication, earlier that year, of Uranga's *Análisis del ser del mexicano*, arguably the most important text in the canon of 20th-century Mexican philosophy—certainly, the most significant and original work in the tradition of *la filosofía de lo mexicano*, or "the philosophy of Mexicanness."

Generally speaking, the philosophy of Mexicanness (alternatively, the philosophy of *lo mexicano*) is a decisive philosophical intervention into *the being of persons* whose existence is formed or informed by or within the complex horizons of "Mexico," understood as a historical, political, spiritual, and ontological space. The persons whose being is in question are nominated in this space as Mexican persons and their *being* as "Mexican" *being*, that is, their existence represents, phenomenologically, *that which is Mexican*, or, in Spanish, *lo mexicano*. Uranga's *Análisis*, which is translated here for the first time, seeks to be the master text in this tradition.

What follows (Part One) is an introduction to and critical reading[2] of this important text, the title of which I have translated as *Analysis of Mexican Being* (hereafter, *Analysis*). As an "introduction," it seeks to introduce *Analysis* to a non-Mexican-, non-Spanish-reading audience; as a critical "reading," it seeks to interpret, clarify, and criticize its methodological commitments, its historical context, and its most significant philosophical concepts.

Mid-20th-Century Mexican Philosophy

Let us begin with what may seem like a controversial statement: Mexican philosophy did not exist before the 20th century. Certainly, Western philosophy itself existed and was practiced, taught, and read in universities and monasteries throughout Mexico and Latin America prior to the 20th century (it is obvious that the Aztecs possessed, created, and practiced philosophy,[3] Scholastic philosophy was taught and published in the "New World" after the Spanish conquest of Mexico and during the colonial period,[4] and the 19th century saw the quasi-despotic rise of philosophy in the form of positivism[5]), but a philosophy conscious of itself as "Mexican" was specifically a product of the 20th century.

The rise of this self-conscious *Mexican* philosophy is a historical story that has been told elsewhere.[6] However, *two key moments* in this story merit retelling: the first key moment is the publication, in 1934, of Samuel Ramos's *Profile of Man and Culture in Mexico*, in which Ramos famously (or infamously) diagnoses Mexican culture in general and the Mexican person in particular, as afflicted with, what he calls after the Austrian psychoanalyst Alfred Adler, a "complex of inferiority."[7] This is a key moment in the history of Mexican philosophy, but it also proves crucial for a proper *reading* of *Analysis*, as it is to Ramos's text that Uranga's book serves as a direct confrontation and response.

The second key moment is the founding of *el grupo Hiperión*, or "the Hyperion group," a philosophical collective that first engages in a sustained and rigorous manner the theme of "lo mexicano," or *the essence of Mexicanness* (the theme of *la filosofía de lo mexicano*) and inspires Uranga's "autognosis"[8] and "ontology" of Mexican being.[9]

We will return to Ramos later. As a means to more adequately frame Uranga's project, however, we begin with the second key moment: the formation of the Hyperion group (hereafter, Hyperion). Hyperion was formed in the fall of 1947 by students of the *transterrado*, the Spanish exile, José Gaos (1900–1969).[10] The group[11] was led by Leopoldo Zea (1912–2004), whose philosophical reputation had previously been established with the publication of his graduate thesis, *Positivism in Mexico* (1943).[12] The group met frequently to read and discuss French and German philosophy, and held conferences and seminars on existentialism and phenomenology in the spring and fall of 1948. In October 1949, Hyperion offered a series of lectures that would cement its cultural and generational significance. These lectures, centered on the question *"Qué es el mexicano?"* (What is the Mexican?), stirred up a great deal of controversy in Mexico City.[13] Young intellectuals took to newspapers and magazines to either answer the question for themselves or declare the question unanswerable and philosophically invalid.

Especially controversial was the charge that Hyperion's interrogations unjustifiably assumed something like a Mexican "essence," namely, that which unified Mexicans despite the plurality of "Mexicos" existing under a common flag (i.e., the multiple experiences, ethnicities, linguistic communities, etc. that make up the nation). Critics pointed to the factual absence of such an essential "Mexican" that would answer the "what is?" and to the apparent circularity of such questioning. By 1951, Hyperion offered courses (not merely lectures) that pushed the controversial issue further. These were given under the title "El mexicano y su cultura" (Mexicans and Their Culture).

Those that recognized the controversy addressed it, proposing that the essence sought was not an exclusionary essence in the sense of a rigid "whatness" (in spite of the wording of the question itself). The essence sought was to be generally inclusive of a plurality of forms of life; thus, it was to be a general essence that captured aspects of both a common or familiar historical experience and a broader *human* experience.[14] In Uranga, the search for an essence broadens into the *howness* of being Mexican, that is, into an ontology of Mexican being.[15]

Hyperion disbanded in 1952. While its questions would not find definitive answers, the philosophy that it births (namely, the philosophy of *lo mexicano*) represents, from a global perspective, one of the most original contributions to philosophy in the 20th century. Uranga's *Análisis del ser del mexicano* is its greatest achievement.

Context and Method: From Ramos to Existential Phenomenology

The radical investigation carried out in *Analysis of Mexican Being* was written between 1948 and 1952. During this time, Uranga published several articles that laid the groundwork for the "ontological" work of the 1952 text.[16] In them, Uranga seeks to philosophically undermine the psychoanalytic cultural intervention undertaken by Samuel Ramos in his 1934 text, *Profile of Man and Culture in Mexico*, wherein Ramos diagnosed Mexicans, as a people and individually, as suffering a "complex of inferiority" (what I referred to above as the "first key moment").[17] Two essays from this period serve as the prolegomena to *Analysis*: the first, "Ensayo de una ontología del mexicano," published in 1948, and the second, "Notas para un estudio del mexicano," from 1951.

In what follows, we briefly consider these two essays. However, a quick overview of Ramos's *Profile of Man and Culture in Mexico* (hereafter *Profile*) is likewise in order, as it is to the central claim of Ramos's book that Uranga is, ultimately, responding.

Samuel Ramos and the Mexican Inferiority Complex

Ramos's *Profile of Man and Culture in Mexico*, published in 1934, applies Alfred Adler's psychoanalytic theory to a study of Mexican cultural life. Its major claim is that after centuries of colonial subjugation, cultural marginalization, and political, moral, and philosophical imperialism, the Mexican people have internalized an inferiority complex that affects all aspects of their everyday life. Believing Western culture to be superior, they adopt an inferior attitude about themselves and their capacities, expressed negatively in everyday life as self-denigration, machoism, rivalry, antipathy, and so on. Ramos puts the matter in the following way:

> The individual affected by the complex of inferiority cannot adapt himself to his world because a maladjustment already exists

within him. ... He is, in general, an individual whose ambitions are disproportionate to his capacities; there is a deficit of power with respect to desire. And this gives rise to the *feeling* of inferiority ... if we were to adjust our desire to our power, then the feeling of inferiority would disappear.[18]

In Ramos's view, the complex of inferiority explains the sense of powerlessness Mexicans feel before more global, cosmopolitan demands; it explains the sense that they "cannot adapt to [the] world" just as they are. It contributes to the sense of worthlessness that leads, ultimately, to inaction and imitation, resulting in the fear of participating in the great human community and seeing themselves as equals with the rest of humankind. Knowing that their individual desires exceed their individual power can only lead to resentment, alienation, and, even, Ramos says, neurosis.

> Wherever there is a feeling of inferiority there you will find an ambition that exceeds power [and] where everything is seen through the optics of superiority or inferiority ... [ultimately] negative attitudes emerge: rancor, hate, resentment, vengeance. ... This fight for power in every sphere of life, in private or in public ... frequently leads to alienation, misanthropy, neurosis, etc., etc.[19]

Ultimately, the complex of inferiority is proposed as constituting the very being of Mexicans, whereby they are unable to be anything other than their feelings or their psychic complexes; that is, Mexicans cannot project themselves, or their ambitions, past the limits of their own psychology.

However, the complex of inferiority is also historical. Echoing Adler, Ramos writes, "In being born, Mexico found itself in the civilized world in the same relation than that of a child before his elders."[20] On its inception into history, Mexico found itself dependent on Spain for its own survival. Before this older, and thus "mature," civilization, Mexicans sought to outdo themselves so as to prove their worth through childlike expressions of power. They, however, found themselves unable to live up to what they claimed capable of doing and *being*, thus developing a *complex of inferiority* before the superiority of their betters. Feelings of inferiority and insufficiency in relation to what is thought to be greater and substantial soon take hold, and more than merely *feeling* inferior, Mexicans *become* their inferiority.

Anticipating a criticism like Uranga's, which would come almost two decades later, Ramos insists that what he is highlighting is a *"feeling* of inferiority," that he is not "affirming that the Mexican is inferior, but rather that he *feels inferior*, which is a totally different thing."[21] This *feeling*, ultimately, results in a "collective illusion"[22] resulting in the propensity to compare oneself to other humans in more advanced cultures. However, this collective feeling of inferiority makes it so that Mexicans believe themselves *to be*, in fact, inferior to other cultures and other peoples; in other words, it is more than a feeling when it becomes a mode of being.

"Ensayo de una ontologia del mexicano" (1948)

When Uranga's critique eventually arrives, its starting point is that Ramos's analysis only superficially accounts for Mexican inferiority, whose true ground is left completely untouched. The complex of inferiority identified by Ramos merely characterizes the empirical or outward behaviors of a much profound *human* condition. In Uranga's view, what grounds the very experience of inferiority is not a collection of psychological moods, mental states, or emotive experiences, but being itself; Mexican existence itself is not a complex of inferiority manifested psychologically as powerlessness before desire; rather, grounding inferiority is the ontological condition of "insufficiency," which Uranga understands as a deficient state of being that gives rise to psychological states of temporal and contingent entities like Mexicans (or human beings in general). Uranga's *Analysis* ultimately endeavors to sublate this (demeaning) psychological self-conception of a characteristic cultural impotence with a more primordial (viz., ontological), and human, self-understanding that, in the process, promises to liberate Mexicans themselves from the paralyzing stigma of inferiority that afflicts not only Mexicans but other colonized or postcolonial peoples. Thinking of oneself as inferior, even if, in fact, one is not, can only but make it easier to internalize other oppressive and marginalizing self-conceptions, thus perpetuating a historical cycle *ad nauseum*.

Uranga's challenge to Ramos's diagnosis of Mexican culture and character is articulated for the first time in his "Ensayo de una ontologia del mexicano" ("Essay on an ontology of the Mexican"; hereafter, "Essay").[23]

The thrust of Uranga's challenge is that Ramos's diagnoses are overly focused on the most obvious aspects of the Mexican character, namely, those found in popular cultural narratives. In those narratives (articulated in songs, literature, popular art, etc.), Mexicans are overly sentimental and melancholic. Uranga agrees that, in their cultural expressions, Mexicans are an emotive people, but adds that Mexican sentimentality points to a constitutive emotional fragility that characterizes their *humanity* and not merely their Mexicanness. This inner fragility represents an existential or ontological "quality of always being threatened by nothingness ... of falling into non-being."[24] It is this *human* quality, Uranga suggests, that is confused (by Ramos) as a symptom of impotence, weakness, fragmentation, and incompleteness in the Mexican character and interpreted superficially as an inferiority complex. The truth, according to Uranga, is that "inferiority is a modality of insufficiency"[25] and the "emotive life psychologically expresses or symbolizes this ontological condition."[26]

It is insufficiency, then, and not inferiority that is at the root of Mexican sentimentality. For instance, Mexican popular culture paints the Mexican person as overburdened by sadness. There is a sorrow and a longing in the music, poetry, and art that *could* be attributed to an infinite melancholy in the essential makeup of a people. Uranga points out, however, that melancholy is tied to the realization that one is not enough, or does not have enough, for the fulfillment of life's demands. Melancholy overtakes one at the first sight of one's *lack*—lack of ability, of power, of prowess, of resources, of history. Uranga calls this lack "nothingness" and says:

> The melancholy individual is trapped in his interior abode from whence he brings to the life of the imagination a thousand worlds to which he bestows value and sense while never losing sight of the fact that those worlds are grounded on nothingness, that they are suspended over nothingness, and this knowledge about the deception regarding the groundlessness of the world is precisely what we are apt to call melancholy.[27]

Melancholy turns one away from the truth of being (which affirms that our insufficiency is ontological) and keeping us in psychological "deception" that seeks to ground us in nothingness. This is a deceptive self-understanding because it arises from our own "interior abode," that is, our imagination, and is thus fatally subjective and relative. If nothingness is the foundation of "a thousand worlds," locating nothingness within us, in our own psychological interiority, can only but break our spirits as the responsibility will be too burdensome to bear. Believing ourselves to be the source of nothingness will only exacerbate our sense of inferiority, since our failure will *feel* inevitable.

If to be melancholic is to be "trapped" within oneself, held hostage by one's imaginings, liberation will come from the recognition that the trap is superficial, that this is not one's *true* state of being. This recognition does not happen without effort, as a sudden religious experience or an epiphany, but results, rather, from a process of self-knowledge, what Uranga calls "autognosis." The first step in the process of autognosis, he tells us in the "Essay," is to come to terms with the deceptions of subjectivity, with the idea that one's condition of inferiority, for instance, is a superficial psychological construct and is not constitutive of our humanity. The second step would then be to attribute the nothingness, or whatever founds inferiority, to the impersonal creative force of being itself. This would mean that one let go of the idealism that says that one creates and is responsible for one's world. It is through this renunciation that one assumes one's place in the impersonal, in the non-subjective, that is, in the *other*. Through this renunciations we also see our "thrownness"; our accidental presence in a world of impermanence and insecurity is revealed as if by "truth" of the heart, what he calls "corazonada." Authentic liberation will come about, however, only after we assume our thrownness and accidentality; that is, once we accept that our being is rooted neither on own creative imaginings nor in a world in which we are thrown, but rather in the impermanence that gives itself as our truth, a fundamental impermanence that is here and in Uranga's *Analysis* called "zozobra." Ultimately, "individuals [must] liberate themselves from things in freedom and assume the condition of 'zozobra.'"[28]

"Zozobra" is further developed in *Analysis* but introduced into Uranga's philosophizing here for the first time (see "Key Concepts," Chapter 3). As a philosophical concept, it is difficult to translate or capture in English, given its specificity to Mexican thought. Uranga will broaden it and refine this in Part IV of *Analysis*, but in his "Essay" the concept is described as akin to the (Western) existentialist concepts of "angst" or "anxiety." Uranga describes it as "the state in which we find ourselves when the world hides its fragility ... in which we are not sure if, at any moment, a catastrophe will overwhelm us or if we will be secured in the safety of asylum. In zozobra we remain in suspense, in oscillation."[29]

Uranga concludes the "Essay" with a reminder that the "danger" of interpretations that "conceal" and "deceive" us into thinking that we are permanently settled in a preestablished identity "lies precisely in closing off the road toward the originary."[30] Closing off the road to the originary means that superficial narratives about who we are will continue to hide our "truth." The key to keeping the road open rests in remaining "immersed in [the] originary possibilities [of life itself],"[31] which means one must remain attentive to one's insufficiency, remembering that "inferiority is an insufficiency that has renounced its origins."[32] Psychological states, such as inferiority, as well as fragility, unwillingness, melancholy, loss, resentment, etc., point back to this lack that affects the being of the human being itself. To forget this is to remain vulnerable to the dehumanization, oppression, and deception of superficial accounts of human life.

"Notas para un estudio del mexicano" (1951)

The ontological approach to the study of the Mexican is introduced in the "Essay," as Uranga seeks a foundational source for the inferiority complex. The next phase of Uranga's project is to settle on a *method*. He settles this in 1951 with "Notas para un estudio del mexicano" [33] ("Notes for a study of the Mexican"; hereafter, "Notas"), noting that "without method we run the risk of losing everything."[34]

The method Uranga chose for his ontology of the Mexican is an appropriated version of existential phenomenology, brought to Mexico by Spanish exiles (*"transterrados"*) fleeing Franco's Spain after 1938. Phenomenology (in its "eidetic" and "existential" forms) is put on the task of "analyzing the being of the Mexican, lending conceptual clarity to that which the Mexican person intuits and that which that person lives in ordinary life."[35]

In "Notas," phenomenology is appropriated in its "eidetic" form, as developed by Edmund Husserl. Particularly useful is the "eidetic reduction," one of three "reductions" to the sphere of essences central to Husserl's method.[36] This reduction relies on the data of subjective experiences (e.g., encounter or presentation of particulars, etc.) that are run through their possible variations in imagination until an essence (or "eidos") of that experience is revealed and grasped.[37] The data to be varied are the behaviors of Mexican persons in their daily life, those behaviors that in their superficiality and everydayness hide a more fundamental ground; for instance, Mexican expressions of resentment, hatred, or enmity, when properly "reduced," reveal an ontological aspect of Mexican being itself. Uranga writes: "All behaviors that are interpreted pre-ontologically as characteristically Mexican set up the field of givenness for the appearance of the being of the Mexican, one that reflection itself struggles to adequately grasp."[38] In general, all cultural or individual behaviors—that is, that which gives itself to everyday interpretation ("interpreted pre-ontologically")—already contain within themselves, in their appearing as individual or collective *doings*, the "being" of Mexicans. Reflection fails to grasp this being in its immediate givenness, that is, in its pre-ontological state, due to the impermanence, relativity, and normality of the doings. Husserl's phenomenological method, and especially the eidetic reduction to essences, steadies the flux, allowing one to grasp what is "essential" so as to "capture it in concepts" (*apresar conceptualmente*).[39]

As we proceed, it is worthwhile to ask about Uranga's "dependence" on European philosophy in order to get at the essence of "Mexican" being. Imperialism and colonialism both have the power to deceive one into thinking that one's discoveries may be one's own, when, in fact, they are already contained in the borrowed methods and ideologies that color our perceptions and inform our pre-theoretical thoughts. We may ask: Is Uranga aware of this danger? The reason for pausing at this question has to do with Uranga's enthusiasm for those philosophies that motivate his analyses and the suspicion that his enthusiasm for them may bias his results. However, it soon becomes obvious that Uranga has considered this and has made a conscious decision to take from his philosophical predecessors only what he needs and no more. A clear example is Heidegger, whose method he appeals to and then quickly abandons as soon as that conceptual arsenal is no longer useful. It holds true here as well, with Husserl, whose reductions to the sphere of transcendental purity Uranga does not accept. That is, while he borrows Husserl's method so as to get to the essence of Mexican life, Uranga does not believe that the essences revealed will be "pure" in the sense demanded by Husserl—a method that demands that essences remain uncontaminated by contingencies and impurities or, what is the same, by accidents. That is, Uranga's phenomenological analysis is not committed to objective purity, since that would require an objective observer, which, clearly, is merely an ideal. He writes: "If we insist on 'objectivity' what happens is that we must still make use of our subjectivity ... [while] leaving it up to the reader to figure out who this objective observer is supposed to be."[40] According to Uranga, philosophical truth cannot be objective in this sense. That is, in the appropriation and application of the phenomenological method, philosophers should not deceive themselves into thinking that their findings will be absolute, or applicable universally and across all human experiences. Like existence itself, Uranga suggests that nothing is permanent and unchanging (all is *accident*). This does not mean that one should hesitate or doubt the results of the method and the investigation. The victory of the phenomenological approach resides in recognizing the contingency of human existence and the presence of, what Leopoldo Zea has called, "the imperial passion"—the dogmatic and *passionate* Western obsession with truth as objectivity.[41]

What is "essential" to Mexican existence will be that which, while found as inseparable from Mexican life, also defines its humanity, namely, an unmistakable concreteness and facticity. This invariant human quality is found by going to the things themselves (Mexican life in its most familiar) and avoiding the allure of secondhand testimonies, for example, "literary, popular, pictorial, and musical testimonies of the characteristically Mexican 'color.'"[42] Uranga does not think that phenomenology can lead us to essences that are pure, universal, and a priori, but it does put us before our own immediate existence, just as it is, in its contingency, accidentality, and insufficiency, which, before the phenomenological reduction, remains hidden, or sedimented in history, language, and habit. This pre-phenomenological state keeps us at the level of the pre-ontological, everyday understanding, where we grasp what we can with nonessential vocabulary, with temperamental grammar; phenomenology, however, brings us closer to our own existential predicament, to our own being, revealing the characteristically Mexican color at its most original.

"Notas" thus seeks to lay out, in a preliminary way, the methodological orientation that will guide Uranga in *Analysis of Mexican Being*. In addition, it also anticipates criticisms of the overall project. One particular criticism, one leveled against Uranga and members of the Hyperion group by his teacher and mentor José Gaos, and ever present in discussions of Mexican philosophy to the present day, is the seemingly relativistic, subjectivist tone of "the philosophy of Mexicanness" (*filosofía de lo mexicano*). The criticism suggests that a "Mexican" philosophy, in being Mexican, will be restricted to Mexicans and to the Mexican experience; that it cannot be generalized to the human experience in general because of its provincialism, regionalism, and subjectivism; and that its lack of objectivity thus limits it as philosophy proper. Uranga anticipates that critics will deem his investigations "illegitimate" because what is said is "limited to specific circles, epochs, classes, and regions of Mexico."[43] At the heart of this critique is the belief that something like a "Mexican" philosophy would fail (in virtue of being Mexican) to approximate the standards of philosophy set out by the Western tradition (i.e., it fails the test of universality and objectivity). Uranga, however, insists that the value of his approach lies precisely in being rooted in his uniquely Mexican perspective, in the Mexican circumstance and Mexican history and culture. He writes: "If it is true that subjectivity inevitably intervenes [in our thinking] it is also true that relying on it to talk about the world is the most honest approach we can take."[44]

Transition: On Method

The previous quote encapsulates Uranga's refusal to dogmatically accept what Zea called "the imperial passion" or what others have called the *view from nowhere*, an ideological assumption stubbornly (Uranga will say "arrogantly") held by Western philosophy since Plato. In contrast, Uranga's desire for authenticity and fidelity to his own, Mexican, experience motivates the entirety of his philosophical program. As we will see later, and as we already saw in his "Notas," Uranga's method of investigation is not meant to be disinterested, objective, generalizing, or purifying; it means to arrive at the concrete, living, experience of human beings in their accidental, insufficient, historical circumstance. He thus appeals to and appropriates the phenomenological method as he finds it in Husserl, Heidegger, Max Scheler, as well as Sartre and Merleau-Ponty—giving it his own spin through the appropriation. This "spin," or what results from the appropriation, promises to accommodate the demands of what he sees immediately before him, a phenomenon that is situated and real, a human existence that, he says in an earlier essay, is not considered "in the abstract, but [is] a situated human existence, in a situation ... a human existence framed in a determinate geographical *habitat*, in a social and cultural frame likewise determined and with a precise historical legacy."[45]

Common to the distinct approaches to phenomenology that Uranga appropriates, and thus central to his own method, is a commitment to the value of what is most familiar in everyday life—a commitment consistent with Uranga's rejection of the so-called imperial passion. He alludes to this methodological commitment in "Notas":

> Nothing is more familiar ... then our own character and nothing prohibits us from taking our subjectivity as an instrument for exploring our reality, since all we have to do afterward is subtract what we take to be the deformations of the instrument in order to get an objective result, as is done in the most trivial and ordinary operations of laboratory physics.[46]

In other words, that which is "more familiar ... our own character" is the space for the investigation of the truths of reality. There is no need to go beyond that, into the unknown corners of a human experience, which cannot be given to me in the realm of my subjectivity. To get to the bottom of things, I just need to "subtract" the vagaries and eccentricities of my own specific personality.

In the case of Mexican philosophy, it need only focus on what is given to the immediate circumstance of Mexicans. Ultimately, Uranga's is not a generalization meant to extend past the boundaries of the realm of justification, that is, outside the range of his experience. His is a pronouncement justified *in principle* given his *phenomenological* starting point, that is, *his specific habitat*.

Commitment to what is closest, to one's habitat or circumstance, is a centerpiece of existential phenomenology as we find it, notably, in the philosophy of José Ortega y Gasset and Martin Heidegger.

Ortega's insistence in attending to the circumstances in his earlier (and influential) works[47] coupled with Heidegger's insistence that that which is nearest and most proximal to "our concern" is what one should attend to is a centerpiece of Uranga's method. It is in sections 14 and 15 of *Being and Time*, where Heidegger says that the "theme" of phenomenological analysis is the "average everydayness," the "world of Dasein which is closest to it," and "those entities which show themselves in our concern with the environment," that is, with our *circumstance*.[48] Uranga echoes Heidegger, writing:

> What is closest to us is what is present in our concern, not what is immediate to us in a geometrical sense. ... The absolute point of reference is not my own body but my "here"; from my "here" significance is given to things and places "there." ... Proximity to the accident, then, signifies always having it present in our concerns. The Mexican continuously lends an ear to the voice of his being through those sentiments common to us ... this being emerges and crosses over into the field of everyday experience. (24)

Uranga spends a great deal of time, especially in Part II of *Analysis*, reflecting on Heidegger's *Being and Time*, especially those sections that are meant by Heidegger as deconstructive of the history of *Western* ontology. Included in this deconstruction is Heidegger's notion that "existence has ... *Jemeinigkeit* as a radical property" (67), which is the idea that existence is personal and individual and is, in each case, *mine*. Simply put, existence is not a general category, belonging to everything that exists, but is mine, belonging to me as that which is closest and most familiar. Because it is closest to me, or proximal, it is also what I can know with the most clarity and profundity. According to Uranga, this intimacy validates the look inward (what he calls "auscultation") into Mexican culture, which is *his* culture, and into Mexican being, which is *his* being. Existence, he affirms with Heidegger, is in each case mine and not "the existence of everyone and no one" (64). "From this perspective," Uranga concludes, "it is legitimate to speak about an ontology of the Mexican" (67).

It is clear, moreover, that Heidegger is just a stepping stone, a point of departure from which the overcoming of the Western way of doing philosophy will take place. As soon as Uranga secures his methodological footing, he unceremoniously moves on from Heidegger, writing,

> Very well then, we think no longer with Heidegger but within our own particular ontological perspective that Being can receive an interpretation that is precisely contrary to that of ancient ontology, that is, to see it and consider it not as substance, but as "accident." (69)

This is a decolonizing, anti-colonial, move; it is a move to distance and disconnect Mexican philosophy from a strict, obligatory, adherence to the tradition of the West (as far as this is possible). This move ultimately depends on existential phenomenology's method and what it implies, namely, an awareness of and a confrontation with our own immediate reality.

The rejection of the imperial passion and the commitment to proximity ultimately inform Uranga's decolonial orientation. That is, Uranga insists that the objective point of view demanded by the Western tradition is unfounded since there is no objective observer to lay claim to it; he insists that there is no access to a humanity in general, a view he reaffirms again in *Analysis*. In "Notas," he says:

> Mexican humanity is precisely opposed to that unbounded sea of humanity in general and the problem that has been posed here is precisely this one: should we continue speaking without differentiating the human or should we determine beforehand that mode of being of persons of which we predicate a particular history?"[49]

Clearly, Uranga's commitments are to "differentiating the human" and determining the "mode of being" of particular persons and not to some objective humanity that resists all differentiation.

Overall, we see in Uranga's methodological commitments the value placed on the first-person perspective, on the value of circumstance, history, and culture. Moreover, insisting on proximity affirms a commitment to principles of openness and respect to the value of other experiences, other circumstances, other histories, cultures, and modes of being. This openness to the other, however, is predicated on a prior openness to ourselves: "What [our method] demands is nothing more than to execute an ontology starting from the Mexican and in not trying to fit the Mexican into one of those ontologies already made."[50]

It is not an exaggeration to say that Uranga's anti-colonial approach to philosophy is ahead of its time, as he seeks to make philosophy fit to the Mexican experience rather than to fit the Mexican experience to philosophy, a project that not only allows Mexicans to see themselves reflected in philosophy for the first time, but also validates the humanity of that experience once and for all. The project, he tells us, "consists in accentuating within the structure of a feeling or lived experience [*vivencia*] that which, in its indeterminate generality, is particularly Mexican."[51]

Finally, Uranga recognizes that the Mexican experience is not the same as other experiences and that there is value in difference. Uranga insists that psychic, cultural, social, aesthetic, or religious experiences are "not lived in the same way by the Mexican as [they are] lived by other types of humans."[52] In Mexico, lived experiences will possess different intensities and different densities, while making possible different possibilities for being. "If with every other human person we share our bad mood, hope, or fear, what distinguishes us is the particular accentuation with which these complex structures are built up within our very selves."[53] That is why it is not enough to list the experiences that pertain to the Mexican person; in addition, it must be shown in what way these are expressed in those persons so that these, in their difference, may be included into philosophy's ever-expanding archive. Once the Mexican experience is shown in its difference, is it then possible to search for and find those eidetic objects that once placed side by side to one another will begin to paint for us a clearer picture of humanity itself as both pluralistic and inclusive?

Uranga's phenomenology thus avoids the commitments of traditional philosophy by beginning with the "ordinary and minuscule,"[54] with what is most familiar to Uranga himself, that is, the Mexican lived experience. It will not remain there, as we will see, but his method demands this starting point. Let us now turn to a reading of the *Analysis of Mexican Being*.

2

Analysis of Mexican Being: A Reading

What follows is a reading of Uranga's *Analysis*. It is an interpretive reading that also aims at clarification and critique.

I take up this *reading* so as to properly introduce it to other readers who would otherwise ignore, avoid, or disparage a work whose title already announces a peculiarity that may seem offensive to philosophy as traditionally understood. What may arouse offense is immediately evident with the title: *Analysis of Mexican Being* (*Análisis del ser del mexicano*). This is a title that, we are taught to think, is not adequate for a *philosophical* investigation. With it, and before any analyses are carried out, Uranga challenges Western philosophy's pretensions to purity and abstract universality; it is already, but especially for the Mexican reader, a rejection of the colonial maxim that says that a pure discipline like philosophy should not trouble itself over the impure concreteness of *Mexicanos*, that it should not be trivialized by nationality, that it should not be restricted by culture. In this way, the title is perhaps the book's most audacious and subversive move, since, in making this move, Uranga is placing in question the very metanarrative that prohibits such moves, a metanarrative that would have revoked David Hume's philosophical credentials on the publication of his *Treatise on Scottish Nature*.[1]

Immediately, the title places us before a specifically Mexican concern, which is the concern for the way in which Mexicans exist as Mexicans, that is, for their being. This was a "generational" concern; in other words, it was a concern that occupied philosophers, poets, and artists in the first half of the 20th century and immediately after the conclusion of the Mexican Revolution (1910–20). A clear indication of this concern is found in the dedication, "For Octavio Paz."

Octavio Paz's *The Labyrinth of Solitude* (1951) is perhaps the most recognizable text from this period. It cemented Paz's reputation as a first-class intellectual, and it lent legitimacy to the "literary" study of the Mexican "character." Paz's analysis provides "reasons" for the faults and triumphs of this character that are historical, cultural, and spiritual. His is an "analysis" of the Mexican character in the strictest sense, and in dedicating the text to Paz, Uranga seeks to place *Analysis* in a similar context—to say, that is, that his own study is at the same level of rigor as Paz's and, perhaps, that it goes beyond Paz's efforts.[2]

Along with Paz, two other figures in Mexican intellectual history make an appearance before we enter the main text of *Analysis*: Ramón López Velarde and Diego Durán.

In two epigraphs, one by Velarde and the second by Durán, Uranga seeks both to contextualize and to signal the trajectory of his intervention. The first epigraph, by the poet Velarde (1888–1921), is a stanza from his celebrated poem, "El son del corazón" ("Song of the Heart"). In the poem, published posthumously in 1932, Velarde lends voice to his heart, which with its rhythmic beating announces a commonality with all who share its pains, its nostalgia, and its laments—that is, a commonality with all mankind. In the epigraph, Uranga has chosen the following stanza:

> My brothers from throughout the ages
> recognize in me their own pause,
> their own laments and their own furies.

With this, Uranga announces a project that will seek to highlight those aspects of Mexican being that connect Mexicans to a universal family and a universal history. It will be a project of unification centered on what is most intimately human: a human heart that beats the same in every chest and a spirit that laments and rages similarly in every person.

The second epigraph is meant to highlight a characteristic about Mexican being that, according to Uranga, turns out to be constitutive of that being. A characteristic that, on the one hand, particularizes Mexicans and, on the other, inserts them in communion with others who are equally constituted. The characteristic (which we will discuss further below and in Key Concepts, Chapter 3) is "nepantla." The epigraph is from the Dominican friar Diego Durán (1537–88) who, in his *History of the Indies of New Spain* (1581),[3] records an exchange with an Indigenous man who, after being rebuked for what Durán thought was frivolous spending, reassures the friar by telling him that they (the Indigenous people) cannot think or behave as he does because they are *not yet* bound to Durán's social and cultural customs or individualistic economic imperatives, nor are they *any longer* bound to their ancient customs, which were, at that time, going through an aggressive process of erasure. Indigenous life, Durán is told abruptly, is in a state of transition (from the old to the new), in transit toward an unknown "yet," suspended "in the middle" of a paradigm shift, moving always farther and faster from familiar ground. "Father," the Indigenous man says, "don't be alarmed, we are still nepantla [*todavía estamos nepantla*]."[4]

Uranga recovers and reappropriates the concept of "nepantla," applying it to modern Mexicans, who, after centuries of miscegenation, colonization, and marginalization, likewise exist "in the middle" of multiple worlds, histories, economies, and existential demands. We can say that the transition begun by the Indigenous man in Durán's chronicle has *never been completed*, either by the Indigenous people themselves or by the modern Mexican, who thus remains always en route, always *in between* unspecified destinations. The concept of "being nepantla" thus becomes the means to articulate and describe a Mexican people whose being is indeterminate and incomplete, neither here nor there, neither this nor that, but suspended in abeyance over unknown possibilities of being.

These two epigraphs set us on our task. The project will be to search for those commonalities that tie us to other human forms of life (as Velarde wants) and, equally important, to highlight an ontological in-betweenness that defines and characterizes the Mexican form of life in particular.

Reading "Part I: Introduction"

The "Introduction" sets up the parameters for the investigation to follow. In the process, it also articulates the urgency of such an intervention. It is widely believed that the mid-20th-century Mexico has arrived at a moment of crisis; it is believed that after 400 years of colonialism, imperialism, civil wars, and revolutions, Mexico must strip itself of its European guises, think past borrowed lenses and philosophies, and finally deal with itself as a unique, world-historical, people. Mexicans have come of age. Uranga understands this moment of maturity as an opportunity for *Mexican* philosophy to speak.

> We have arrived at that historical and cultural age in which we demand to live in accordance with our own being; and, from that demand, arises the imperative to clarify the morphology and the dynamics of that being. (10)[5]

Arriving at this "historical and cultural age" in which such a "clarification" is "demanded" is itself a historical accomplishment. The imperative to clarify the morphology of "that being" could not have been articulated or heeded at any other time or by any other people. This is an imperative made possible by Mexican history, the work of Samuel Ramos, and a generation come of age.

The imperative for clarification is thus a "generational theme." What is to be clarified is the morphology of Mexican being, that is, the *form* of being Mexican, what Mexican philosophy itself calls "lo mexicano." This form appears to Mexicans as an "unmistakable air of familiarity in everything" (12). In everyday life an "air of familiarity" is *unmistakably* recognized, immediately and with a certain degree of certainty; in ordinary language, confidence in our ability to recognize that which is most familiar is captured by the statement, "I know it when I see it." "Lo mexicano" is recognized by Mexicans who *know it when they see it*, and know it before they "know" it, namely, in its pre-theoretical familiarity and pre-propositional givenness. A habit, a custom, a way of performing a task, a song, a joke, a wedding, a boxing strategy, or funeral could all be said to hold something of "lo mexicano," recognized not by anything explicit or propositional, but by the "air" that "surrounds it." Ultimately, "lo mexicano" is said to be "constitutive" of what it means to be Mexican. As such, the generational theme is to clarify the meaning and morphology of "lo mexicano."

In a more specific sense, "lo mexicano" can be understood as referencing a more or less "essential" quality of persons, things, or states of affairs recognized as Mexican. He says later in *Analysis* that "lo mexicano" refers to "the essence of the Mexican person, that is, of a particular style of life, of a radical project of existing that only belongs to Mexicans and that distinguishes them from Spaniards, North Americans, and Europeans" (45). In philosophical terms, "lo mexicano" is thus the "whatness" or "howness" of that which is Mexican, those existential and ontological qualities that will ultimately differentiate Mexicans from and unify them to all others.

Uranga's *Analysis* seeks to make the phenomenon of "lo mexicano" explicit and describable, to reduce it to its most basic, ontological, ground. Two philosophical approaches appear suitable for this task: phenomenology, which will allow a *return to the things themselves* (Mexican existence itself), and historicism, which will allow for those things (viz., Mexican existence) to speak through and in virtue of their own history.

The value of phenomenology for the analysis is evident (see "Transition: On Method," Chapter 1). But even more valuable is historicism. Its value resides in its implicit rejection of the universalist pretentions of Western philosophy and the simultaneous vindication of the value and necessity of history and circumstance for an adequate account of human existence in its concreteness. Historicism, Uranga believes, allows the concrete to have a voice. The underlying idea is that if history and circumstance matter to philosophy, then so do the people who can define themselves only through that lens. Uranga writes, "In becoming conscious of our particularities, historicism has motivated non-European cultures to interpret their own and most intimate ways of conceiving the world and man" (10).

Ultimately, Uranga understands historicism as a liberating philosophy. Somewhat paradoxically, it *frees* non-Western thinkers to think outside the confines of history and tradition (particularly, European history and *its* philosophical tradition). As it frees one to think outside Western history, it *allows* one to think within one's own—to vindicate, validate, and assume one's historical position. This is a transformative move: philosophy in the service of one's historical situatedness and circumstance means that one can dig into and deal with what truly matters to one's particular being in the world.

A Transformative Project

The permissions afforded by historicism to look philosophically into one's particular and concrete experience make possible the transformation of much more than one's worldview. Accordingly, the purpose of *Analysis* is much more ambitious than merely *analysis* for its own sake. Uranga writes: "what brings us to this kind of study is the project of bringing about moral, social, and religious transformations with that being" (10).[6] Having *arrived at that cultural and historical age* where Mexicans demand to live in accordance with their own being, it becomes imperative that this being is revealed, an operation that will ultimately demand the transformation or transfiguration of moral, social, and religious life.

This revelation of being is the task of philosophy, a philosophy that, although guided by historicism and existentialism, and thus bound to the concrete, will reveal essential truths.

> Far from moving about in imprecision and dispersion we are bound by a very constant and even rigid structure that, although it allows for secondary variations, which are perhaps limited, and offer the

possibility of differences, point to an "essential" characteristic of that structure. (12–13)

Said differently, the Mexican experience will be shown to be *rigid*, or constant, and, moreover, "bound" or limited to a very specific *manner of being* that, in spite of the different "Mexicos" or the differing experiences of being Mexican, points to a common truth, or essence, that unifies them all. Finding that essential constant is a primary goal of the analytic project (the other being the transformations previously announced). However, seeking to avoid exclusionary essentialism, relativism, or the pitfalls of Ramos's project, Uranga does not believe that the essential constant will be something superficial, such as a common social behavior, a known cultural mannerism, or one of the many psychological complexes that could be attributed to Mexicans; rather, the constant will be a manner of being that is *unmistakably familiar as* indicative of "lo mexicano"; that is, the constant is an ontological reality. At this point, the investigation becomes an ontological investigation.

Calling his investigation "ontological" poses a historiographical problem for Uranga. The problem has to do with his use of the concept of "ontology" itself and refers to an insistence, particularly in the Western philosophical tradition, that ontological concepts should be universal in scope and should refer to "being in general," and not to specific modes of being belonging to specific entities like "Mexicans."[7] Uranga shrugs off this problem, arguing that while ontological concepts do indeed only to refer to being, in either a universal or a regional sense, their *usefulness* becomes apparent only when they capture specific forms of being. He puts this in the following way:

> What is clear is that whatever the field may be from which ontological concepts are extracted and first coined, what matters is their dimension of being [*dimension de ser*]. ... The abstract nature of these categories does not really permit us to treat them in their purity, which is why we refer ourselves, a bit out of fatigue and a bit more due to the effort that abstraction itself demands, to those regions in which we first find them. (15)

Uranga's "ontology" thus means to refer to a situated, "regional" being; it is a regional ontology of Mexican being.[8] This regional ontology of Mexican being seeks to make sense of the way in which these beings exist in their uniquely historical, cultural, and geographical *being there*. Invoking Heidegger, Uranga proposes that "existence has ... *Jemeinigkeit* as a radical property" (67), that is, that existence is in each case mine and not "the existence of everyone and no one" (67). "From this perspective," Uranga concludes, "it is legitimate to speak about an ontology of the Mexican" (67). Uranga's methodological commitment to that which is nearest or most proximal to one's existential concerns is clear (see Chapter 1, "Transition: On Method").

Corazonadas

Uranga's phenomenological project is ambitious, especially considering that it seeks to take as its object a form of life circumscribed by history, politics, geography, customs, and so on. This sort of object does not easily give itself to intuition, perceptual or intellectual, and so it poses a problem for philosophical analysis. Uranga further complicates the issue by broadening the field of analysis to include, what he calls, the "air of familiarity" that points to a Mexican essence. Even more problematic than customs or history, "airs of familiarity" are not objects that can be intuited by perception, intellectual or sensuous, regardless of one's distance from it. Philosophical intuition, like that proposed by Descartes, Kant, or Husserl, seeks to grasp definitive objects (whether ideal or real) given in immediate experience, so that they may be intelligibly articulated with concepts. In Kant, for instance, knowledge comes about when intuitions (which are of sensuous phenomena) adequately correspond to their concepts (which are in the mind); outside of this fit, there is no "knowledge," per se.

The problem for Uranga has to do with capturing objects that are not sensuous in this, Kantian, way, but which one nonetheless "sees" in their familiarity or in their nonconceptual givenness. Thus, Uranga broadens his phenomenological methodology to include more than what the philosophical tradition has previously authorized; he says that we need to *feel* our way into those things that intuition cannot give. Borrowing from the poet López Velarde, the instrument for capturing the nonconceptual, immediate, givenness of Mexican life he calls "corazonadas," which I translate as "intimations." Uranga describes this expansion of method in the following way:

> We should also not allow ourselves to be overwhelmed by the conditions imposed by a rigorously crafted ontological terminology. There are analyses that do not appear ontological, but that when looked at more closely show themselves almost immediately as direct "translations" of lived experiences, [we can call them] ontological "intimations" [*"corazonadas" ontológicas*]. This is the case with poetry. Being speaks through the poet in its own language. Poetry does not translate the being of its experiences into terms alien to being itself, but comes to the reader in an almost pure form. This is why the ontology of the Mexican has to lend attention to the work of our poets with a degree of attention that will never be sufficient. Poetry has spoken more than the historians, psychologists, or sociologists about the being of the Mexican. (16)

With this, the methodological framework of *Analysis* is set. It is an ontological investigation aided by phenomenology and historicism and an expanded epistemic arsenal borrowed from poetry that includes the "corazon," the heart, that delivers through "intimations," or *corazonadas*, the truths of "instinct and thought," which would otherwise escape philosophical intuitions as traditionally understood.

A genuine and authentic Mexican philosophy will be grounded on these considerations. Sure, the *ontological* approach will be criticized because of its defiance to standards of "purity," or its deviance from or defiance of the Western model. But, if the project is to found a "Mexican" philosophy, Uranga has no choice but to deviate from the authorized philosophical approach; he *must* change it, disrupt it, and contaminate it: "Without such 'contamination' or 'borrowing of meaning' we do not believe there is any possibility of taking a step forward in our thematic" (16).

Reading "Part II: Philosophy"

"Part I: Introduction" thus orients us to the task at hand, namely, the grasping through intuition and/or intimation of those ontological characteristics that constitute Mexican being.

As an epigraph to "Part II: Philosophy," Uranga once again turns to Diego Durán: "To be so without foundation, and thus without being, in all things" (17). The Dominican friar's words prefigure the ontological description of Mexican life that Uranga seeks to articulate, namely, that a *lack* of foundation for Mexican persons likewise points to a lack of being. This lack, however, rather than pointing to, what Durán calls "without being, in all things," points to an insufficiency of being and an insufficiency of substance. It is a lack of being and substance that in traditional ontology characterizes non-substantial properties, or accidents.

Accidentality and Insufficiency

Uranga introduces accidentality as descriptive of Mexican being in his "Essay." He returns to it here, affirming it as a historical and ontological characteristic of Mexican being, one which is revealed in the fragility of Mexican existence as understood in its temporality and grasped by *corazonadas* as if in the "air," or intimated as "familiar" by ordinary Mexicans. Understood as a defining ontological characteristic (as characterizing *being*), accidentality defines beings that "in all things" lack in being and foundation. In other words, "Every modality of being grounded on accident is characterized by a lack of ground, grounded on an shifting and fractured base" (17).

At this point in the text, Uranga returns to the first "key moment" that precipitated Uranga's *Analysis*, namely, the controversial thesis of Samuel Ramos's *Profile of Man and Culture in Mexico* that says that Mexican persons are characterized by psychological "complex of inferiority" that explains powerlessness and marginalization. Against this thesis, Uranga argues that it is not a psychological complex that defines Mexican being, but something deeper, namely, an "insufficiency" of being that itself serves as a foundation for both psychic and cultural life. Like accidentality, insufficiency, as an ontological determining factor, determines the being of accidental beings and is, in fact, an existential and human characteristic that defines all beings (and not just Mexicans) in their being human.

What does it mean to say that Mexicans are accidental and insufficient? First, it means that Mexicans are temporal beings and always in the process of becoming, and so not complete or fulfilled in their being; second, it means that the foundations of Mexican being are not settled, they are *nepantla* (as announced in the epigraph attributed to Durán); and third, and perhaps more importantly for social and political transformation, it means that Mexicans are, indeed, the negation of Europeans, who in their historical posturing have proclaimed themselves to be "substantial," existing in the "fullness" and "plentitude of being" (17) (namely, the opposite of insufficiency and accidentality).

Indeed, Uranga suggests that Mexicans have come to understand themselves as *other* to a specific narrative of human dignity. It is narrative that equates value and dignity with European being. The Mexican consciousness of its own otherness is born in the confrontation with that narrative and the realization that, as non-Europeans, they are also non-substantial. Being non-substantial does not mean, however, that they are nothing, or pure negation. Rather, between the two extremes of substance and nothingness, Mexicans are accidents. Uranga puts it thus: "[Accidental being] is non-being when it gazes upon substance and a being when it returns its gaze toward nothingness" (18).

Understanding oneself as the negation of substance is an accomplishment. Being in the middle (nepantla) between substance and nothingness, or being accidental is, in fact, the most authentic form of human existence. Recognizing oneself in this middle ground means that one has likewise understood that substance *cannot belong* to man (but perhaps only to God or man's imaginings). According to Uranga, this recognition already puts Mexicans at an advantage, as they, more than the Europeans, *understand* the truth of their being as accidental.

Aside from being more in tune with the truth of one's being, being accidental is also an opportunity; it is an opportunity to live in accordance with one's being. Uranga presents this opportunity as a *project*. The project (which promises to bring "social, moral, and religious transformations") is to reaffirm one's accidentality so as to not lose touch with one's *ontological* reality. This project takes the form, Uranga says, of "having to be accident" (19).

Affirming that "having to be accident" is the project of Mexican being sets up a clear front in Uranga's confrontation with Western reason. Since the conquest, and certainly during the colony, Europeans (Spanish Catholics in particular) rationalized their existential project as "having to be *substance*." This project took an institutional form with the church, which framed existence in terms of a divine duty to repent and purify one's soul so as to achieve the goal of substantialization. This project, however, assumed that only "the chosen of God" had a soul to save and to purify, while those not so chosen lacked it; it mattered that the chosen of God were the European colonizers, the evangelizers themselves, because this meant that "having to be substance" as project was reserved for them and them alone. Uranga insists, however, that contingent, historical, beings cannot be substantial in the sense rationalized by the colonizing Christian narrative. Rather, he says, "the being of the human being is ontologically accidental" (18), which means that European Christians, too, insofar as they share this human truth, are likewise accidental.

Consequently, the proposal is this: accidental being, and not substantial being, is the true ontological reality of the human being. To be accidental is to be human, and to be human is to be accidental. However, only those human beings that recognize their accidentality will become conscious of their authentic humanity. Because they readily do, Mexicans are thought by Uranga as the model form of the human. Mexicans *intimate* their accidentality (it has an "air of familiarity") and pre-theoretically understand their insufficiency, their lack of ground and being. Mexican persons are thus not less than Europeans, as the colonizing narratives had insisted; since Europeans also lack the being they believe themselves to have, they are, similarly, ontologically insufficient and accidental. What applies to Mexicans as accidental thus also applies to Europeans as accidental: "The insufficiency of the Mexican is the insufficiency of his *being as accident* and only this" (18).

In this context, substantialization is an ideal to which the accident may aspire, although this would be to live in bad faith and inauthenticity. The project of "having to be substance" is (for either Mexican or European) inauthentic. Uranga writes: "Inauthenticity would be to flee the condition of accidentality and to substantialize oneself; the Mexican person falls into this temptation almost by necessity when her originary constitution is 'too much to bear' " (19). It is tempting to flee the facticity of our accidentality and lose ourselves in objectivizing myths regarding our own permanence, immortality, and destiny, especially when the task of "having to be accident" requires one to constantly affirm one's metaphysical and existential shortcomings. Uranga proposes another route to authentic living, one built on the basis of our accidentality (which serves as foundation and project). Rather than aspire to substantiality, one could aspire to "sufficiency." Uranga writes: "That 'sufficiency' towards which we aspire cannot be a 'substantiality', but a sufficiency that emerges from the same insufficiency, an emergence that is the only legitimate and properly moral goal" (20). Sufficiency thus refers to doing as much as we are capable of doing given the lack of being that always already constitutes us; that is, sufficiency is achieved by doing what we can do and accomplish in accordance with our being.

Western Arrogance

Consistent with his apparently anti-Western stance, Uranga suggests that the *imperial passion*, that is, the demand for objectivity, universality, substantiality, and purity, is a clear manifestation of philosophy's Eurocentric arrogance. It is the arrogance of a historical people that insists that Europeans, and only Europeans, have a privileged access to the truth of being to the exclusion of all other peoples. Western reason itself becomes arrogant reason, and as such, it labors to close itself off from the ontological primacy of history, subjectivity, and concrete life. Uranga summarizes this in this crucial passage of *Analysis*:

> We are not very certain of the existence of the human being in general ... [since] whatever passes itself off as human being in general [is merely] generalized European humanity [which] does not appear to us to define itself as accidental, but precisely as arrogant substantiality. (20–1)

I say this is consistent with Uranga's "anti-Western" stance because, ultimately, Uranga seeks to distance Mexican philosophy, as he conceives it, from the (arrogant) pretentions of European philosophy as it is traditionally understood and practiced. The project of "generalizing" from the particular to the universal characterizes a colonial gesture to reaffirm the colonizer's superiority, one that justifies an "arrogant" belief that European existence is the archetype of all existences, that European thought is the model for all thought. But in line with the project of "having to be accident," Uranga refuses the ploy, challenging the generalization and the arrogance of Western thinking.

Martin Heidegger

The remainder of the "Philosophy" chapter attempts to affirm and overcome those Western influences that, in their arrogance, deny the humanity of nonconforming points of view. A principal figure to affirm and overcome is Heidegger.

Uranga carefully read and studied Heidegger's works, especially his famous *Being and Time* of 1927. His teacher, Gaos, had been a student and translator of Heidegger, and Uranga studied first with Gaos, as one of his first Mexican students, and years later with Heidegger (in 1954), albeit to his great disappointment. In *Analysis*, Heidegger's existential phenomenological insights into human Dasein, that is, into human existence as a *being there*, are laid out and appropriated for the sake of his ontology of Mexican being. In fact, *Being and Time* justifies Uranga's attempt to ground his investigation on the being of the Mexican. He says: "When we speak of the Mexican as person we mean to refer to an interpretation of the Mexican as person from the starting point of her being" (22). The ontological approach thus begins not with psychological, anthropological, ethnographic, or characterological facts and observations, but with being, the concrete being in the world that, as Heidegger insists, each person is as a particular focus of existential concern.

Mexicans as Humanity's Hope

Uranga finds that history and ontology go hand in hand; that is, history informs his ontology. From the perspective of historicized ontology, Mexican persons reveal themselves as accidental and insufficient. It is an accidentality and insufficiency that is revealed in the way they relate to themselves and each other, in their relation to non-Mexicans (especially, Europeans or North Americans), and in attitudes toward morality and mortality. As such, accidentality and insufficiency are pretheoretically understood by Mexicans as constitutive of their very being, although, as was the case with Samuel Ramos, psychologically misinterpreted as inferiority or sentimentality. However, even when misinterpreted, Mexicans know without knowing, i.e., in their *heart* (through *corazonadas*), that their being in the world, their thrownness in the sociohistorical landscape with which they are so familiar, is uncertain, unsettled, random, and indeterminate; in other words, Mexicans understand that their being in the world *is* accidental. As Uranga makes clear: "We know what an accident is even if we cannot concretely formulate what we mean by 'know'" (25).

Together with the understanding that Mexican being is accidental is the "intimation" that it is not alike that which is non-accidental, namely, that it is *not substance*. Uranga's claim here can be understood as an anti-colonial affirmation that defies a 500-year-old metanarrative that says that *some* human beings are endowed by history and divine right with substance—an endowment conveniently reserved for those who conquer and subdue accident and randomness. Uranga's declaration that Mexican being is accidental and not substantial is thus meant to overturn the dehumanizing narrative of prevalent since the conquest. Uranga elaborates:

> It appears to us that considering the Mexican person in his being, or in his ontological aspect, serves or functions as a source for a sense of the human applicable to anything that pretends to represent itself as human. It is not about articulating *lo mexicano* (that which particularizes us) as human, but the opposite; it is about articulating the human in terms of *lo mexicano*. *Lo mexicano* is the point of reference for the human; whatever resembles *lo mexicano* calibrates itself as human, disposes itself of whatever is dissimilar or distant from this kind of being. In ontological terms: any interpretation of the human as substantial creature seems to us inhuman. At the origins of our history we suffered a devaluation for failing to assimilate ourselves to European "humanity." In a similar spirit, today we reject that qualification and, thus, refuse to recognize as "human" any European construction that grounds human "dignity" in substantiality. (23)

Prima facie, one reads this passage (what could be one of Uranga's most controversial claims in *Analysis*) as suggesting that the being of the Mexican is *the most* human and that the human itself cannot be understood without first understanding that which is Mexican ("lo mexicano"). Moreover, as "the point of reference for the human," no other forms of humanity can be understood without first understanding the form of humanity that belongs to Mexicans. However, what Uranga means is, simply, that to be human is to be accidental and insufficient, and so to understand oneself *as* the Mexican understands himself is to understand oneself in the right light.

Narrative of Substance

The European narrative of substantiality can be seen as dehumanizing in two ways: first, it dehumanizes Europeans themselves by convincing them of a substantiality that they cannot possibly possess, hence cutting them off from the truth of their humanity; and second, it dehumanizes non-Europeans by denying them a substantiality that would apparently allow them to be properly human, thus denying them humanity from the start. This is why Uranga says that "any interpretation of the human as substantial creature seems to us inhuman" (23). The *re*-humanization of all comes when humanity is understood in its most ordinary sense, as that which is most proximal to the accident, to impermanence, and to concrete life.

Uranga's anti-Western, anti-colonial motivations are slowly revealed throughout the "Philosophy" section of *Analysis* as he seeks to establish an obvious difference between Mexican and European conceptions of humanity—a difference that ultimately boils down to what one thinks of oneself *ontologically*. It is a phenomenological difference between humanity as accidental and humanity as substantial. However, when we go to the things themselves, that is, to existence as it gives itself in its immediate and most proximal givenness, it is obvious that none of us is substantial, that our lives are random and accidental, indeterminate, and absolutely finite. For Uranga, this "data" of human experience is enough to say that Mexican being, which to him reveals finiteness and accidentality most clearly, is the model of the human. These are truths that, in contradistinction to European self-certainty, are given to Mexicans to "know," even if that knowledge is not cognitive or intuitive but given in "corazonadas." Uranga's method is ultimately meant to be deconstructive of traditional philosophy. He is clear on this: "We endeavor to overturn the teachings of the Western tradition" (25).

Of course, not all the teachings of the Western tradition are overturned, nor does Uranga's anti-colonial stance seek to overturn them all. What we find in our reading is not an "overturning," but rather a desire to *open* and expose a tradition previously closed and blind to other modes of being.

Accidentality: Seven Modalities

A means to open and expose the Western philosophical tradition to the otherness of Mexican being is by appropriating Western philosophical concepts and applying them to the Mexican experience. In this process, concepts that have been previously denied to other experiences and other modes of being are enriched and "transformed" in their application and appropriation. "The 'application' [of a concept] to a determinate material region 'clarifies' the concept, it 'enriches' it, but at the same time, it 'transforms' it" (28). One such concept is "accidentality," appropriated by Uranga for a task previously closed off to it, namely, the ontology of a particular form of life. The idea is that when applied to Mexican being, "accident" as a concept will be clarified, enriched, and transformed.

Subsections 2.9–11 *clarify* the "mode of being as accident." There are seven modalities of the accident, which Uranga enumerates in section 2.10 (31).

(1) Inherence, or being-in: "the being of the accident is not being in the 'proper' sense, or simply 'being,' but rather, finds its formulation in the complex expression of 'being-in' (we must conceive of this notion of accident as the unity of these two elements)" (30).
(2) Contingency, or being-in-and-not-being-in: the accident is "oscillation between being and nothingness" (30).
(3) Dependence, or of entity: "the accident ... depends on, or belongs to, another being" (30).
(4) Absence (*Ab-esse*), or un-being: "the accident is privation, lack, penury, a defect or absence of subsistence, and insufficient being" (30).
(5) Surprise, or being-over: "the accident is that which suddenly appears, what is not expected" (31).
(6) Adhesion, or being-proximal, or attached: "the accident sinks into or embeds itself in substance" (31).
And (7) Projection, or being-toward: the accident "tends toward being, it pulls and projects itself toward it" (31).

In sum, for something to *be* an accident, it will (1) be part of, (3) depend on, or (6) adhere to another being; moreover, it will (4) lack sufficient being so that it is (2) something rather than nothing; it will (5) interrupt being, and, finally, it will (7) always intend or be intentionally directed to being. Uranga's appropriation, which enriches, clarifies, and transforms this notion, seeks to show that Mexican being is part of, depends on, and adheres to European/Spanish being; that, as a being, it is insufficient, hence, it is contingent and random; and, finally, that in its authentic state it intends "having to be accident" as a fundamental project of existence.

Meta-Philosophical Interlude

In section 3, the text deviates into something of an "interlude," a break in the reflection, where Uranga seeks to address an obvious, predictable, and unnecessary criticism. It is the kind of criticism that investigations such as these naturally invite. The criticism can be formulated in the question: Can a "Mexican" philosophy possibly obey the philosophical demands for purity and universality and still be both "Mexican" and "philosophy"? This question is loaded with an "obvious" critique that says that philosophy is not supposed to hint at origin, place, or, even worse, nationality—it is supposed to be transcendent in its aims and universal in its scope. It is a "predictable" critique in the sense that anyone who takes historicism (and history) seriously (as Uranga does) must expect it, and it is an "unnecessary" criticism as it wrongly (and perhaps unjustifiably) assumes that the philosophical investigation will stop at the boundaries of "Mexico"—as place and idea—saying nothing about what lies beyond it, what transcends it, or what has lasting, human, value. Internal to this (unnecessary) critique is the belief that in being subjects of colonization, and hence *late* to philosophy, Mexican philosophers do not fully understand what "philosophy" is or how it works. Notwithstanding this (implicitly racist) colonialist critique, Uranga tells us that focusing on the immediacy of "lo mexicano" is merely a beginning, the point of departure for a philosophizing that will eventually speak about and from the Mexican circumstance to all similarly constituted peoples, Mexican or not.

> *Lo mexicano* must be conceived as a juncture or nexus of multiple paths, and the work of the philosopher resides in clearing up those paths, in highlighting their place on the map, and of articulating their direction. When we speak about the search for the being of the Mexican, what we mean is that we seek to arrive at a system of communicative relations, an ontological crossroads, a means of relating ourselves to the great currents of humanity; it does not refer to constructing a repository wherein we will hold a minuscule portion of humanity, particularized for our exclusive use, aggressively purified and protected against the incursion of any foreign element. (34)

Uranga is aware of the possible charge of relativism or provincialism that his philosophical approach to the problem of Mexican being naturally invites. Some would even call his a "national" philosophy. But in this elegant passage, Uranga assures us that the philosophical search for "lo mexicano" does not mean to enclose a "miniscule portion of humanity" under some relative observations or a contructed nationality; rather, the articulation of "lo mexicano" will reveal new possibilities for communicative interaction with the rest of the world, new ways to relate to the "great currents of humanity," and new ontological highways never before explored (see "Transition: On Method," Chapter 1).

What the ontology of Mexican being will inevitably accomplish is an opening and an enrichment of our conception both of philosophy and of humanity itself. The Mexican person stands as a testament to the influence and power of European colonialism and an instance of its overcoming through a "special or exceptional ontic particularity." Uranga says,

> I am aided in my intervention by the conviction that our character enjoys a special or exceptional ontic particularity. ... More fragile, but better clarified than any other aspect of our character, is our way of being an excellent lens through which to look at the way the West has constituted the human being. The goal of my work can thus be reduced to this. It could be said that any other character [besides the Mexican] allows for the same kind of operation, but I have my

[Mexican] character ready to hand and it would be absurd to appeal to something other than myself as a means to find the truth—it would be like cleaning my neighbor's glasses so that I may see better. (36)

If anything, rather than a relative investigation into Mexican being, *Analysis* is meant to be a reflection on and, ultimately, *of* Western thought, as Mexican being itself is a "lens through which to look" at Western history, philosophy, and culture. What it sees when it looks through itself at the West, however, is the extent of its difference and the ways in which Mexican being is other to it, accidental rather than substantial, insufficient rather than a fulfilled totality, and thus closer to the truth of being than any Western conception.

Radical Humanism and Nationalism

Uranga wants his contribution to the "great currents of humanity" to be a radical humanism, or a humanism that is truly rooted in his own Mexican experience. In this radical and rooted humanism, the genuinely human is elevated and placed as an aspiration. Since the genuinely human (what being human is in actuality) is accidental, insufficient, and particular, the hope is that all peoples should seek this genuine humanity by assuming "having to be accident" as an existential project. Unconsciously, or in the ordinary course of life, the Mexican person has accepted this aspirational project, living her accidentality and her insufficiency and, in the process, modeling what it means *to be* genuinely human. In this ontological state, the Mexican person is closer to the truth of humanity, a truth that philosophy and history have previously tried to cover up with substantializing, Eurocentric narratives.

A radical Mexican humanism will, consequently, affirm accidentality and insufficiency as an everyday state of being. It will, moreover, propose this way of being as a human way of being, which, although found in the particularity of a Mexican ontological truth, reaches beyond to "the rest of humanity." Uranga writes:

> Our being is not a private essence that cuts us off from the rest of humanity and gives us an incomparable profile, but, on the contrary, it is a common "essence" that unites us and brings us closer to that which is human, empowering us to recover it in its fundamental dimension and detaching it or clearing it of certain unfortunate characteristics in which we lose ourselves and, once lost, fail to recognize what is uniquely human or different ways of being. (37)

Mexican humanism, in other words, is not satisfied with humanizing Mexicans, but seeks to transcend its enclosures and reveal commonalities with "other ways of being," commonalities that humanize all beings in their "different ways of being."

Naturally, this sort of openness to others is a vulnerability; it exposes one to the possible violence of strangers, to death and dissolution of what is uniquely one's own. Nationalism becomes the safeguard against this threat. The reason is simple: nationalism preserves our imagined differences by substantializing them as common characteristics of a unique people, so that whoever does not possess the common characteristic is excluded, thereby eliminating the threat and ultimately protecting our vulnerability. In the Mexican case, the lure of joining the great currents of humanity is trumped by a desire to protect "lo mexicano." Uranga observes that "with equal originality the Mexican refuses the human and closes himself up ... in his nationality" (39). Not just the exclusive achievement of religion or tribal logics, nationalism "hardens and reinterprets" Mexicans, covering them over with ideological layers that "substantialize" them, justifying a forgetfulness of their human condition as accident, contingency, and randomness. Even if, as Uranga writes, "it is degrading to be a nationalist when one can simply be a man" (41), the promise of a substantial identity, in spite of its superficiality and fragility, is a temptation that is hard to resist.

Opposed to nationalism, radical humanism of the kind Uranga proposes urges one to "open [oneself] up, without defense, to the human condition in a profound way ... to that which is human" (41). While nationalism assumes the inevitable violence of the other, and thus seeks to protect and secure one's difference, humanism assumes accidentality, a vulnerability that comes with being cast into a world of chance and randomness, and so insists on openness and generosity toward others. This being open to others in empathy, sympathy, or generosity makes possible, what Uranga calls, following Edmund Husserl, "pairing" (Spanish: *emparejamiento*; German: *Verkoppeln*). This willingness to "pair" with others makes it possible for Mexicans to "transfer" their accidental condition to others, which means to sympathize and empathize with other accidentalities and, thus, share the originary human condition. Of course, this is not an exercise in erasure; that is, in pairing, in empathy, or in sympathy, one does not lose oneself in sameness—one's differences remain intact: "If the Mexican person is compassionate, demonstrating with that compassion that he feels a universal similarity with all others, he likewise intuits that his fate is not completely shareable, that there is a center on which is impossible to communicate" (43).

A radical Mexican humanism thus insists on both the preservation and the sharing of one's unique difference in the communal act of "pairing." Nationalism only seeks to preserve and entomb, a nationalistic desire that proves unnecessary, since one's unique difference will be preserved as a matter of fact. Uranga notes that "there is a remainder that cannot be overcome, that does not avail itself" (43). However, while this remainder is what nationalists exploit as the source of nationalist pride or cultural uniqueness, it is not *essential*—the essential, what is human, is what is shared, what "is familiar to the Mexican person because it is with him as that other extreme with which to establish meaningful communication" (44); what is familiar is accidentality.

Internal to Uranga's radical humanist critique of nationalism is the anti-colonial rejection of the West that underlies *Analysis*, manifested here and there as a desire to overturn the ideology of political insularity inherited from Europe. It is a rejection that follows, ultimately, Uranga's a critique (although partially muted) of the Eurocentric tendency for abstraction, substantialization, and objectivity.

"Philosophy" thus sets up general parameters for the investigation into Mexican being and seeks to unburden itself of those pretentions internal to the Western tradition that would demean, defund, and debunk a philosophy that dares to call itself "Mexican."

Having shown how philosophy has contributed to the covering-over of the truth of being through a one-sided humanism that pits substance against accident, Europe against its other, and so on, Uranga now seeks to show the role that history has and must play in this evolving story.

Reading "Part III: History"

"Part III: History" begins with a brief outline of the major moments in 20th-century Mexican philosophy and concludes with Uranga's argument for the historicity of ontology.

20th-Century Mexican Philosophy

The first major moment in 20th-century Mexican philosophy is the "bankruptcy of positivism and the pretensions of natural science to establish themselves as guides for human life at the exclusion of art, religion, and philosophy" (45). The 19th century had witnessed the adoption of positivism as the doctrinal ideology of the state, whereby positivism (in its Comtean and Spencerian versions[9]) had become the national philosophy. In the early years of the 20th century, this state-sanctioned ideological program became an object of intense scrutiny by an intellectual collective known as the *Ateneo de la Juventud*.[10] Members of *Ateneo*, like members of *Hiperión*, who would come 30 years later, exposed positivism as philosophically "bankrupt" by showing the manner in which it devalued Mexican cultural life and, consequently, Mexicans themselves.

The second moment Uranga highlights is the "elaboration of an aesthetic and sensuous vision of the human being and of the world" (45). This contribution was related to the first and had to do with what was added to philosophy after the delegitimization of positivism, namely, an unparalleled artistic expression exemplified by the muralist movement led by Diego Rivera, José Clemente Orozco, and David Alfaro Siqueiros. These and other artists of the time sought to capture, through historically saturated paintings, the very soul and personality of Mexico and Mexicans—a project that positivism would have previously deemed unfit and unproductive for social progress.

Finally, the third moment Uranga considers is "the most significant of all" (45). This is the project formed around the philosophy of lo mexicano, of which *Analysis* is meant to be the most profound expression. The aim of *la filosofía de lo mexicano* was to determine the particular style of life, or "radical project of existing that only belongs to Mexicans" and that differentiates them from "Spaniards, Europeans, and North Americans" (45). That is, with the philosophy of lo mexicano, Mexican philosophy sought its difference and its validation by capturing a historical, ontological, and existential uniqueness that is both Mexican and human. The premise of the project was that the "radical project of existing" that "belongs" to Mexicans represents human truths that have value and connection, truths and ways of life that point to a genuine humanism. As Uranga puts it, "The originality of the Mexican's lived experiences allows a repositing, from its own ground, the *general sense* of humanism" (49; my emphasis). The philosophy of lo mexicano ultimately vindicates and validates Mexican existence as truly valuable to human history and, thus, truly deserving of recognition.

Insufficiency, Redux

In the conclusion of Part III: History, Uranga proclaims that the "elaborations" carried out here are for the sake of "the project of 'historicizing' our ontology" (75). Against Eurocentric conceptions of ontology concerned strictly with being in general, Uranga seeks to situate, particularize, and temporalize ontology. As an instance of ontology historicized, he looks at the way in which insufficiency has been "lived" by Mexicans at different historical moments.

> Insufficiency, as a central theme of the ontology of the Mexican, requires history; it requires it for the illumination of those "historical moments" in which, in an extreme way, insufficiency is lived authentically or inauthentically; that is, it requires the repetition of those historical periods in which insufficiency is made explicit or is covered over [*se acusa o se sepulta*]. (75)

In this way Uranga aims to make sense of the way in which insufficiency is a lived experience. For this purpose, it is necessary to differentiate between insufficiency and inferiority, to underscore that while something can be insufficient, it does not mean that it is inferior, and vice versa. Food makes for a good example. A bowl of *pozole* can be insufficient insofar as it does not satisfy my hunger, but this does not mean that it is inferior; on the contrary, it may be the most delicious, and superior, *pozole* I have ever tasted. On the other hand, a different batch of this Mexican delicacy may be fully sufficient, but inferior in quality. It may satisfy my hunger, but not my taste. The same holds for the sufficiency–superiority distinction.

On its own, the sufficiency–superiority distinction is unproblematic. We make it daily. It becomes culturally and existentially problematic, however, when deployed in the realm of politics, ideology, or morality—when it is used to justify or legitimize the value we place on ourselves, our culture, our history, or our preferences. In other words, insofar as "sufficiency" and "insufficiency" are used to make everyday value judgments and distinctions of personal taste, "insufficiency" will be unproblematic. It becomes a problem when it is used for representing an objective measure between two things, in this case, Mexican culture and non-Mexican culture. Uranga says:

> Sufficiency and insufficiency represent an "immanent" or "intrinsic" value scale. But if we compare Mexican culture with European culture, if we look for an "extrinsic" criterion of valuation, the problem of "superiority" and "inferiority" is automatically introduced. (52)

Affirming the existence of such objective criteria can certainly put one in the position of devaluing oneself with the recognition of something that seems greater than or better than. However, this ability to recognize something or someone as superior does not mean that one is, with the same breath, recognizing one's own inferiority. Against Ramos, Uranga argues that rather than exhibiting a "complex" of inferiority, in recognizing something that is superior, one exhibits a normal, healthy, and "generous" (53) attitude toward the world—a capacity, to put it in colloquial terms, to give credit where credit is due. In fact, the "complex" of inferiority, like resentment, appears only when one tries to deny the superiority of something that is, in fact, superior. This, he says, is a "deficient" existential situation (54).

The recognition of one's insufficiency overcomes deficient situations such as resentment and inferiority complexes by underlying and highlighting one's accidental, imperfect, and always already nonsufficient being. Knowing that one is ontologically insufficient allows one to put whatever is deemed factually "superior" in its proper horizon (a horizon where nothing is absolutely sufficient but only relatively so), thus avoiding the complexes that psychologically corner one into thinking that one can never be sufficient enough to be like that which is absolutely fulfilled and substantial, but rather work "to give [oneself] the sufficiency that [one] lacks" (54), specifically the sufficiency that I require for myself, in my specific particularity, and for my own life. This sufficiency will not be absolute, but relative to my own particular life, and it will be enough.

On Cynicism

In considering how insufficiency is *lived through* in Mexican life, Uranga wonders how the recognition of one's ontological insufficiency can be deployed or weaponized for the sake of a liberatory project of historical overcoming? The answer is cynicism.

The diagnosis that Mexicans suffer from an inferiority complex whereby they deem themselves materially and spiritually inferior to other, superior cultures means that, on the one hand, they must either surrender or resign themselves to their inferior situation or, on the other, demean or demote what they perceive as superior in acts of resentment and envy. In either case, whether one choses resignation or resentment, the end result of that choice is impotence, a feeling of powerlessness before others and the world.

In response to the powerlessness associated with this perceived inferiority, Uranga argues that one should adopt an attitude of cynicism, which, unlike resentment and resignation, is a confrontation with the world that exudes "virtue and power" (58). Echoing Nietzsche, Uranga proposes that inverting values, or turning value structures on their heads, or "replacing superior values with inferior values" (58), is a willful and powerful act. Unlike those for whom inferiority is what defines their personality, for whom submission and impotence is the only response to that which is superior, cynics are defined by an "attitude of dignified rebellion"; they are "carefree and bold" and always motivated by a "desire to put 'the world upside down'" (59). However, this boldness in the face of what is commonly considered great, noble, worthy, or superior (usually values and value schemes dogmatically acknowledged as fully rational, essential, and substantial), is rooted in the recognition that the highest values define only substantial (and abstract) beings and not insufficient and accidental beings such as (concrete) human persons. Recognition of one's accidentality, of one's temporal and situated being, frees one to confront the arrogance of what pretends to be greater and better by virtue of its representation through the prism of essential or substantial values.

Ultimately, cynicism is the triumph that comes with accepting the truth of one's being. It is the conscious affirmation that we can only do so much, that substance is not for us and inferiority is not a state of being. Cynicism is the power of insufficiency.

> Cynicism is clarity; it is always intellectual labor due to its transparency and the cold-bloodedness of its decisions. The force and brutality associated with it is not born, however, from a sense of sufficiency itself, but, rather, from that of insufficiency, although cautiously veiled to the eyes of others. (60)

Because "cynicism is clarity" and "intellectual labor," it is "in its pure form, philosophical work" (59). And since philosophical projects such as the one Uranga undertakes seek to liberate, "it is the cynic who saves us" (61).

The saving power of cynicism should not be misunderstood. The cynic cannot "save" us in the sense of giving us a way out of our predicaments, nor does the cynic redeem; the cynic "saves" by "proposing," through the "cold-bloodedness" of value inversions, a "mission, a destiny to be realized." The inversions themselves reveal the ground of value, and as the cynic inverts, he un-conceals and, in so doing, liberates and uproots.

> To be saved means that we wait for something that we lack to be given to us, that we must be fulfilled with possessing a certain thing, with something that is given (*gegeben*), but to be liberated does not depend on waiting for a gift, on being fulfilled by something given, but, and simply, it depends on a proposal (*aufgegeben*) as a task, a mission, a destiny to be realized. ... Cynicism does not promise wealth or riches, but work. (61)

Thus, a cynic will behave in opposition to one who is convicted of an inferiority complex. The former will seek freedom through labor; the latter will seek salvation by others. Uranga tells us, then: "Cynicism calls for action, but salvation is expected by a creature who is unwilling, apathetic and lethargic" (62).

The Negation of the Spanish

If cynicism represents a path to liberation, then the liberation sought must be liberation from oppression. The most oppressive relation for Mexicans is the historical relation between Mexico and Spain, or between Mexico as a colonized, dependent, accidental entity and Spain as the colonizing, independent, and substantial totality. It is this historical contrast that nourishes inferiority, dependency, and that negative sense of self-worth that maintain Mexicans in the peripheries of world history.

Ultimately, the relation between Mexicans and Spaniards is one of opposition, and the opposition is constitutional and constitutive, revealing, once again, insufficiency as an ontological truth. Uranga writes:

> The negation of that which is Spanish is in the Mexican person [*del mexicano*] the determination of that which is Mexican [*lo mexicano*]. Every other opposition is derivative or secondary and always presupposes the originary and radical negation of Spanishness [*lo español*]. The Mexican chooses himself as "accidental" or precisely as the negation of Spanishness, which presents itself as "substantial." This originary election of accidentality before a determined substantiality gives direction to an entire history of that which is Mexican and, of course, to our relations with the world and with Spanish men. (72)

From a purely *philosophical* standpoint, the being of "lo mexicano" is constituted by this relation of negation to Spanish substantiality. Mexicans in their accidentality are the negation of the Spanish in their fullness. From a purely *historical* standpoint, moreover, Mexicans have created their cultural and historical identity through choices ("elections") that determine their identity and culture as different from what the Spanish colonizers attempted to impose.

Ontology and Autognosis

At this point, we can indicate seven propositions that make up Uranga's ontological program:

(1) History has produced a unique way of life, the Mexican way of life;
(2) The Mexican way of life can be generally described as *a way of being Mexican* or a manner of Mexican being;
(3) Mexican being, as historical and circumstantial, is accidental;
(4) Mexican being, as accidental, is insufficient;
(5) Mexican being, as insufficient, is the negation of the European;

(6) (1) through (5) can be given in intuitions or intimations;
(7) So, given (1) through (6), a Mexican ontology is possible.

The end of "History" anticipates a criticism of proposition 7 and the ways in which a historicized ontology can be possible.

A grounding premise (proposition 1) of Uranga's ontological program, and philosophy of "lo mexicano" more generally, is the fact that Mexico and its people are historical accidents. Were it not for the accidental "discovery" of the "New" world, the Mexican person would not have emerged on the historical scene; that is, were it not for the economic demands for trans-Atlantic trade routes, the randomness of ocean currents, the happenstance of contact, the violence of miscegenation, conquest, and settlement, Spanish colonial ambitions would have met a different fate and the being captured by the term "Mexican" may have been an entirely different being, or there would be no such being at all. In spite of, or because of, these historical contingencies, Uranga finds a non-accidental truth about the Mexican person, namely, that Mexican people are the product of an opposition.

In opposition to Spanish colonial power, to the challenge of a mixed identity, and to precolonial history itself, the Mexican person emerges as accident, insufficiency, and negation (proposition 5). Uranga translates this insight into the philosophical affirmation that the Mexican person is closer to the truth of human being because she lives her life in intimate contact with accidentality and insufficiency, characteristics that constitute the limits of her worldview and her identity (proposition 4). This philosophical affirmation is not one that merely touches on her psychological makeup, on her character; this philosophical affirmation is more than "autognosis," or self-knowledge, it is philosophical *par excellence*, it is ontological (proposition 7).

Uranga foresees that philosophical critics will seek to protect the sanctity of Western philosophy as a pure and uncontaminated discipline, one free of history, temporality, and the *accidental*. According to Uranga these same critics will seek "to deny that there can be an ontology of Mexicanness" (66). They will insist that "ontology can only refer to being in general and, in the case of a fundamental ontology, to the analysis of not a particular type of man, but of 'man in general'" (66). To this, Uranga counters that "man in general" does not *exist* and that the question of being is "always a question asked by man himself; moreover, asking about being seems inconceivable if it is not grounded in man" (66). Therefore, ontology only makes sense as a study of *human being* if it begins with the human being in particular (and not in general), since

> the link between man and being is not made as a link between being and man in general, but is made with concrete modalities of man, one of these modalities being that of the Mexican. The being of man is not a generic being in which diverse types of human beings would appear as subordinate species. (66)

Insisting, then, on the philosophical value of avoiding the jump from human being in particular to "being in general" and, instead, justifying the perspective of "being in particular," Uranga is able to affirm Mexican philosophy as both "Mexican" and "philosophy." In this way, Uranga unhinges Mexican philosophy from the standard history of European philosophy, thereby refusing assimilation so as to execute an appropriation and move forward with the project of a *Mexican* ontology. The moment of the unhinging is here:

> We think, no longer with Heidegger but within our own specific ontological perspective, that Being can receive an interpretation that is precisely contrary to that of ancient ontology, that is, to see it and to understand it not as substance but as "accident" precisely because we have placed it in its proper horizon, which is temporality, and which we must also interpret, consequently, also as accident. (69)

Heidegger's existential phenomenological analytic had provided the motivation necessary for Uranga's undertaking to get underway. Now, however, having taken advantage of Heidegger's insights into the "temporality," that is, the historicity and concreteness, of individual humanity (to which accidentality belongs), Uranga is able to move beyond Heidegger and affirm the value of his own existential and conceptual resources.

Returning to his version of ontology, the concluding lines of "History" reaffirm Uranga's commitment to the value of history for ontology: "An ontology that understands itself cannot be anything but historical" (74). History, he believes, serves to reveal those characteristics of the *how* of Mexican being, characteristics that repeat themselves and, in that repetition, reveal accidentality and insufficiency as "essential" characteristics of temporal (i.e., accidental and insufficient) beings. He concludes:

> Ontology cannot do without the history of problems that repeat themselves. Through repetition we understand the immersion of a problem in its essential possibilities. Maintaining a problem in those originary possibilities and nourishing it in those possibilities is repetition. Insufficiency, as central theme of the ontology of the Mexican, requires history; it requires it for the illumination of those "historical moments" in which, in an extreme way, insufficiency is lived authentically or inauthentically; that is, it requires the repetition of those historical periods in which insufficiency is made explicit or is covered over [*se acusa o se sepulta*]. (75)

Reading "Part IV: Poetry"

Toward the end of the 20th century, Richard Rorty sought to break philosophy's stranglehold on truth and justification by insisting that the "quarrel" between philosophy and poetry was unnecessary, and due mostly to philosophy's conceit. Whereas philosophy prides itself on always being ready to "transcend" human contingency, poetry, even when it seeks transcendence, always finds itself rooted in its moment, since by its very nature it is a "recognition of contingency."[11] It is an unnecessary quarrel, however, since neither can really overcome the human experience. Rorty writes: "philosophy and poetry can coexist peaceably if both sides are willing to give up on the attempt to transcend human finitude."[12] Rorty's point is, ultimately, that humanity can speak through poetry just as well as it can through philosophy.

Part IV of *Analysis*, titled "Poetry," anticipates Rorty's claim that philosophy and poetry have been forced into a precipitous divorce due to perceived irreconcilable differences. Uranga writes that a "malicious conviction, sanctioned without end by common sentiment ... [holds that] to poeticize and to think [to philosophize] are opposed just as things which have too little or too much of some quality are opposed" (76). This opposition is due, he continues, to the view that "thought wanders through regions inaccessible to poetry and what the poet reveals is set apart (with almost religious care) from the dominions accessible to [philosophical] thought" (76). However, "today, we begin to suspect that the tradition has imposed on our minds a separation of [philosophical] thought and poetry that in more ... original epochs would not have even been considered" (76). In fact, poetry and philosophy ought to supplement each other in our analyses of the human experience, especially because they widen the horizon of what can be gathered from that experience: "poetry and thought communicate with each other via robust connections that due to the narrowness of our vision we think as impalpable and subtle. Poetic thought reveals itself as rigorous as philosophical thought" (76).

Like Dante's Virgil and Heidegger's Hölderlin, the poet that leads Uranga into the profound depths of ontological truth, and that best exemplifies poetry's ability to communicate the "inaccessible" to philosophical thought, is Ramón López Velarde. According to Uranga, "to appeal to a poet like López Velarde has been, for us, a task imposed by our obligation to return to the origin," and this because, in his poetry, Velarde

> speaks of our character ... with a pristine echo that lends dimension to his observations, that does not reduce or obscure them to their simplest meaning, but rather "aggravates" them and casts them once

again into the sea of their own possibilities ... [he] does not allow himself to be deceived by first impressions, everything that is said stands within a horizon of signs and significations that can mean or refer to any possibility. (99–100)

Particularly insightful is Velarde's poetic articulation of the Mexican Revolution. As Uranga sees it, Velarde lays the groundwork for a possible poetic philosophizing that will finally capture the "meaning" of the revolution and, as a result, of Mexican identity, while making sense of a political and cultural trauma that continues to endure. Placing the burden on philosophy, he asks: "Is not our philosophy guilty of a radical blindness if it does not translate what poetry has taught us about the revolution?" (77)

According to Uranga, it is in the analysis of the Mexican Revolution where poetry showcases its power of revelation. The Mexican Revolution, a singular world-historical event marking a permanent fracture in Mexican history, signals the birth of modern Mexico and, simultaneously, a profound historical and ontological deficiency in the being of the Mexican person. Poetry, but especially the poetry of López Velarde perfectly captures the "sense" of the revolution as bringing this deficiency to consciousness or, better yet, of allowing Mexicans to finally be at home in their ontological and historical accidentality.

Velarde himself talks of the revolution as making possible the creation of a "homeland." But Uranga reads this "homeland" not as a nation, but as a state of being. He tells us that "with the revolution, López Velarde sees the emergence of a homeland which is 'not historic, not political, but intimate'" (77). This intimate homeland is the place where one achieves a confidence in knowing oneself, where one is at home in insufficiency, accidentality, and deficiency. For Mexicans, then, the homeland is not Mexico as a nation, but Mexico as a lived experience. Uranga laments that, 30 years after the fact, "the modesty of the human condition revealed by the revolution is forgotten" (77), and so is Velarde's message.

Clearly, the revolution (and the violence, death, and destruction that it wrought) performed an ontological service that was never fully appreciated. The "modesty of the human condition" may have been revealed, but it was not assumed—that is, internalized and made one's own into a *homeland*. It is now the task of philosophy, following the intimations of poetry (read: *corazonadas*), to seek a way to appropriate these lessons, which are "modest" existential and ontological revelations about the "human condition" itself.

The philosophical insight, gathered from history and arrived at the end of the previous section, points to repetition as a method for the appropriation of the lessons of the revolution. The task is to keep fast, always and repeatedly, to the ground that the revolution uncovered, that is, to what Velarde called the "homeland."

> Transforming the novelty of the homeland is an everyday affair, and so is tirelessly repeating its possibilities; otherwise forgetfulness will dispel it and confuse it. The task is, then, vigilance and watchfulness so that the essence of what the revolution has produced may be transformed into an everyday reality lived and repeated in ordinary situations. (78)

What's repeated is not a political manner of being, nor is it the trauma of death and violence that constituted the event of the revolution; what is repeated is the being that such an event made possible, the humble, modest, and non-grandiose manner of being that is closest to the human origin. Nearness to the accident and insufficiency is what must be reiterated. This call for repetition, however, is a personal call; it is a call made to concrete persons with concrete relations to a real historical event. And to heed the call is to recognize oneself in the call, to find one's facticity intimately concerned and invested in the appropriations and repetitions that must be undertaken.

The project that invites one to repeat the possibilities of history mirrors the project that asks one to accidentalize oneself; the "having to be accident" involves repetition, as one must continuously, and repeatedly, accidentalize oneself. This invitation, or this call, however, is made to each person individually. It is not a general call made to the mass of humanity. Uranga insists, after all, that he *does not* seek to address humanity in general, which is a generality he has no right to presume; he demands that his readers understand that "the matter concerns them" in their particularity, as individuals, in their concrete, temporal, facticity. It is *their* urgency to assume. Following Kierkegaard, Uranga adopts a maxim from Horace, "*tua res agitur*," explaining that "it is about something that concerns each one of us, not to an anonymous and social mass" (78).[13]

There is a lot in play in the final section (Part IV) of *Analysis*. While the style and tone of the writing betray a "genuinely" philosophical project (the writing is poetic, its tone somewhat distractingly mimicking the poetry being analyzed), what we get is philosophical intervention into Mexican poetry that reveals the accidental being of the Mexican person in its obvious familiarity. Ultimately, what poetry reveals is a being in "zozobra" and "nepantla"—uniquely singular terms in Mexican philosophy.

Nepantla and Zozobra

The second definition of "accident," according to Uranga's schematization in the "Philosophy" section (subsection 2.9–10), is that the accident is "oscillation between being and nothingness" (30). The "oscillation" that formally belongs to the accident, Uranga will also call "nepantla" and, after Velarde, "zozobra" (the subtle differences between these terms are further considered in "Key Concepts," Chapter 3).

The concept of "nepantla" is mentioned only twice in the main text of *Analysis*, yet it is arguably the most significant "ontological" concept in Uranga's philosophical arsenal. The concept first appears in the second of the epigraphs that open up the study. We see there that "nepantla" is a Nahuatl term that refers to a being "in-between" two possibilities of existence; it is akin to a hovering over two world spaces, over two distinct modalities of being, but being committed to neither.

It reappears in this final part of the *Analysis* only to set the stage for another significant operative term in Uranga's philosophy, "zozobra."

Uranga defines "nepantla" as follows:

> The mode of being of the Mexican is oscillatory and pendular, moving from one extreme to the other, making simultaneous two instances while never sacrificing one for the sake of the other. The Mexican character does not install itself over—for lack of a better term—two agencies, but between [*entre*] them. The Nahuatl term "*nepantla*" captures this phenomenon perfectly; it means "in between," in the middle, in the center. We thus have before us, in all its purity, the central category of our ontology, autochthonous, one that does not borrow from the Western tradition, satisfying our desire to be originalists. (81)

Although this definition falls in line with the second definition of accident previously mentioned, it is meant to be more than that; it is meant to capture the *being* of the accident, its "in-betweenness," its lack of ground or substance. As "the central category of [Mexican] ontology," nepantla defies the Western tradition by insisting on transition, movement, and suspension as possible foundations for being itself. It is, ultimately, the state of being *uninstalled*, ungrounded, and unfinished ("in the middle" referring, in this way, to being between points, to transition).

As in the epigraph that opens the text, nepantla appears as suspension or as the "being in between" a transitional movement (from the ancient to the modern, the pre-Hispanic to the Hispanic, the pagan to the Christian). Nepantla, however, is devoid of emotional content; it is simply an original or originary state of being. On the other hand, zozobra captures nepantla *plus* the emotionality of existence. Uranga borrows the concept of zozobra from Velarde, and it is meant to designate the dynamic, becoming structure of a being that is emotionally conflicted in regard to bringing about, or "making simultaneous," one's existential possibilities (as limited as these may be).

Together, nepantla and zozobra ontologically characterize the being of an accidental being. Both are ontological designations of Mexican life, and both are formal schemas of Mexican being. Their difference, simply put, rests in the way that they are lived through. While the former can be described as a categorical in-betweenness, or a permanent transition without destination or point of origin, the latter is an active searching for its end points, an emotive and frustrating searching; the former is resignation in an ontological purgatory, the latter is resistance and suffering; finally, the former is oscillation over an abyss of being, while the latter oscillates over sentimentality and emotive fulness. Uranga calls zozobra "an emotive to and fro":

> Zozobra finds itself suspended in a sentimental limbo, or to put it differently, it does not oscillate inside an obscure and simple space, but rather, the space is colored, or painted, with a sentimental atmosphere. That is why we have said that more than a movement of will, zozobra is an emotive to and fro, it is sentimental. (88)

Uranga's characterization of nepantla and zozobra is one where time, or temporality, is key. Both are movements or transitions, both point to characteristics of beings that are in the process of becoming, of creatures in the process of a perpetual figuring things out. Moreover, both are thought as *formal structures* of that being-becoming, although nepantla's structure is abstract and filled only with uncertainty and in-betweenness, while zozobra's is saturated or "colored" with a "sentimental atmosphere."

Zozobra, Existential and Ontological

The sentimental coloring of zozobra would have us believe that zozobra is just an emotion, like dread, anxiety, or fear (terms in existential philosophy commonly used to translate zozobra). However, since zozobra and nepantla share a similar structure, Uranga wants to say that zozobra is much more than mere anxiety, for example. Anxiety, it turns out, is one of various ways in which zozobra can manifest itself; in other words, anxiety, dread, fear, and melancholy are *contents* of zozobra *as structure*.

Uranga makes this clear, affirming that zozobra is a schema of being as accident that can be filled up with emotive content original to the experience of Mexican being: "The content within which our being oscillates is, suddenly, indifferent in regard to its matter; there is, for its part, nothing that would invalidate the form that binds it together" (81). That is, zozobra has *form* and this form, or schema, has content. Uranga continues: "What must be kept in mind as decisive is not, I insist, the content, but the schema, one that we preliminarily refer to as logical, pendular, oscillating, and zigzagging. In a word: zozobra" (83).

Zozobra can thus be understood in an *existential sense* (manifested as anxiety, indecisiveness, or melancholy) and in an *ontological sense* (its pendular, logical, or oscillating schema or form). This ontological sense is suggested in passages like the following:

> The coming together of a heterogeneous series is randomness; zozobra is nothing else but the naked skeleton of that universal to and fro that allows creatures of all kinds to communicate one with the other. (86)

In this sense, zozobra points to the very being of beings in general. Thus, Uranga calls it a "universal" movement, one that, moreover, escapes dialectical or formal logic.

According to Uranga, zozobra in this ontological sense has its very own logic; he calls it "the logic of oscillation."

> What we say about the logic of oscillation corresponds to what we may say about zozobra. This peculiar ontological movement that is zozobra does not correspond either to a linear formal logic or to spiral dialectical logic. Contradictory terms exclude themselves in a formal logic, and in order to construct an image of a justifiable character, one must reject one of the terms in order to preserve the other. In a dialectic, both extremes are overcome and are synthesized so as to give birth to a third moment that will absorb the contraries, sublimating them perfectly in a new term. (82)

Zozobra is thus not compatible with Eurocentric logic; it conforms neither to the linearity of the syllogism (simply: if A is B, and B is C, therefore, A is C) nor to the law of excluded middle (simply: a proposition cannot be both true and false at the same time) nor to dialectical logic (simply: X, the negation of X, the negation of the negation of X, which is a new X). Zozobra's logic is the logic of randomness and accident, refusing form and linearity, dialectic and synthesis, taking the form of *perhaps, certainly, never, always, yes or no, and yes and no* (P *and* not-P). Uranga describes this logic as an accumulation and a "not letting go" of extremes:

> In contrast, zozobra is a "not knowing what to depend on," or what is the same; it is to simultaneously depend on both extremes, to accumulate, to not let go [*no soltar presa*], to hold on to both ends of the chain. The incessant rocking to and fro, the coming and going, has no end; we could say with López Velarde (who will always have the last word in our ontology) that "our lives are pendulums." (82)

Ultimately, this "rocking to and fro, the coming and going" of zozobra characterizes the transitional, that is, the temporal structure of being as accident. If our "lives are pendulums," then the struggle, the transit, and the oscillation are constant and random according to their temporal and inconsistent logic.

The remainder of "Poetry" is dedicated to an examination of Velarde's poetic works that will reveal more about the ontological structure of zozobra as constitutive of the accidental being of Mexicans but, more importantly for the transformative project, as foundational to genuine human intersubjectivity.

Returning to existential zozobra, we see zozobra manifested as anxiety, resentment, inferiority, melancholy, or other behaviors/attitudes that accentuate themselves in certain communities of people. This "content" will be different in different times and cultures. Despite the content, however, zozobra, as an ontological schema/form, stays the same.

In Uranga's reading of López Velarde, existential zozobra as it relates to the being of the Mexican is most clearly revealed in the poem, "The Weaver." In that poem, Velarde proposes melancholy, randomness, and guilt as expressions (i.e., the content of the schema) of zozobra (84–7). "The Weaver" speaks of a woman weaving an intricate fabric without a prefabricatred pattern before her; she weaves the pattern as she goes, randomly arranging threads and satisfying no prearranged plan as to how the final product is supposed to look. The final product betrays the randomness of its construction.

Uranga *reads into* this poem, suggesting that the "weaving" of the weaver symbolizes the accidental and contingent logic of zozobra as lived through (or expressed) in the being of Mexican life. Randomness and chance appear as gifts of a God that haphazardly sets His universe in motion and, once in motion, abandons it to accidentality. However, randomness itself finds a way. Rather than resulting in chaos and disintegration, zozobra and accidentality converge in the harmony of a pattern. Although it seems as if all is randomness, human beings nonetheless communicate, socialize, and form communities. The possibility for such coalescence is made possible by zozobra itself as ontological and existential.

> The thread of life that in its zigzagging movement weaves opens the wound. The thread is not spun by a providential hand, or a logical one, but an adventurous and random hand. The weaver is not the omniscient predictor of effects and causes, but is the abandoned inspiration of accidentality. ... Randomness [*el azar*] is, in essence, what is hybrid, the pairing of incompatible kinds, of contradictory kinds. ... As in the Epicurean universe, the vertical fall of atoms have to endure an inflexion so that their encounter comes about; this clinamen, this breeze that twists but communicates, is the home of randomness; it is the crooked furrow that in a sudden crisscross brings together the heterogeneous, connecting the specific and particular in a rigid definition. (85–6)

Lives in zozobra will eventually converge with one another, just as in an Epicurean universe "the vertical fall of atoms" eventually encounters itself so as to form matter. This convergence is community and togetherness, a space of communicative action and dialogue, a space for the sharing of individual zozobra. Although "incompatible" and "contradictory," individuals will recognize their own zozobra in one another; they will recognize that they belong to a similar suffering, just as individual threads belong together in the pattern randomly created by the "adventurous" weaver. Consequently, Uranga suggests, zozobra makes intersubjectivity possible, since it is "nothing else but the naked skeleton of that universal to and fro that allows creatures of all kinds to communicate one with the other (86).

We thus imagine a community of persons of different backgrounds brought together by historical accident and random circumstances; their togetherness is accidental, it lacks predetermination, a fixed direction, or a purpose. As defined by their encounter, they are beings without essence or substance, but they commune through their ontological zozobra, through that "universal skeleton that allows creatures of all kinds to communicate," sharing the content of their existential zozobra as they communicate, for example, sharing their suffering and their anxieties.

We note that the way the schema is filled, the way this universal to and fro is manifest, will be different in different communities and with different historical experiences. But the fact that this schema is universal means that it is already shared, it is already (pre-theoretically) familiar despite the particularities of the sentimentality expressed, and can thus serve as the point of departure for any type of intersubjective interchange, cooperation, sympathy, caring, or creating.

Like accidentality, zozobra is thus a project of existence, a "having to be zozobra." Taken to its limit, however, the project that calls us to "forge our character as zozobra" takes us to the *end of ourselves*, to the non-I, outside of our solitude and to community.

> To forge our character as zozobra is a call to randomness, to chance, it is an invocation or incitation. ... To submerge oneself in originary zozobra *seems to be* a movement that brings us closer to darkness, toward the annulment of consciousness. But, at the extreme point when we are about to give ourselves over to twilight, our wakefulness

shines, a subtle antenna readies to receive the message. (p. 87; emphasis added)

To submerge oneself in zozobra is to surrender to indeterminacy, to unsettledness, and to the ignorance of not knowing what to depend on. This is why Uranga suggests that this submersion in "originary zozobra" "seems" like *death*, like twilight, or the "annulment of consciousness." At the moment before death, however, the annulment of consciousness is suspended in the interaction with other consciousnesses, with other beings in zozobra. In other words, a submersion in zozobra makes possible a reaching out from the self to other selves or, what is the same, of listening to others in zozobra who reach out to me.

Community and Love

It is not enough for community building to communicate our suffering (our existential zozobra) on the basis of a common ontological ground (ontological zozobra). Something more grounding, more profound, than zozobra, nepantla, accidentality, or insufficiency is required in order for different solitary subjectivities to converge: this is *love*.

> In truth, the situation clears up if we look at the movement of the weaver, which seeks to bring about the synthesis of different consciousnesses, or that seeks to bring about intersubjectivity: the getting out of insular consciousness and arriving at communal consciousness. This is the end of the movement, when randomness no longer captures our attention ... we are aware of this movement from the solitary to the popular, from the individual to the collective. According to López Velarde, this power of extroversion and communication is love. (87)

Accidentality, randomness, zozobra, or nepantla are lived through in the sanctity of our subjectivity, and so they do not tend outward—they keep us in ourselves. So, how does love accomplish what these essentially cannot? The simple answer is that in love we are lured out of ourselves, invited out of solitude, an exposure that delays the "annulment of consciousness" by awakening us to the consciousness of others. In this capacity, love transcends contingency and the lure of insular consciousness (i.e., of an ego trapped by zozobra in the darkness of itself) and makes possible an intersubjective pairing that *appears* necessary or predetermined, even if this pairing or coming together is in truth merely random and accidental, just as the seemingly purposeful pattern that emerges from a weaver's random weaving.

Although "universal" like zozobra love, however, is not frantic or chaotic, it is not a not-knowing-what-to-depend-on. The logic of oscillation is still in play, but love makes it so that those ruled by this logic, that is, by zozobra, may be able to exhaust their being in meaningful and selfless acts. Uranga agrees with the poets that to be in solitude is a waste of being: "The interrupted operation of intersubjectivity [is] a squandering of being, [it is] decay" (92). The preservation of being, which here just means living one's life free of oppression (e.g., from inferiority complexes), marginalization (e.g., from arrogant substantiality), or self-sabotage and bad faith (e.g., from the lure of waiting to be saved by Europeans or North Americans) is only possible in community and solidarity with others. When in solitude, in selfish insularity, "being itself escapes ... it slips through one's fingers" (92) as one tries to fulfill a borrowed vision of what one should be. Community preserves being by affirming our own vision and assuring that this vision is enough.

> Solitude puts us in the presence of the decay of our within, of our irreparable un-being [*deserse*]. One of the most criminal disfigurement we can think of is one that invites us to remain in our solitude with the hope of coming into contact with a firm foundation, or of coming to possess an imperishable flow. But solitude is not a means for the preservation of being, but, rather, is a way to perdition. Only community "assures"; only community affirms. (93)

The affirmations and assurances of community are what Velarde means by "homeland," which is the point of convergence, the home, the familiar destination of beings whose being is homelessness, transition, temporality, or, as Uranga puts it, nepantla and zozobra. Community is the homeland as the ontological space of convergence, where random strings will be woven into a pattern. It is the ontological space where the affirmations and assurances of love offer respite from the incessant to and fro of zozobra and the indeterminacy of nepantla. Lacking a home, lacking community, the lack of being that defines beings in zozobra becomes nothingness. Zozobra needs love; otherwise it exhausts being: "The process of squandering being is a result of the dizzying pendular movement of zozobra. In this case, zozobra operates as a true bleeding, as a hemorrhage" (93). One stops the ontological hemorrhaging by sharing one's existential suffering in acts of love.

The Imperative

As it concludes, *Analysis* comes full circle. At the beginning, Uranga's hope was that an investigation into the ontology of Mexican being would make possible "moral, social, and religious transformations" in that being (10). As we approach the final pages, he is confident that he has clarified this being sufficiently enough to affect those transformations.

The transformation begins, first, with a return to what is most familiar, namely, the Mexican circumstance in its everydayness, where an essential difference is intimated (made known via *corazonadas*): Mexican being is insufficient, accidental, zozobrante and is always already nepantla. Uranga envisions these insights into the being of Mexican being as pragmatically valuable for the sake of the transformative project, one that involves accepting, affirming, and appropriating the truth of being human as an existential imperative. "In confronting our manner of being we cannot escape the imperative to assume ourselves as we are" (97).

In a moment of prescription (the descriptive project presumably complete), Uranga lays out the elements necessary in order "assume ourselves as we are":

> This means, *first*, that we should not be ashamed of ourselves, *second*, that we should not allow ourselves to feel marginalized and negated, and *third*, that we should avoid the blind man's stick that in the darkness seeks to destroy our character and "change" us. (97)

Uranga articulates this apparently moral imperative in the negative, as a "should not." Mirroring this "should not," however, is a positive "should," which we can schematize in the following way:

(first) *demand recognition* (moral transformation)
(second) *take a stand against your own oppression* (political/social transformation)
(third) *protect your difference* (political/social/religious transformations)

Thus, from the intimation of lack and contingency one generates the resources necessary (1) to take a stand on one's subjectivity, (2) to demand recognition, and (3) to fight against erasure. This is Uranga's imperative for Mexican being.

The Catastrophic

Ultimately, if change is required, Mexicans themselves must bring it about through self-critique, analysis, and philosophy. In this way, they will serve as an example for other peoples, in other times, who struggle or may struggle in similar ways. In the end, the Mexican experience, the characteristics of Mexican being, and the imperatives for transformation will transcend the Mexican people, as they will ring familiar to others whose lives are, Uranga says, "framed by the catastrophic":

> The image of man that will emerge here will not be original, but it will be originary, which means that in it one will be able to recognize those others that through a thousand accidents of history, of culture or society, have been framed by the catastrophic. But this "morbidity" and this "catastrophism" are only negative if one's focus is squarely on consecrating their contraries as positive. Originality would consist in being incommunicable, in defining only the particular, the irredeemable. Character as zozobra is not an enclosed pool, but an open channel. (99)

History, and its accidents, frame "the catastrophic." "Catastrophism" is a type of historical being that is not isolated (original) to Mexico, but which has been experienced by colonized peoples for centuries (it is communicable). Mexicans have dealt with the catastrophic by recognizing their accidentality, insufficiency, zozobra, and nepantla and by making this recognition the basis of a transformative project.

Because these catastrophic peoples are also constituted by zozobra, by a "permanent crisis," it is then easy to teach them the transformative project and communicate the required imperative."[14]

> Our character contributes a permanent crisis that will never be normal. Our normality is our crisis, not that which is transitory. People from other cultures that contemplate us exhaust themselves in explaining how it is that we have survived all these centuries, or to put it more crudely, how we have "progressed" and how we continue to "progress." We have a lesson to teach, we owe the world a lesson of a vital crisis, one that is virile, that is brave. And on this sense of what is radically human, we must construct our humanism. (99)

The Value of Philosophy

The final two paragraphs of *Analysis* seem out of place. In fact, they serve as a postscript to Uranga's philosophy, an addendum that points to (1) Uranga's views on the value of poetry for philosophy and (2) his appropriation of phenomenology. The penultimate paragraph (100) can be broken down into three moments:

1.1 The first, that poetry is capable of breaking through the sedimentations and ideologies that language nurtures so as to get us to the truth of the matter. It is language, or the ideologies and metanarratives that it expresses, that keep Mexicans in the dark about their own reality. He writes that "our language," which "has sought to speak about the character of the Mexican person … confuses us and alienate us."

1.2 The second, that philosophy needs to be inclusive not exclusive, especially of poetry if the task is to successfully arrive at the true being of things. The divorce between poetry and philosophy has been to the detriment of philosophers, who "in their insistence to exclude [the poets], did not grant them any rights," leading to a blindness in the pursuit of being. The suggestion here is that to truly get at the truth, philosophy itself needs to be open and inclusive of diverse points of view.

1.3 And, the third, that *Analysis* has achieved a broadening of philosophy to include the poetic voice. *Analysis* has shown that it has "heeded the voice of the poets" and arrived at a picture of Mexican being that philosophy alone could not paint. A poetic philosophizing thus liberates philosophy from its enclosures and grants access to regions heretofore unexmplored. "Freeing the Mexican from speaking in that manner has not been an easy task; today, however, we can speak of that task as realized."

These three moments highlight what Uranga thinks is the uniqueness and value of his philosophical project in general and Mexican philosophy in particular. Unlike "Western" philosophy as traditionally understood, *this* philosophy is open to what is beyond reason (*corazonadas*) or logic (poetry, zozobra) and, as a result of returning to the familiar and intimate, ends by being liberating and transformative.

The final paragraph adds to the anti-colonial impetus that Uranga carries out with his critique of Eurocentric, "arrogant," reason. Not only is poetry allowed to speak ontology, but phenomenology is allowed to speak *without* purity and in an "unhealthy" way. In a final break with the Western philosophical tradition, Uranga reiterates his commitment to a phenomenological method that attends to the particularity of Mexican being, disregarding a search for generalized, eternal, essences or the dictates of the tradition itself.

> Much has been said lately regarding our eidetic attitude, regarding our "unhealthy" insistence to contemplate the essence of our character. Phenomenology itself has been unjustly reduced to an investigation of essences and it has been forgotten that it is radically something else, a something else that can be described as an advance toward the nutritive and originary roots of our character and not toward fixing

a limiting and particular structure. This level of depth has been our principal preoccupation and our earliest writings on these themes testify to this commitment. (100)

And with this, *Analysis* ends with a final, decolonizing and distancing, postscript or "note"; the final sentence reads: "Let this important clarification [about phenomenology] remain here simply as a note." Uranga believes himself to have accomplished, or "realized," what had not been accomplished before: namely, capture the ontological "roots of [the Mexican] character" in a philosophical analysis that simultaneously identifies a Mexican uniqueness (a life in intimate familiarity with accidentality, insufficiency, zozobra, and nepantla) and reveals the possibility that this uniqueness is what is most truly human. That is, the characteristic that defines Mexicans in their Mexicanness is also that which defines humans in their humanity. But since we are prohibited by our methodological limitations to speak about humanity in general, we are forced to claim that those revealed truths that capture Mexican existence are truths that other human communities, with different histories and different catastrophes, may share and, ultimately, build upon.

3

Key Concepts

The following is a list of key *thematic* concepts[1] operative in Uranga's *Analysis of Mexican Being*. By no means is this list exhaustive, nor are my efforts to define or explain said concepts. The definitions, or explanations, I offer here are preliminary (in some cases, brief) yet, I believe, sufficient for a richer and more informed reading of the text.

Accidentality

Accidentality is the most significant thematic concept in Uranga's existential ontology. Uranga insists upon it as the defining characteristic of Mexican being, but also as the defining characteristic of temporal, nonessential, and non-substantial beings more generally. Broadly speaking, accidentality refers to beings whose relationship to substance is one of lack, contingency, or dependence. As he puts it: "The accident is a *minus* of being, a being reduced or 'fragmented' due to its mixture with nothingness, a mixture in which being and nothingness communicate" (emphasis in original) (17). According to this definition, Mexican being is accidental due to an ontological *insufficiency* in relation to European humanity, as well as the fragmentation, and mixture (*mestizaje*), of its being by history itself (a history of conquest, colonization, and Eurocentric reason). However, it is its accidentality as a constitutive characteristic that allows Mexican being to claim its value and humanity. Uranga thus confidently asserts that "the being of the human being as ontologically accidental is the most important affirmation we make in *Analysis*" (18).

In virtue of Uranga's definition, we can understand accidentality in a metaphysical, historical, and ontological sense. Metaphysically, to say that a being is accidental is to say that its being is to be an accident or property of substance. It is to say that the being that is a property or an accident *lacks* being, is not substantial in and of itself, or, put differently, its existence is defined by its relation to that which lends it its basic reality, to that which completes it as the thing that it is. In the case of the Mexican person, her *being Mexican* depends on a relation to the Spanish or the Indigenous, which lends her reality *as* Mexican. This points also to the historical sense of accidentality, which refers to being a by-product of an accidental encounter between uniquely distinct worlds and cultures. According to *Analysis*, the Mexican is an accidental, or unnecessary or unessential, by-product of the confrontation between historical peoples that already existed in the fullness of their being. However, because she is merely a property or an accident that resulted from that confrontation, her existence, or her being, lacks fullness and reality; when she looks within, she finds fragments of the two worlds, sprinkled in the mixture (in her *mestizaje*), as insufficient representations of a substantial otherness. Ultimately, this makes possible the complex of inferiority that plagues the Mexican psyche, making possible an ever-frustrated desire to be European or Indigenous and the failure to be either.

Ontologically, "accidentality" (*accidentalidad*) refers to the way of being of an insufficient being, which is a way of being for another or a way of being subservient to or dependent on something of greater being than itself. In the history of philosophy, Uranga follows Leibniz in this characterization, who proposes that "an accident ... is a being whose notion does not include everything that can be attributed to the subject to which the notion is attributed."[2]

These three senses of accidentality converge into an interpretation of Mexican being as unessential to substantial cultures, histories, and peoples and, as such, as essentially lacking in being and foundation, as by-products of European conquest and colonization, and as fragments of an Indigenous past no longer recoverable. As by-products and fragments, Mexican existence shows itself as incomplete and dependent, determined always, on the one hand, by a perpetual distance to and a desire for intimacy with the Spaniard, who represents European totality, permanence, and universality, and, on the other hand, to the "Indio," who represents cultural purity and original history. In relation to these, the Mexican is a *mestizo*, that is, a contamination of purity—a mixture, inessential and unnecessary.

Accidentality, however, proves to be more than a phenomenological description of Mexican being. It is also *a project of existence*. This is due to the fact that in accidentality Mexicans exist vulnerably, as perpetually threatened by erasure or extermination.

> The accident is fragility: oscillation between being and nothingness. ... The accident is constantly threatened by displacement. Implanted in being, it can always be uprooted from its "there," that is, exterminated. Whatever it holds on to, whatever handle it grabs on to, can be removed. It was born to be in and at the same time to not be in. (30)

The threat of extermination is tied to the nonessential being of the being as accident. If, in contrast to substance, the accident is as "a *minus* of being" (emphasis in original), then its erasure is likewise a matter of accident. Not only this, but the history of philosophy itself has endowed substance with a "greater rank'" than accident and relegated accident to "an entity of 'lower class'" (18), an interpretation that can be transferred to the social realm, whereby people considered accidents are "naturally" subject to social and political marginalization or deprived of socioeconomic status. To this threat of erasure and marginalization the accident must respond in a project of affirmation that denies the privilege (and reality) of "arrogant substantiality" and affirms the phenomenological and ontological truth of accident,[3] namely, that it is *not* nothing, but always something and, as something, valuable. Uranga writes, "If the accident is nothing before substance, it is something in relation with nothingness" (18).

The project of "having to be accident" is a project of resistance, subversion, or transformation (19). This having to be accident involves an appropriation of one's ontological condition, which involves the recognition (in the form of a conscious repetition) of accidentality, which is the only authentic *way to be*. Uranga says,

> To realize oneself as accident means that one must maintain oneself as accident, on the horizon of possibility of the accident itself. Inauthenticity would be to flee the condition of accidentality and to substantialize oneself; the Mexican person falls into this temptation almost by necessity when her originary constitution is "too much to bear." (19–20)

To "maintain oneself as accident" is to willingly submit oneself to the precariousness of life, to face one's contingency without fleeing into substantializing metanarratives or, what Manuel Vargas has most recently called, prearranged "normative packages."[4] Uranga writes:

> We are talking here about a being that has to accidentalize itself, that has to place itself in a situation of a radical "not knowing what to depend on" insecurity, and unpredictability. Every "existential" or "characteristic" of the being of the human being is located beneath the inevitable formality of being accidental. (20)

In this way "having to be an accident" is a "project to be realized" (19), one where accident understands substance as a delusion of permanence and security while the unstable, the random, the precarious is kept plainly within view.

Although Uranga applies the metaphysical, historical, and ontological conceptions of accidentality to Mexican being, he also characterizes the being of the human being in general. However, Uranga believes, history has reserved the everyday *intimation* of accidentality to Mexicans in particular, an intimation that in its immediacy opposes the Eurocentric narrative of substantiality, where those that are accidental are subject to erasure and extermination.

Auscultation

Uranga abandoned the study of medicine in order to pursue philosophy under the critical eye of José Gaos. It is no surprise, then, that he believes his analysis of Mexican being to be a kind of "auscultation." Auscultation is a medical term that refers to the act of carefully listening to the internal processes of the human body, for those internal movements that signal its health or its disease (in existential terms, its *dis-ease*). In Uranga's analytic, the auscultation reveals the being of the Mexican in its temporality as unessential and without foundations (it is accidental), as constituted by an essential internal conflict (it is a being in nepantla and zozobra), and, in its accidental and historical becoming, as a "minus of being" (it is insufficient). While the term itself appears only once in the text, it is, in fact, one of the names Uranga gives to his project:

> Our character, that structure of our being that history has bestowed upon us, has been "executed" from the impressive depths of ontological auscultation. It has been revealed to us as permanently fatalistic, in a dangerous communication with limit situations, and from this unending dialogue with the physiological and foundational aspects of human being there has emerges a *mode of being* on which we find an original layer of being that has been informed by everything, that absorbs everything—this is its most characteristic symbol. (italics in original)

Autognosis

Uranga seeks to distinguish his *ontology* from autognosis. The term "autognosis" means "self-knowledge" or "knowledge of one's self," from the Greek *auto*, self, and *gnosis*, knowledge. Uranga uses the term as both a verb and a noun—as a process and as what is achieved in the process, so that, so to speak, through an autognosis we may achieve an autognosis. As a process, however, it is a process of self-discovery that stays at a superficial level of investigation. Thus, "autognosis can and must be, with equal right, philosophical and non-philosophical knowledge. In contrast, ontology designates philosophical knowledge *par excellence*" (italics in original) (63).

Corazonadas (Intimations)

In the context of *Analysis* we can distinguish a unique epistemological commitment that goes against the grain of standard theories of knowledge. While referred only a handful of times in *Analysis*, the epistemological commitment is clearly operative in the auscultation of Mexican being. This is a commitment to what Uranga calls "corazonadas." In philosophical terms, corazonadas are an *affective source of immediate epistemic justification and truth*. I translate corazonadas as "intimations" (16, 33, 80, 86).

At its root, the Spanish term "corazonada" derives from the word "corazon," meaning "heart." This suggests that the heart, and not the mind, is the operative epistemological mechanism. The Spanish word itself is technically identified with "presentiment," "foreboding," and "a certain interior movement that foretells that something will happen."[5] We could thus define it in English in the same way as presentiment, "hunch," "forewarning," or "premonition." However, both in English and in Spanish, the suggestion is that a corazonada (for instance, as foreboding or forewarning) is tied up with "suspicion," fear, or some kind of knowledge of *things to come*. But Uranga wants it to have a specific technical meaning that is not strictly tied to negative feelings of anticipation toward, or arising from, what is to come, or the future. He writes:

> There are analyses that do not appear ontological, but that when looked at more closely show themselves almost immediately as direct "translations" of lived experiences, [we can call them] ontological "intimations"

["'corazonadas' ontológicas"]. This is the case with poetry. Being speaks through the poet in its own language ... in an almost pure form. (16; italics in the original)

The poet's access to being is not one of foreboding or presentiments. It is not restricted to *anticipations*, but is broader and more encompassing. In this context, a "corazonada" is an immediate affective encounter with one's "lived experience" in "pure form." It is an immediate access to *being* itself.

In a strictly *philosophical* sense, the term could be translated as "intuition"—which is one of the dictionary definitions given for corazonada. However, Uranga implicitly discourages this translation, since he says that intuition, when previously employed in the history of philosophy, is a "confusing concept" (16).[6] In order to heed Uranga's reluctance, I have thus translated corazonada as "intimation," a term that preserves Uranga's insistence that the sort of knowledge gained is not strictly cognitive, but includes the entirety of the "lived experience," which involves, among other things, "instinct and thought" and an "intimate familiarity" with the circumstance under consideration. Intimation retains, I believe, its character of being grounded on the heart.

In *Analysis*, Uranga seeks to grasp Mexican being in an adequate and all-encompassing way. For this purpose, he commits himself to the phenomenological imperative to allow the things to speak for themselves. Because the being of anything at all will always overflow our human abilities to conceptually grasp it (being will always overflow the concept), Uranga seeks to expand the field of comprehension to include that which is given in affective interaction (love, feeling, emotive intuitions) with that being.

> Before arriving at [the being of the Mexican], we are completely at a loss, and it seems that when we have gotten close to a shadow or region of the appropriate horizon, we have done so only by "intimation" ["*corazonada*"]. But now we are in the right context from which the "things themselves" can speak. (33)

Hence, a corazonada, or an intimation, is what gets us closer to the being of the Mexican *before* the intervention of concepts. Moreover, the proper context, or "appropriate horizon," has been arrived at in "intimations," in pre-theoretical "translations" of the lived experience of Mexican persons given nonconceptually. In this sense, intimations are akin to nonconceptual recognitions of our most unique human characteristics, viz., accidentality, zozobra, nepantla, and insufficiency.

Corazonadas grant access to the mysteries of (Mexican) being; they are immediate graspings that reveal the secrets of a situated existence. The upside of corazonadas as sources of truth, moreover, is that the emotional *habitat* or circumstance is as significant as the material habitat or circumstance, so that those *modes of being a Mexican* are given immediately to anyone who can invest, or inhabit, or dwell in the Mexican circumstance.

Insufficiency

Uranga conceives the notion of "insufficiency" in three senses: the first is metaphysical—insufficiency refers to a lack of substance; the second, historical—insufficiency refers to a lack of history or culture; and the third, ontological—insufficiency refers to a lack of being. He uses these three senses to refer to Mexican persons as lacking the same substance claimed by "arrogant" European reason, as historical by-products of European conquest and colonization, and as human beings that in their temporal becoming always already lack substantial fullness.

It is this multidimensional sense of insufficiency that Uranga deploys against Samuel Ramos's seemingly superficial autognosis of Mexican persons as burdened by a constitutive inferiority complex. Whereas "inferiority" refers to a demeaning self-conception grounded on feelings of powerlessness, inadequacy, or subordination before others, seen and felt as representing power, substance, totality, or superiority, insufficiency refers to human existence itself, specifically to that state of being belonging to human beings that is temporal and contingent, which is a minus of being or accidental before being. That is, ontologically speaking, human beings, in a general sense, are never fully sufficient in themselves, existing always in a state of dependence, unfulfillment, and incompleteness. In traditional philosophical language, whereas substance is sufficient in and of itself, human beings are non-substantial and, in their accidental being, always being for others (18).

> Insufficiency, ontologically speaking, determines the accident in relation to substance. Every modality of being grounded on accident is characterized by a lack of ground, grounded on a shifting and fractured base. (17)

On such grounds, Uranga rejects the idea that Mexicans can be defined by a superficial psychological complex that sets a *feeling* of inferiority as the constitutive feature of their character. Instead, he argues, from a philosophical point of view, Mexicans are not inferior in the sense that they are empirically less than other peoples; rather, their feeling of inferiority is only the outward manifestation of a deeper, yet entirely human, existential or ontological condition of unsettledness and lack.

Generally speaking, the underlying claim of Uranga's *Analysis* is that *our* natural human condition is that of insufficiency and not of substance. The suggestion is that the possibility of being substantial characterizes a philosophical delusion perpetrated by European colonizers to justify a dehumanizing agenda. Mexicans, in historically coming to know themselves as insufficient and insubstantial, are thus closer to a truth that says that human beings in general, as temporal beings, are accidental, groundless, defined by absence and impermanence.

Nepantla

Nepantla refers to being "in between," being "in the middle," or being "neutral." Nepantla is the "in between" temporalities, worlds, processes; it is being "in the middle," as in "on the way," in transit from one place to another, or "in the middle," as in "in the midst of" a crisis or a paradigm shift; it is "neutral," as in noncommittal, that is, suspending judgment or action regarding one's obligations, loyalties, or commitments.

According to Uranga, nepantla describes Mexican being in its in-betweenness, namely, in its perpetual in-between the Indigenous and Spanish worlds. Nepantla describes Mexican being as "in the middle" of a seemingly endless journey, always in transit, migrating and immigrating always further away from its Indigenous roots and toward a European lifeworld to which it is destined never to fully arrive. Mexican being is nepantla, moreover, in being neutral in response to claims made on its identity by others, on the one hand, or by its own conscience, on the other—in nepantla, that is, Mexican being suspends its allegiances to whatever seeks to define it rigidly as either this or that.

The term "nepantla" appears only twice in the entirety of *Analysis*, yet it is arguably the most significant ontological concept in Uranga's philosophical register. "We thus have before us," he writes, "in all its purity, the central category of our ontology, autochthonous, one that does not borrow from the Western tradition, satisfying our desire to be originalists" (81).

Nepantla is first mentioned by Uranga in the second of the epigraphs that open up *Analysis* (more on my interpretive account of nepantla can be found in Chapter 2). There, Uranga quotes the 16th-century Dominican friar Diego Durán, who records it as a Nahuatl term used by Indigenous people to refer to their being "in between," or "in the middle," of their ancient ways of being (i.e., the Mexica or Aztec way) and a new way of being to which they were being subjected by the Spanish (the European-Christian way). Nepantla was the Mexica way of saying that they were still uncommitted to either.

In his accounts, Durán himself fails to appreciate the significance of nepantla, that is, of the Indigenous attempt to express their sense of in-betweenness or neutrality, condemning it as just another variation of "that abominable excuse" on the part of the "savages" to disobey the mandates of the church. Durán writes: "Incited by the devil … these miserable Indians remain perplexed and neutral regarding matters of faith … they believe in God and at the same time adore still their idols and appeal to their superstitions and ancient rituals, mixing one with the other."[7] In Durán's frustration, however, we note a subtle recognition of the Indigenous people's ontological homelessness, which they express as an *inability* (after all, the devil himself "incites" the resistance of the "miserable Indians") to be at home in the Spanish worldview.

For Durán, nepantla thus refers to a new state of being, a being "in between places" and "in between times." However, it is a state expressed even today by immigrants, exiles, or the displaced, who exist always in transition, in between an origin to which they cannot return and a destination to which they may never arrive, that may never welcome them, forcing them, then, to be "neutral" as to their commitments, "in the middle" as to their loyalties, and "in between" as to their being.

In colonial historiography, the term "nepantla" is first recorded in Alfonso de Molina's *Arte y la lengua Mexicana*, written in 1547. Molina also defines it as meaning "in between" and "among" [*entre*] and likewise attributes it an Indigenous self-understanding, which is one of homelessness and indecisiveness.[8] It is Durán who popularizes it in his *Historia*, written in 1581, as the term used by the Indigenous people to refer to their own (post-conquest) reality of unsettledness, of always being in transition, of being neutral or uncommitted, and of existing in the tiring process of becoming.

In our own time, we can understand nepantla as an ontological category referring to being *out of place* and *out of time*. Take the plight of Mexican Americans as one example. One is out of place in not properly belonging to North American history, on the one hand, or Mexican history, on the other. One is out of time in being historically orphaned by both, a phenomenon that explains an attitude of neutrality toward or abstention from ideals essential to the first, for instance, ideals of American individualism and mass consumption, or essential to the second, for instance, Mexicans ideal of family and community. In Uranga's account, nepantla describes the uncentered center of Mexican being, one that, in its instability and unsettledness, harmonizes with other ontological characteristics that define the Mexican (and, ultimately, all human being) like insufficiency, accidentality, and zozobra. Or, as

James Maffie describes it, it is a "betwixt-and-betweenness ... order-disorder, being-nonbeing, life-death ... tension-ridden, reciprocating balance between being-nonbeing [where] human existence is defined by inescapable processing, becoming, and transformation."[9]

The introduction of the concept of nepantla as an ontological category represents a moment of rupture between Mexican philosophy and the Western tradition, as it is supposed by Uranga to be a category uniquely emergent from the Mexican, mestizo, and colonized, insufficient, and accidental circumstance. In recent times, the term has been appropriated most prominently by the Chicana feminist philosopher Gloria Anzaldúa. As in the work of Durán, Molina, and Uranga, Anzaldúa deploys the term in an effort to characterize the condition of in-betweenness of Latinx and Chicanx peoples in the United States:

> Nepantla, a psychological, liminal space between the way things had been and an unknown future. Nepantla is the space in-between, the locus and sign of transition. In nepantla we realize that realities clash, authority figures of various groups demand contradictory commitments, and we and others have failed living up to idealized goals. ... In nepantla we hang out between shifts, trying to make rational sense of this crisis, seeking solace, support, appeasement, or some kind of intimate connection ... we fall into chaos, fear of the unknown, and are forced to take up the task of self-definition.[10]

As with the Mexican manner of being, as described by Uranga, or the Indigenous manner of being, as described by Durán, Latinx peoples are caught "in the middle" of "contradictory" forms of the human (contradictory commitments to ways of life), a condition of homelessness or suspension ultimately rooted in insufficiency, accidentality, and zozobra (ontological and existential).

Thus, of the thematic and philosophical concepts we find in *Analysis*, nepantla has the most to offer for contemporary social and existential philosophy.

Substance

Understanding that authenticity lies in "accidentalizing oneself" requires seeing the truth of substance, namely, that substance is not something one can be. Substance is, after all, what is independent and entirely in and for itself. Uranga's Aristotelian/Leibnizian understanding of substance, namely, as an autonomous, self-determining, non-relational, totality is obvious. With Leibniz, for example, he thinks of substance as that on which all accidents depend. As Leibniz defines it in his *Discourse on Metaphysics*, "the nature of an individual substance or of a complete being is to have a notion so complete that it is sufficient to contain and to allow us to deduce from it all the predicates of this object to which this notion is attributed."[11]

Uranga's critique of substance (or the narrative of substance) follows that of the French phenomenologist Jean Wahl.[12] According to Wahl, substance is that which "stands under—i.e., under the appearances"; it is "something permanent beneath change," "unity behind the multiplicity," and "also a kind of perfection."[13] Uranga echoes Wahl, claiming that "substance does not imply change of any kind; it places its stability beyond the limits of transformation; it rests in itself, indifferent to all mobility, alteration, or decomposition" (18). Wahl's understanding of substance, however, is destructive, and Uranga's critique of substance reflects this understanding. Wahl argues that the traditional conception of substance as wholly independent is wrong and, turning the tables on the tradition, considers substance to be dependent on accident: "There is substance only in relation to something that is not substance. The idea of substance would have no meaning in the absence of something that differs from substance."[14] Thus, Uranga rejects, what he calls, "arrogant substantiality" (21), or the idea that substance may refuse its own essential relation to that which is particular, different, or, in Uranga's case, Mexican.[15]

The question becomes as to *why* Mexicans have internalized a demeaning and superficial self-interpretation. The simple reason is that consciously or unconsciously, Mexicans have accepted the Eurocentric narrative of substance, where, although substance belongs to God, it can also belong to man—if he is worthy. As accidental, Mexicans have been told by colonizing narratives that they are not worthy; hence, substance is not something to which they can or should aspire. The Eurocentric narrative is articulated by Uranga as follows:

> All, or almost all, of the Western philosophical tradition has thought of being in terms of substance. To be is to be substantial; if one wishes to be genuine, one must refer to substance, since the accident is but a "shadow" of being, a "quasi-being." It is true that the Scholastic tradition proposed that "being" was "transcendental," which means that being "hovers over" [encima] substance and accident. But "Being" itself is considered by this tradition as the "Supreme Entity," more than substantial, super-substantial in virtue of eminence, which allows the Scholastics to say that, in order to grasp it, the concept of substance itself must be extended to its limits; haecceity [la haceidad[16]] is, in this way, "substantial substance," quintessential substance. Man, for his part, figures as a "creature," but also "substantial like his Creator." Everywhere we notice, then, the radical tendency for substantialization on the part of the Western philosophical tradition. Man is on this historical account "being for substance," being that must make itself substance. (18–19)

Uranga thus insists that a feeling of inferiority is merely a manifestation of the internalized belief that one can never become substantial like the Creator, who can be either God or the Spanish colonizer.

In the effort to overturn this ideological self-understanding, Uranga characterizes the being of the Mexican in ontological terms as insufficient in its being as accident. The auscultation of Mexican persons and culture as inferior misinterprets this being as accident as a psychological complex rather than an ontological state. Thus, when Mexicans, in their everyday behavior, show themselves as inferior or inadequate, they are merely living through, in a momentary and temporally determinate way, a mode of their insufficiency and not a permanent psychological condition. Recognizing this, namely, that they are not determined in their humanity as inferior but are simply instantiating an ontological aspect of existence as such, is enough, or sufficient, to overcome the perniciousness of the narrative that pegs an entire culture as inferior without justification. This recognition, moreover, is enough for transformation to begin.

Zozobra

The dictionary definition of "zozobra," which follows its colloquial use, is that zozobra is "uneasiness, anguish, or anxiety."[17] According to this definition, zozobra would describe the state of unease felt upon finding oneself in the brink of war or a in the midst of pandemic, the anguish on learning about the death of a loved one, or the anxiety about one's own impending demise. In this, its colloquial use, zozobra is a *feeling*, and, depending on one's psychological fortitude, one could find oneself gripped by it to the point of paralysis or one could simply ignore it without suffering much of a disturbance. However, Uranga believes that zozobra characterizes being itself in a profound way, which is to say that zozobra characterizes the being of Mexican being foundationally and at all times and never depending on one's emotional resilience. He thus seeks to broaden the definition of zozobra by ontologizing it so that it refers to a state of being and not just a psychic state.

Uranga looks first at its etymology, pointing out in his "Essay on the Ontology of Mexican Being" that *zozobra* derives from the Latin "*sub-supra*" (under-over).[18] *Sub-supra*, or *sots-sobre* in Old Catalan, can refer, literally, to the behavior of a boat in the process of capsizing or, when applied to persons, to that feeling of *drowning* and breathlessness experienced by one who, in the throes of anxiety, hyperventilates, comes in and out of consciousness, etc. Uranga suggests that Mexican being exists in this constant anticipation of drowning, of capsizing, of going over and coming under:

> Zozobra is the state in which we are not sure, if at any moment, a catastrophe will overwhelm us or if we will be secure in the safety of asylum. In zozobra we remain in suspense, in oscillation, as its etymology clearly announces. ... We are at the mercy of whatever may come, we are constitutively fragile. ... We must always know what we can count on, but the belief that we can never know what we can count on constitutes our restlessness or zozobra. (173)

Uranga's "earlier" description of zozobra (from 1951) reminds one of Søren Kierkegaard's characterization of anxiety in *The Concept of Anxiety*. There, Kierkegaard defines "anxiety" as "the dizziness of freedom" triggered by the uncertainty and burden of one's infinite possibilities of existence.[19] In a similar sense, zozobra is the state of being overwhelmed when confronted by multiple (however, not "infinite") possibilities of life (or ways of being). There is in zozobra that sense of desperation that "dizziness" implies, one that points to coming face to face with "the possibility of possibility" that defines anxiety for Kierkegaard.[20] For Uranga, however, this is a desperation or "restlessness" rooted in the sense of *impossibility* before those same possibilities of life, that is, in the sense that none of the possible avenues of existence (which are always finite) are available *to me*. Hence, in zozobra we remain in "suspense," always "in oscillation," since the world itself appears indeterminate, full of unwelcome surprises, threats, and catastrophes. Our fragility is exposed since we never know what we can count on.

With *Analysis*, Uranga moves further away from the Kierkegaardian conception that would conceive zozobra as merely the dizziness of freedom and to a conception found in the poetry of López Velarde, which allows him to define zozobra in a more ontological way, namely, not in terms of absolute freedom but as a "mode of being" sentenced to the perpetual indeterminacy of an indeterminate world. (More, of course, can be said about Uranga's debt to Kierkegaard, but this I leave for others.) Inspired by López Velarde, Uranga defines zozobra in the following way:

Zozobra is a "not knowing what to depend on," or what is the same; it is to simultaneously depend on two extremes, to accumulate, to not let go [*no soltar presa*], to hold on to both ends of the chain. The incessant rocking to and fro, the coming and going, has no end; we could say with López Velarde (who will always have the last word in our ontology) that "our lives are pendulums." (82).

We thus have two slightly distinct conceptions, or variations, of zozobra: *existential* zozobra and *ontological* zozobra. The first, existential zozobra, is anxiety, angst, disquiet, fear, etc. before the unknown, a not knowing what to depend on (this falls in line with the earlies definition). Existential zozobra is inspired by Kierkegaard and closely resembles what Gabriel Marcel called "metaphysical unease," which the latter described as similar to "the bodily state of a man in a fever who will not lie still but keeps shifting around in his bed looking for the right position."[21] In its existential guise, zozobra is that particular unease we carry into our everyday encounters with the world and our own finitude.

Ontological zozobra, on the other hand, is suggested by Velarde when he says that "our lives are pendulums" (this is the definition we find in *Analysis*). If life itself is a pendulum, then zozobra is not a psychic state, but a way of being. Uranga goes on to call zozobra "the bare skeleton" (86) onto which anxiety, angst, disquiet, fear, and unease are added as "matter." It is the *form* or structure of the "incessant rocking to and fro," of a pendular movement, of the "not knowing what to depend on." It is "ontological" because it refers to a characteristic of being and not to a psychological state. Uranga says that zozobra, when ontological in this sense, is a "[universal] schema, one that [is] logical, pendular, oscillating, and zig-zagging" (82). Zozobra as schema, or skeleton, is pure oscillation, permanent zig-zagging, and the constant movement to and fro of our being.

It is in this way that the already insufficient and accidental being of the Mexican is likewise constituted by ontological zozobra. In the everyday being of the Mexican person, this ontological skeleton is filled out by psychic attitudes of sentimentality, melancholy, anxiety, fear, "metaphysical unease," and the paralyzing hesitation of "not knowing" who or what to trust. Mexicans cannot escape their zozobra, as it is grafted onto their being. Mexican life reflects the schema:

> Zozobra refers to a mode of being that incessantly oscillates between two possibilities, between two affects, without knowing on which one of those to depend on, which justifies it, indiscriminately dismissing one extreme in favor of the other. In this to and fro the soul suffers, it feels torn and wounded. The pain of zozobra is *not obviously identifiable* with fear or anxiety, it takes from both in an emotionally ambiguous manner. (95; my emphasis)

We notice here a distancing away from the earlier, Kierkegaardian, reading in Uranga's characterization of zozobra as including within itself both fear and anxiety in an "emotionally ambiguous manner." In other words, ontological zozobra is different than the fear and anxiety that would characterize existential zozobra, and the difference is that ontological zozobra is ontologically neutral regarding the specific emotions one feels as one oscillates from one possibility to another.

Although the possibilities to be fulfilled are not infinite (they are finite, as with existential zozobra), the movement of ontological zozobra nonetheless paralyzes, nails one in place, and, as such, is grounding. But although "this ground is not a fixed and firm foundation, but rather it is unstable quicksand upon which nothing firm can stand" (95), it is a *place* that, although moving, is the site on which existence unfolds. Zozobra is, in this way, groundless and unstable and, as such, the source of our *felt* disquiet, discomfort, and unsettledness. Uranga writes, "To constantly refer to that region in which possibilities face and confront themselves creates a spiritual state that is nothing close to tranquility" (95). Our lives, as pendulums, are unstable and random, reflecting our being as accidents perfectly.

As ontological, zozobra refers to a human condition that Mexicans, through accidents of history, are conditioned to quickly recognize. However, it is also a characteristic of human being. In this way, zozobra connects us with one another across time and space. Uranga thus lends it a constitutive role in the formation of community and sociality. He writes that "in zozobra we find foundational moments in the formation of intersubjectivity, with all of its modalities" (94). It is, thus, not simply and exclusively the idiosyncratic experience of Mexicans. Unlike its existential formulation, which appears to isolate the individual in an existential solitude (thrownness and angst), ontological zozobra makes community possible. It does this by being a kind of permanent internal suffering that we seek to communicate, that we sing about, that we write about, that lends us an external and visible profile. We also recognize it in others, in *their* visible profile. We see their interiority in what they say or in how they behave. As Uranga says, zozobra, in its "emotive to and fro … makes creatures of all kinds communicate one with the other" (86). What is communicated, what fills out the schema, will, of course, be different to different people. However, the *schema*, the form of our experience, will be recognized and will be recognized in others.

Part Two

Translation: *Analysis of Mexican Being*

Emilio Uranga

A TRANSLATION OF *ANÁLISIS DEL SER DEL MEXICANO*
BY CARLOS ALBERTO SÁNCHEZ

For Octavio Paz

My brothers from throughout the ages
recognize in me their own pause,
their own laments and their own furies.

—Ramón López Velarde

As I listened to an Indian tell me of certain things, and in particular that he had dragged himself on the ground picking up money on bad nights and worse days, and once he had, with much effort, collected a certain amount of money he had a wedding and invited the entire town, and as I rebuked him for the evil he had done he answered: "Father, don't be alarmed, since we are still *nepantla* [todavía estamos nepantla]." And while I understood what he meant to say with that vocabulary and that metaphor, which means to be in the middle, I turned and insisted that he tell me what middle it was in which they were. He told me that, since they were not very well rooted in faith, that I shouldn't be alarmed since they were still neutral in the sense that they neither depended on one law or another, or better put, that they believed in God and at the same time relied on their ancient customs and demonic rites [*costumbres antiguas y ritos del demonio*], and this is what he meant with that abominable excuse that they still remained in the middle and were neutral.

—Friar Diego Durán

I. Introduction

1. *Lo mexicano* as Our Culture's Central Theme

A perceptive observer of Mexico's current cultural activities will not fail to notice a remarkable phenomenon: *Mexican culture has taken the Mexican himself as its central theme* [9].[1] *Our culture is Mexican in subject and in object.* Urged on by certain compelling necessities, the intellectual labor of our researchers has focused on the task of analyzing the being of the Mexican (*el ser del mexicano*). Attention to the theme of *lo mexicano*[2] lends an almost perfect unity to every meditation carried out by our intellectuals. This phenomenon must have an explanation; otherwise it will be seen, and regrettably so, as merely an effect of a momentary intellectual fashion that lets go of the theme as soon as another appears, taking it up with equal disinterest and superficiality.

The "Hyperion" group (*el grupo "Hiperión"*) cannot help but rejoice at the attention given to the theme of that which is Mexican (*del mexicano*).[3] The problem of what it means to be Mexican (*lo mexicano*) cannot be said to be merely *contiguous* (*próximo*) with our concerns; to be exact, we must say that this problem *constitutes* us; with it we have arisen and, if it were to fall, we would also fall. We have become so intimately connected to its demands that we cannot avoid feeling that, whenever the theme is approached, we are also intimately and personally approached. But more than acknowledge the appearance of this phenomenon, we must ask ourselves about its motivations, the reasons as to why the theme of what it means to be Mexican (*lo mexicano*) has now come to occupy such a central place in our culture.

This all happens as if our researchers have decided to join a trend begun by the "Hyperion" group. And thus, as it was said three years ago,[4] quite falsely, that the Hyperion group had given itself over to a fad when it took up the theme of existentialism, it now seems that everyone else has given themselves over to a fad, but this one imposed by Hyperion. But just as the study of existentialism was shown at that time not to be just a trend, the same is perhaps the case today and, perhaps, it could now be shown that those for whom Mexico is an object of study (*mexicanistas*) do not allow themselves to be dragged around by whatever is in fashion, but rather that their orientations are always motivated by much deeper currents [10].

The interest in *lo mexicano* has been awakened by the broader movement of consciousness known as historicism. This mode of thinking emphasizes the circumstantialist relations of all thought regardless of how universal it pretends to be. To historicism we owe the ability to limit the pretensions of one particular culture to set itself as the sole model of culture. Every culture has its own values, values that are worthy of study and attention, as are those of that culture that pretends to be the archetype, namely, European culture. In becoming conscious of our particularities, historicism has motivated non-European cultures to interpret their own and most intimate ways of conceiving the world and man (*el mundo y el hombre*).[5] *We have arrived at that historical and cultural age in which we demand to live in accordance with our own being, and from that demand arises the imperative to clarify the morphology and the dynamics of that being.*

But we must not allow ourselves to be seduced by a purely theoretical analysis of the being of the Mexican. As brilliant as that analysis may turn out to be or as much care as one may take in clarifying methodological maneuvers that validate it, it is never enough. Clarifying the mode of being of the Mexican is only a premise—certainly, a necessary premise—in order to bring about a reformation and a conversion. More than a straightforward and rigorous meditation on the being of the Mexican, *what brings us to this kind of study is the project of bringing about moral, social, and religious transformations with that being*. And this is what distinguishes a superficial from a deep and meaningful approach to this theme; we cannot, we must not, be the same before and after we have executed our autognosis.[6] The theme on its own will *save no one*; however, once we have immersed ourselves in it, the task of saving others falls on us. Let us not turn our reflections concerning that which is Mexican into a new form of imitation, as before we imitated Europeans on such matters; rather, let us understand, once and for all, that the analysis of *lo mexicano* imposes upon us a moral task, one of purification and responsibility, a moral task that will not be satisfied with merely allying oneself, at the last minute and conveniently, with what (through the efforts of many) goes by that name [11].

Another reason that explains the notable popularity and priority of our theme is, without a doubt, that it has been taken up by the present generation of young people. The theme of Mexicanness is a generational theme. And we know what it means—as Ortega y Gasset has taught us with all the clarity that this matter requires—for a problem to become a theme for a generation. *The Mexican person about whom we speak is the Mexican of our generation; we speak about the mode of being of the Mexican that lives every day in the existence of the new generation.* In truth, what has happened is that to live the Mexican reality (*lo mexicano*) has been elevated by reflection into a theme about which meditation is aware. But not just any kind of meditation, but meditation of the philosophical kind.

The Mexican person has been analyzing himself almost from the day of his historical birth. We have been a fundamentally introverted people, in the sense that we have tirelessly been searching for ourselves from within. This secular tradition of self-knowledge has allowed a glimpse of, or outright revealed, the richness of the Mexican character, while at the same time pointing to its radicalization, although radicalization here does not mean anything other than the search for a method of exploring ourselves guided by philosophical principles. Philosophical wisdom is, according to its perennial definition, knowledge of causes and ultimate principles. The knowledge that the Mexican has of himself is already so voluminous that it allows the philosopher to throw himself straight into the depths in search of that being or that mode of existence that the Mexican person gestures toward or makes obvious through his ordinary, extraordinary, historical, literary, political, religious, and moral conduct.

The younger generation has thus made philosophical knowledge of the Mexican person the defining theme. "Philosophical" here refers to radical, fundamental, and decisive analyses carried out before reflections that would be content with remaining superficial, with loitering at the entrance of the theme, but without forcing their way and opening the path, decisively, with philosophical instruments as their guide [12]. Even those generations that occupied themselves with Mexican themes could not elevate them to a central preoccupation, much less develop them with philosophical methodology.

Finally, it is worth mentioning another reason for the popularity of this theme, namely, teamwork (*el trabajo en equipo*). The new generation has understood, to their benefit, the limitations involved in research undertaken in isolation. Without undervaluing individual talent, we have come to the belief that the labor of research demands teamwork; that is, it demands the necessary submission of oneself to specific and yet flexible general philosophical orientations that align what are mere gestures to very specific coordinates. A team devotes its attention to a wide area, inexhaustible by just one researcher, and can execute the analysis of that sector from a variety of points of view, attending to the personal idiosyncrasies of each of its members, and in a relatively short time. The unity of the investigation is thus assured, in addition to that offered by the philosophical method itself that serves as its base as well as by a number of well-posed questions that cannot be capriciously invented but that represent a catalogue of main concerns that are unique and deserve attention in virtue of their contemporaneity and depth, since nothing is more regrettable than to see the work of researchers go by the wayside and get lost with questions about which "no sleep is lost" [36].

For anyone who has taken up this theme, nothing seems clearer than the unifying outline being draw around the mode of being of the Mexican. Of all the analyses that have been made, one common denominator stands out: *There is an unmistakable air of family* (aire de familia) *in everything that our investigators tell us about the Mexican.* Thus, the family relationship between this or that aspect proclaimed

I. Introduction

as crucial is a clear guide for the systematization of the findings. The comparative method, more than any other, allows us to approach that common nucleus in which our "character" is found. *Those who have not gone to the extremes (to which we now go) may think that things that are said about the Mexican person are disparate and contradictory, but whoever familiarizes themselves with our theme arrives at the opposite conclusion.* Far from moving about in imprecision and dispersion, we are bound by a very constant and even rigid structure that, although it allows for secondary variations, which are perhaps limited and offer the possibility of differences, points to an "essential" characteristic of that structure [13].

Everything that has so far been affirmed regarding the being of the Mexican converges or points to the same thing, and the task of the philosopher is made easier by the proper management of multiple observations and ideas that, to put it simply, immediately reveal their underlying family resemblances. The convergence itself has to be seen as an unequivocal sign of objectivity.

We have previously indicated that the interest for the present theme seems to us to be one of the consequences of the historicist movement. This observation allows us to delve into the very meaning of the concern over *lo mexicano*. Promoted at its roots by historicism, the analysis of the being of the Mexican has to be historical, keeping in mind that not every investigation into the Mexican person (*el mexicano*) is of this kind. One epoch distinguishes itself from another in the way in which it chooses to talk about basic human facts or events. There are ages in which everything is reduced, all things human, to religious or theological terms; in those epochs it was necessary to clarify the personal or collective situation in relation to orthodoxy or a fundamentally religious morality. Other epochs, in turn, are fundamentally psychologistic. What matters is then to define oneself in terms of psychological complexes or traumas and look for psychological normality. Psychology has the last word, and so long as reality is not reduced to psychological factors, it is not thought to have touched on the depths of the question. The same thing happens when everything is dominated by the sociological perspective, where problems of class and community rise to the surface right away. Bourgeois and proletarian attitudes toward life are classified as truly authoritative, and everything else is but an accessory. To truly explain something, then, you only have to call it bourgeois or proletarian.

It is clear that historicism reduces everything human to historical factors, and so long as the historical ground of any particular question is left untouched, it appears as if the real issue is left untreated. Thus, history has to say, if not the last, at least the penultimate word with respect to the being of the Mexican [14]. On that basis, the investigation into our intellectual past should achieve an extraordinary reach. In history we shall read the structure of our being, or differently stated, the study of our history should teach us who we are.

It is difficult to say if history, or historical science, just as it is, can satisfy what historicism demands. Historical methodology is, perhaps, incurably flawed by prejudices. Tied to the worship of the document, it insists in conceptualizing the work of the historian as making past events speak without an orienting a priori. And it is obvious that past events do not speak since, propped in a corner of the archive with a tag that says "past," they do not willingly avail themselves for the recitation of their lessons, especially if one has not previously submitted them to a systematic and ordered interrogation.

It is often said that history is the science of the past. The past has accumulated all sorts of documents, testimonies, and facts. But the past is historical only when it ceases to be merely the past and animates itself with the breath of the human. *The truly historical is not the past, but what the past contains of the human*. History does not seek the past, but seeks the human in the past. *The theme of history is humanity*. That is why it finds its grounding only when it is defined authentically or, better, when it is identified with the theme of philosophy. Historicism leaves this question unanswered: Is the truly human historical? The reason for this is that it cannot answer without returning to the phrase: the truly historical is the human. Thus conceived, history can have, if not the last, at least the penultimate word regarding the being of the Mexican. It is the penultimate word because the question that is placed before us is precisely one that asks if man is historical by virtue of finding himself in history or, better yet, if history is what it is by virtue of emerging from man.

The being of the human being is of such a kind that it demands history; it is of such a kind that it gives the condition for the possibility of history. *History is, at its foundation, a mode of being human, and, moreover, it finds its definitive expression in terms of being, that is, in ontological terms.* The language of being is thus the ultimate basis of reduction, the one that gets closest to the foundation [15]. Thus, everything that we previously said about theology, psychology, sociology, and history would have to be restated in its relation to ontology. In its origins, philosophy understands that to speak in terms of being is to speak in the language of the things themselves, a fact that also gives it its status as originary; the things themselves are saturated with and formed by being. *Things are made of being, but so long as one speaks of them in the very same terms as their "materiality," our speech slips and remains in the realm of appearances.*[7]

Ontological analysis is, then, of a very particular kind. Its categories, or very general concepts, are the widest possible designations of class, types, or modes of being. Only when one speaks and holds fast to these categories is the analysis a proper analysis. If the analysis is not carried out on these terms, everything takes on the aspect of metaphor and image. Ontological concepts, for instance, those of substance and accident, are not notions that can be reduced to terms belonging to other, not strictly ontological, spheres, as many think. Hence, it has been said that when Aristotle speaks of a "true" ontology, he is merely talking about biology, since the notions that he deals with as purely ontological are nothing other than concepts derived from the dominion of living things, making his application unique in that it is adequate. *What is clear is that whatever the field may be from which ontological concepts are extracted and first coined, what matters is their dimension of being* (dimension de ser) *and not the basis of their emergence.* The abstract nature of these categories does not really permit us to treat them in their purity, which is why we refer ourselves, a bit out of fatigue and a bit more due to the effort that abstraction itself demands, to those regions in which we first find them. However, we must not lose sight of the fact that we have descended from abstraction and that what matters is to keep ourselves and our concepts exclusively directed toward the ontological.

If we propose an analysis of the being of the Mexican, it is obvious that so long as we do not speak of that being in terms of being itself, everything stays the same. The ontology of the Mexican person requires us to refine the catalogue of our ontological concepts, to clarify its categories, since without this previous work of setting and formulating our philosophical instruments, we run the risk of splashing about in vagueness and of baptizing in the name of an analysis of the Mexican being an investigation that, undoubtedly, is an analysis of that being, but is not ontological, since it speaks with concepts and ideas not ontologically defined [16].

However, we should also not allow ourselves to be overwhelmed by the conditions imposed by a rigorously crafted ontological terminology. *There are analyses that do not appear ontological, but that when looked at more closely show themselves almost immediately as direct "translations" of lived experiences, [we can call them][8] ontological "intimations"* ("'corazonadas' ontológicas").[9] This is the case with poetry. Being speaks through the poet in its own language. Poetry does not translate the being of its experiences into terms alien to being itself, but comes to the reader in an almost pure form. This is why the ontology of the Mexican has to lend attention to the work of our poets with a degree of attention that will never be sufficient. Poetry has spoken more than the historians, psychologists, or sociologists about the being of the Mexican.

In this way, the contributions of the poets will be of immense value to the analysis of the being of the Mexican—analyses such as those that we find in Octavio Paz's *The Labyrinth of Solitude*. The poet lives in a most intimate familiarity with being; he has being ready to hand, so to speak. It is clear that we cannot give a formula that will teach us with mathematical regularity in which way the philosopher will translate what the poet says into properly ontological terms. It is a work of instinct and thought—two things, that is, that allow us to save ourselves from the confusing concept of intuition—and of flexibility and rigor. In any case, it is true that poet and philosopher, as well as philosopher and historian, must live in constant communication and nourish one another when it comes to the elaboration of the ontological analysis of the being of the Mexican. Without such "contamination" or "borrowing of meaning," we do not believe there is any possibility of taking a step forward in our thematic.

II. Philosophy

To be so without foundation,
and so without being, in all things

—Friar Diego Durán

2. The Accident and the Mexican Person [17]

In a previous essay dedicated to the ontology of the Mexican,[1] we *have sought to define a certain constitutional insufficiency in our manner of being*; at the same time we have discussed a project, first studied excellently by Samuel Ramos, of elevating insufficiency over and above the so-called complex of inferiority. Presently, we take up once again that line of thought and undertake on its basis the following reflections:

2.1. The insufficiency of a particular "reality" is equivalent to inconsistency or to the lack of foundation. Insufficiency, ontologically speaking, determines the accident in relation to substance. *Every modality of being grounded on accident is characterized by a lack of ground*, grounded on a shifting and fractured base. The accident is a *minus* of being, a being reduced or "fragmented" due to its mixture with nothingness, a mixture in which being and nothingness communicate. As an unstable combination, the accident perpetually refers to its extremes, its excesses call and reject each other at the same time. Being posits nothingness and nothingness posits being, which means that in the accident there exists that *Werden* (*to become*), that transit and movement that Hegel elevated to the condition of "true" reality, inasmuch as the extremes as such, on their own and in their isolation, are "abstract and ideal." What is concrete is the movement itself, the expanding of being that turns it to nothingness and the relaxing (*distención*) of nothingness that ties it to being. It is worth noting, however, that for

Hegel that movement is not an "accident," a notion that his system does not recognize. On the other hand, substance is plenitude or fullness of being, entity without fissures or edges, to put the matter graphically [18]. Substance does not imply change of any kind; it places its stability beyond the limits of transformation; it rests in itself, indifferent to all mobility, alteration, or decomposition. Substance is sufficient and not insufficient. Traditionally, substance has been endowed with the status of being of greater "rank" entity wise, while accident has been seen as a degradation or reduction, as an entity of "lower class." But, in spite of this, the accident has not been placed beneath nothingness since, according to Aristotle, if the accident is nothing before substance, it is something in relation with nothingness; it is a relative nothing; that is, it is nonbeing when it gazes upon substance and a being when it returns its gaze toward nothingness.

2.2. That the being of the human being is ontologically accidental is the most important affirmation we make in our essay.[2] *The insufficiency of the Mexican person is the insufficiency of his being as accident and only this.* Any other sense that may be given to the word "insufficiency" falls outside our ontology. If critics insist on interpreting our affirmation of the insufficiency of the Mexican being as "weakness," "impotence," "defeatism," "hopelessness," and thus continue to criticize what we have affirmed, they show themselves to be perverse, incapable, or bad intentioned. When we say that the being of the Mexican is accidental, our purpose is to take such an assertion seriously, which means that our purpose is to clarify the problems entailed by the characterization of being *as* accident.

All, or almost all, of the Western philosophical tradition has thought of being in terms of substance. To be is to be substantial; if one wishes to be genuine, one must refer to substance, since the accident is but a "shadow" of being, a "quasi-being." It is true that the Scholastic tradition proposed that "being" was "transcendental," which means that being "hovers over" ("*encima*") substance and accident. But "Being" itself is considered by this tradition as the "Supreme Entity," more than substantial, super-substantial in virtue of eminence, which allows the

Scholastics to say that, in order to grasp it, the concept of substance itself must be extended to its limits; haecceity (*la haceidad*)[3] is, in this way, "substantial substance," quintessential substance [19].[4] Man, for his part, figures as a "creature," but also "substantial like his Creator." Everywhere we notice, then, the radical tendency for substantialization on the part of the Western philosophical tradition. Man is on this historical account "being for substance," being that must make itself substance.

We define the being of the Mexican in precisely opposite terms. As a "being for accident," its being is a *having to be an accident*. Due to our historical situation within the Western tradition, it appears "comprehensible," as an idea belonging to that tradition, that man "must" become substantial. However, prima facie, we fail to understand (although this is what is pre-ontologically the most immediate) what the meaning is of the affirmation that man "must" accidentalize himself. To help us understand this, it is convenient to recall that when the being of the human being is thought to be accidental or "substantial,"[5] it does not mean that these are properties or attributes that it "possesses" or that it *already* "has," properties of which it can avail itself as with others already part of his fixed or inalterable reality, rather that the being of the human being must be made or it must appear as a "project." This condition of the being of the human being is expressed by Martin Heidegger with much rigor and precision in the following formula: "The 'essence' of this entity (of man) consists in its having to be."[6] The being of the human being is not something given (*gegeben*), but something proposed (*aufgegeben*). My being is a having to be my being. If one then says that the being of man is substance, then we must understand this statement as also affirming that we must substantialize ourselves. Similarly, if we say that the being of the human being is accidental, what we mean is that it must accidentalize itself, that the accident is not "given," but "proposed," as a project to be realized; we would say, "it must be realized." *To realize oneself as accident means that one must maintain oneself as accident, on the horizon of possibility of the accident itself* [20]. Inauthenticity would be to flee the condition of accidentality and to substantialize oneself; the Mexican person falls into this temptation almost by necessity when her originary constitution is "too much to bear." That "sufficiency" toward which we aspire cannot be a "substantiality," but a sufficiency that emerges from the same insufficiency, an emergence that is the only legitimate and properly moral goal, as we will show later. For now, it is enough to say that being as accident already contains within itself the "essential" possibility to accidentalize oneself, a possibility that can also be clarified as a bringing of all human conduct to a radical horizon of accidentality.

In speaking of the being of the human being, Heidegger defines it as "*Sein zum Tode.*" This celebrated formula has given rise to a multitude of inadequate interpretations. "Being toward death [Ser para la muerte]" better approximates the truth of what Heidegger means to say (perhaps better than any other translation). But much more precise than this would be to translate *Sein zum Tode* as "*being that has to die*" (*Ser que tiene que morir*). The being of the human being is perishable, mortal, is meant for death, for an ending. That being assumes as ontological the "obligation," "duty," "imperative" to die or to be no more. The same happens with *being toward accident* (*ser para el accidente*). We are talking here about a being that has to accidentalize itself, that has to place itself in a situation of a radical "not knowing what to depend on" insecurity, and unpredictability. Every "existential" or "characteristic" of the being of the human being is located beneath the inevitable formality of being accidental. In what follows we will see some of the consequences that result from this radical ontological positing.

2.3. It has been raised as an objection against our ontology that in affirming that the being of the Mexican is accidental we have defined the human condition in general, one in which the Mexican person participates. It is said that in "truth" the human being is what is accidental and not just the Mexican person. We should then not be talking about an ontology of that which is Mexican, but an ontology of the "human being in general." The accidental constitution of the human being would have been read by us in the Mexican, but it would not be specific to the Mexican, but to the human. To these objections we respond, first, that *we are not very certain of the existence of the human being in general and, second, that whatever passes itself off as human being in general, namely, generalized European humanity, does not appear to us to define itself as accidental, but precisely as arrogant substantiality* [21]. A different yet truly difficult problem is one that tries to demarcate the human from the ontological, but there is no problem in separating that which is Mexican from "humanity in general."

The nature of what Heidegger called "fundamental ontology" has been the focus of discussion ever since the publication of his *Sein und Zeit* in 1927; however, not much clarity has been gained from those discussions. In that work, Heidegger proposes to take up once again, and on a new basis, the decisive ontological question, namely, what is being? An analysis of the question just formulated reveals the need, overlooked by the tradition, to rigorously specify the entity that has to respond to the question. Bordering on the confusing, he proposes that only a person can ask, and eventually answer, the question of being. But Heidegger really does not propose that a person is the entity chosen to ask and answer the ontological question, and the source of many false interpretations of the author of *Being and Time* is found here. What he really says is that *in persons there is a most particular structure of being, Dasein*, which is precisely the where the ontological question must be posed and answered; it is not, then, *a person* who is the interrogated subject in a fundamental ontology, but *Dasein in the person*. If one insists that Dasein can only be human, or that only in persons is it possible to find a structure as that of Dasein, one incurs an unforgivable inversion of terms, since Heidegger's intention is precisely to approach a definition of ontology as prior to anthropology or humanism and not, as it is commonly interpreted, to subsume ontology into a philosophical anthropology. Humanism rests on a fundamental ontology, and not the other way around.

Clearly, it is equally important to ask oneself, what is being?, as it is to ask oneself, what is man?, but inevitable methodological demands force us to first posit the ontological question and then the anthropological question. Only when we have appropriated the ontological formula of

Dasein is it legitimate to return to man and inquire about his "essence" [22]; if we want to do this first, we would find ourselves without the indispensable guiding thread of the investigation and all of our efforts would frustrate themselves with imprecision and the artificial piling up of materials, facts, theories, opinions, etc. Such has been the destiny of Max Scheler's "philosophical anthropology," which he proposed more than a quarter of a century ago. Despite the brilliance of his proposals, Scheler's philosophical anthropology has helped us advance but little in regard to the knowledge of man. The efficacy, on the other hand, of "existentialist anthropologies" is due to their ontological foundations.

2.4. The ontology of the Mexican being must be prior, methodologically, to any and all investigations into the Mexican *person*, her *life*, and her *soul*. When we speak of the Mexican as person, we mean to refer to an interpretation of the Mexican as person from the starting point of her being. More radical than any talk of the Mexican as a person is talk of the Mexican as a being, "talk" with which ontology specifically occupies itself. The ontological formula "a Mexican as a being and not as a person" nevertheless sounds paradoxical. For many, this formula just means this: *the Mexican is subhuman*. "The ontology of Mexicanness doesn't treat us like men," some will say. Others will say: "They define the Mexican as a creature that does not participate in the human." And in this tone we will hear other phrases that point to the "ineptitudes of an inept culture." But to refer to "the being of the Mexican," we do not refer to a state of being wherein the Mexican person is *not yet* a person, in which he exists in a kind of ontological primitiveness, a state stupidly interpreted as an "epoch" or a historical "time" in which the Mexican lives in a happily state of ontological innocence. The Mexican as being and the Mexican as person are *contemporaneous* interpretations (they arise simultaneously); however, the investigation distinguishes them without isolating them abstractly and without turning them into independent and self-sufficient realities. This does not mean that their relation does not pose a problem for the investigation; the relation involves a very peculiar problem, one of immense importance.

We have already put forth some ideas regarding these relations in an essay specifically dedicated to this theme [23].[7] It appears to us that considering the Mexican person in his being, or in his ontological aspect, serves or functions as a source for a sense of the human applicable to anything that pretends to represent itself as human. It is not about articulating *lo mexicano* (that which particularizes us) as human, but the opposite; it is about articulating the human in terms of *lo mexicano*. *Lo mexicano* is the point of reference for the human; whatever resembles *lo mexicano* calibrates itself as human, disposes itself of whatever is dissimilar or distant from this kind of being. In ontological terms, *any interpretation of the human as a substantial creature seems to us inhuman.* At the origins of our history we suffered a devaluation for failing to assimilate ourselves to European "humanity." In a similar spirit, today we reject that qualification and, thus, refuse to recognize as "human" any European construction that grounds human "dignity" in substantiality.

2.5. If the human being is constitutionally accidental, then it becomes understandable why the Mexican has to be described as authentically human given that he exists in immediate proximity to the accident. This is another way to say that the Mexican is authentic because life is lived as originally ontological or in proximity to his own being. Any distancing from being as accident implies a certain effort at substantialization, and all proximity to being as accident implies a certain effort at accidentalization. Of course, we admit that it is difficult to define what it means to be "proximal" to the accident. There seems to be a scale of approximation and a scale of distancing. Already in the tradition whatever is accident is placed in its position in the scale relative to substance. The relation "*as accident*" was the furthest removed from substance; it was the "accident of accident," the accident closest to nothingness and further removed from substance.[8] This distance is not understood as "spatial," yet it is difficult to understand what these terms mean without reference to space, especially now that it seems appropriate to remember that existence enjoys a certain *sui generis* "spatiality," which is not the order of positions and locations but of places and sites of everyday preoccupation [24]. We live immersed in a space framed in terms of the distribution, or "placement," of its places and our everyday concerns over persons or things.

What is closest to us is what is present in our concern, not what is immediate to us in a geometrical sense. Existence, Heidegger says, "de-distances";[9] it destroys distances and brings closer. The absolute point of reference is not my own body but my "here"; from my "here" significance is given to things and places "there." But existence as a "de-distancing" cannot get close to annulling all distance; it cannot concentrate everything in a "here" without a correlative "there" relative to which it can be, at least, *minimally* at a distance. Proximity to the accident, then, signifies having it always present as a concern. The Mexican continuously lends an ear to the voice of his being through those sentiments common to us such as "sorrow" (*pena*), the analysis of which we have dealt with elsewhere. "Sorrow" is the voice of conscience in the Mexican person, a voice that we must interpret as surging from the very same being that constitutes us—this being emerges and crosses over into the field of everyday experience. In the Mexican person there is a sensation that there is never enough being. Our life offers clear examples of powerlessness over existence, of not "understanding" it, to put it in one of Heidegger's well-known terms. Life becomes difficult, and, more than feeling joy or power before the difficulty, a vague and obscure absence overtakes it. Swiftness or ease in our everyday living is not, then, one of our characteristics. We are situated in the antipodes of a "sportive" and "festive" conception of man and world. This life, which weighs and "drags" is not, I must insist, a load that will never lighten, as happens with extreme melancholy, but, rather, it finds itself inserted in the horizon of accident in which, suddenly, it is dissolved by death. As a matter of fact, it could be argued that death is sought as "liberation."

The eagerness to "saturate life with randomness" is, perhaps, the most obvious manifestation of freedom for a being as accident [25]. This being's irritating and convulsive search for a way out of the insufferable monotony of a routine, the desperate wait for a miracle or for a winning lottery ticket testifies, to that will to accident in which we recognize our own ontological particularity. If, then, the accident constitutes the being of all human beings—a reason for which we endeavor to overturn the teachings of the Western tradition—the Mexican person, in the act of accidentalization, approximates the originary condition of our proper and authentic constitution, even if at the same time there is a distancing from a manner of existing that has already become comfortable. The "untrustworthiness" (*desconfianza*) with which the Mexican person deals with everything, and the unwillingness that colors all his doings, are manifestations of a closeness to the accident, just as "confidence" and "generosity" in other modes of life are symbols of a mastery over accident and of a certain security felt in being on a path to substantialization.

2.6. Until now, we have avoided, and intentionally so, to entangle our affirmations with methodological reflections. We had first to put in motion, and without obstacles, the thesis that we now propose, and only after that turn our attention toward the serious problem of its methodological legitimacy. It is time now to attend to those issues of methodological clarification. For those who have read us carefully, it will be easy to make out two sharply delimited areas of inquiry. Our primary purpose has been to arrive at a definition of the being of the Mexican, and we have found that definition in the ontological notion of accident. But we still know nothing about "accident." In introducing the notion, we have made a tacit call to that pre-ontological experience that nourishes the use of the notion. We know what an accident is, even if we cannot concretely formulate what we mean by "know." When we affirm that the being of the Mexican is accidental, a horizon of meaning opens up for our meditative thinking, but one that is still vague and obscure. On the other hand, in speaking of the accident, we have appealed to a confrontation between this traditional ontological notion and the, not-so-traditional, but only recently elaborated, notion of existence.[10] We have explained the accident through the idea of existence and, at the same time, existence through the idea of accident [26]. An immediate demand is thus placed on us, namely, that of clarifying the notion of accident involved in the pre-ontological experience of that idea and of justifying the assimilation or approximation of accident and existence. Once the notion of accident is clarified and shown in its kinship to existence, we should once again return to the theme of Mexicanness so as to "repeat" through the notion of accident existence those behaviors, or modes of being, that we have highlighted as characteristics of the Mexican person.

2.7. Traditional philosophical thought (and here we could refer to St. Thomas Aquinas's commentary on Aristotle) does not understand the notion of *existence* illustrated by Søren Kierkegaard in the 19th century. It has been noted, mainly by Heidegger, that what the tradition means by "existence" (*esse*) has nothing in common with the idea of "existence" (*Existenz-Dasein*) that "existentialists" discuss (e.g., Heidegger, Sartre, Jaspers). We have here an "equivocal" notion, such as the notion of "Leon," which refers to or signifies equivocally to a city (León, Guanajuato, in Mexico) and an animal (a lion) [48].

A different problem arises if we ask how traditional philosophy itself would understand the notion of "existence," what place it would assign to it in its categorical archive. Our previous indications, although negative or prohibitive, would (if they are legitimate) bar us only from placing this notion where we currently find the notion of "existentia." But, if we cannot find it elsewhere, is that the only place in which it could be, thus remaining irremediably without a categorial place of its own? This is unlikely. We are aided by the belief that its location in that archive is achievable. We have to find it elsewhere and this elsewhere exists: we locate it in that region of traditional thought in which notions such as accident, evil, and privation are discussed. But the purpose of our efforts has to be understood. We will demonstrate how, through the clarification of accident, of evil, and of privation, as these notions are understood in our tradition, we have a means to ignite the idea of existence, as this concept has been understood in existentialism. It is not simply a matter of identifying existence, lack, evil, and accident, but in studying their reciprocal changes in meaning, their lending and borrowing of sense, and to do this in such a way that the notion of existence is clarified and enriched by its confrontation with lack, evil, and accident; moreover, these notions will themselves be clarified and made virtual in the confrontation with existence.

If to explain is to identify, as we have been previously taught by Emile Meyerson,[11] then our confrontation, even if it explicitly avoids identification, will be an identification in spite of itself. For the most part, the clarification of concepts brings about their identity through the explication itself. In other words, in explaining concepts, one identifies them, whether one wants to or not. But it also differentiates, since, as Hegel judiciously observes in his *Logic*, if those propositions emanating from understanding inevitably formulate as identical the subject and the predicate of those judgments that they pronounce, even if tacitly, since it is not within their power to do so explicitly—that is, since in doing so it would seem that they are referring to some other distinct thing previously mentioned, when in fact they are repeating the same thing—they likewise inevitably formulate as diverse the subject and the object of their judgments. That we fail to see that difference, as we see identity, is due to "defects" in our mode of expression, and we shouldn't assign them, if we are to be fair, to thought itself that in its purity, and not undermined by its formulation, has before it at the same time both identity and difference.

But we have said that it is not only about identifying or differentiating but also about something else suggested by words such as "clarification" and "enrichment." Heidegger, in his *Being and Time*, uses a methodological device that comes from phenomenology, and which he calls "deformalization" (*desformalización*).[12] When phenomenology is defined as "a descriptive science of essences in the phenomenological attitude," many translate the formula in the simplest way, in favor of brevity and due to certain prejudices, as the science of "essences," the science of empty and formal concepts. "Essences," however, as described by phenomenology, are not left to float in the region of pure formalism, but are projected toward "material" regions where the task is to uncover their regional variations, the *transformations* they undergo through the process of "deformalization" [28]. Heidegger demonstrates this through the notion of "end" (*fin*). A formal "definition" of "end" is not enough for the purposes of phenomenological description, the concept must be "materialized," assigning it to determinate regions of entities, such as the region of inanimate things (the full moon is the end of the crescent), the region of life (fruit is the end of the fruit tree), the region of the human (the last brushstroke that brings to an end a work of art), and the region of existence (death is the end of "being there"). This kind of materialization, each case peculiar of this notion of end, should make the meaning of end precise, one previously understood in its formal or most general structure. The "application" to a determinate material region "clarifies" the concept, it "enriches" it, but at the same time it "transforms" it. This in a double sense. First, it transforms the formal notion into matter, it concretizes it, and second, it transforms the reality to which the concept is applied, since it makes possible the opening of new ontic dimensions of its own structure, which before this confrontation was fixed or bounded in virtue of its reference to other horizons distinct from those horizons opened up by the application of our new notion.

At the beginning of our investigation, the notions of existence and accident are merely formal, empty in themselves, isolated; they know nothing of each other. But in their "communication," as we put them in contact, their structure is altered. In "communication" they face each other already materialized or concretized, and it is in such a state that the interchange of meaning of which we previously spoke takes place. Thereafter, we think of the accident in the horizon of existence—we open new dimensions in its ontological structure that was hidden until now and, as a matter of fact, could not give itself in a virtual way—and we think of existence in the horizon of the accident. In this process of confrontation, we find ourselves finally before the "problem" of existence as accident, with the problem, that is, and not with the solution, which with its mere mention here lacks all sense.

2.8. The notion of accident, as any ontological notion, offers to our analysis a rich and structured complexity of constitutive moments [29]. Heidegger has called our attention in numerous occasions to the unjustified prejudice that motivates all terminological investigation and notation when dealing with the definition of ontological realities. We feel justified to end the investigation as soon as we grasp a simple and uncomplicated formula that characterizes a mode of being, but before achieving that simplicity, we distrust all complexity as inauthentic or definitive. However, being does not approve of the reduction of its essence (*meollo*) to a simple and rudimentary element. The being of man is formulated in a layered and complicated expression. We recall here Heidegger's definition of "care" (*Sorge*) as the being of existence *(Dasein)*: "being-ahead-of-itself-in-already-being-in (the world) … as being-alongside (the "world")" (*Sich-vorweg-sein-im-schon-sein-im … -als Sein-bei*).[13] Just as the being of existence is not simple, neither is the definition of the accident simple (this is not simply a causal correspondence). If we seek to fully grasp what this idea means, we have to proceed slowly and cautiously, pausing before each of the successive significations that the analysis may give us. However, we must also avoid dismembering the notion and dissolving it in a myriad of aspects lacking any obvious connection. Unity from diversity, as with any concept, applies also to the accident and is achieved by the gathering of multiple moments that must be attended to individually so as not to lose any of the richness that in itself such a fluid notion contains.

2.9. So as to orient ourselves in what follows we propose a very general characterization of the accident as being, or as a mode of being as accident, which will orient us as we proceed.

2.9.1. The "essential" characteristic of the accident as a being is expressed in that formulation that contrasts accident to being in the proper sense. The accident is not being, the accident is being-in. Being, without this prepositional addendum, is authentic being, being par excellence. Every modulation, declination, of that precise and correct reality which is being must be explained and, above all, not violently reduced to being in a simple sense, but preserved in its originarity [30]. The being of the accident is not being in the "proper" sense, or simply "being," but rather finds its formulation in the complex expression of "being-in" (we must conceive of this notion of accident as the unity of these two elements). But what lends the accident its peculiarity is its having had modulated simple being in accordance with the demands of the preposition "in" or the demands of any preposition whatsoever.

2.9.2. The accident is fragility: oscillation between being and nothingness. This means that its "fit" in being, its adhesion to being expressed in the modality of being-in, is not protected by an inalienable right, but rather whatever may be the form of its inherence, it is always revocable. The accident is constantly threatened by displacement (*desalojamiento*). Implanted in being, it can always be uprooted from its "there," that is, exterminated. Whatever it holds on to, whatever handle it grabs on to, can be removed. It was born to be-in and at the same time to not-be-in.

2.9.3. The accident hangs on to, or depends on, or belongs to another thing. It is not enough in itself for itself. Its interiority points (*su entraña alude*) to a reality that "sustains" it and without which it would disappear into nothingness. The other toward that the accident points or tends to is substance. The accident does not possess its own being, it enjoys it (*lo usufructúa*), but it does not possess it as its own—it is a gracious "loan." The accident's dependency is of the most radical kind that can be imagined, since it is a dependence on being. Substance "gives" it whatever being that it has.

2.9.4. In a negative sense, the accident is privation, lack, penury, a defect or an absence of subsistence, and insufficient being. "To be so without foundation, and so much without being in all things" ("*Ser tan sin fundamento, y tan sin ser en todo*"). Accident is, to put it simply, a fleeing, an escape, a slipping beyond being. The accident refers to a defect of being. More than con-sisting, it is an ex-sisting, a de-sisting. In the confrontation of the notion of substance with that of accident, one proves that the notion of accident is a "decompression," or a loosening of being. Being in the accident has distended itself; it has untied itself. The tight mesh of being has "slacked" and that distension is the accident.

2.9.5. The literal definition of accident is that of a happening or the occurrence of chance [31]. The accident is that which suddenly appears, what is not expected. The accident is being that supervenes; it is not simply an addition, but the addition itself, and not the thing added. The accident is the "subject" of the verb "to happen"; it is the pure action of being extra, of being outside. To this we add the idea of that which is bursting out and arriving to itself in all purity: pure ecstasy, pure and constant bursting in itself and toward itself.

2.9.6. Being accidental expresses an essential adhesion to something else. The accident sinks into or embeds itself in substance. It refers itself to its final resting place as its radical support. It lives to adhere to or attach itself. Its alteration is an impregnation or a preparation. It is inserted or projected as if toward a target on which it attaches itself "in a highly viscous manner" (*viscosamente*).

2.9.7. Finally, the accident is in relation to being. It tends toward being; it pulls and projects itself toward it. Its "consistency" is exhausted in its relation to being. It is pure allusion, intentionality, index or vector of being. Substance does not have a true relation to being; rather its proximity or nearness to being is so extreme that it has transformed itself into identity or fusion. But the accident expresses a relation to being and not fusion or identity.

2.10. Let us bring together these seven characteristics or modalities of the accident so as to fully understand this notion; let us reunite them and thus understand their nuances so that the impressive richness of the idea of accident can appear before us.

The accident as being, or the mode of being accidental, is (in accordance with 2.9).

    2.9.1. *In-esse* (being-in)

    2.9.2. *In-esse-non-in-esse* (being-in-not-being-in)

    2.9.3. *Entis* (of the entity)

    2.9.4. *Ab-esse* (un-being)

    2.9.5. *Super-esse* (being-over)

    2.9.6. *Ad-esse* (*Ser-cabe* [being-proximal])[14]

    2.9.7. *Ad-esse* (Being-toward)

The accident as adherence (*ad-esse*) expresses a reference to substance, not simply a relation (*ad-esse*); it is stuck to it, clinging to or next to substance (it is near to [*cabe*]). It is together with, infused in substance (here we recall what is already contained in the German prepositions *bei* and *zu*), it is in proximity to substance [32]. The most formalized notion of reference is relation, but the notion of accident conjugates both meanings. If we express it in "specialized" terms, we can say that the accident is in the vicinity or is in nearness to substance, that it is close to or in proximity to substance, or attached to substance.

For reasons not clearly known, these modes of being find expression in the formula of accident as *ad-esse*. Thus, for the sake of clarity, we must distinguish between them by highlighting the *ad* when it occurs in the meaning of *proximity* (*cabe*) as being-in (*impregnado*) and not as relation. In saying that it is being-in, embedded, absorbed, or "sucked in" ("*chupado*") (as in the sponge that "sucks in" the ink), by substance we allude to the signification that Heidegger gives to *Besorgen* and *Fürsorge* as "to cure oneself of" or "to procure" and of the project of "viscosity" in Sartre.[15] But just as the accident, by virtue of one of its dimensions, is imprinted in substance, so does it find itself originally at a distance, alienated, detached. This condition of its being finds its expression in *ab-esse*.

Accidentality is that which is distant, being somewhere else, being always in a different place (*ailleurs*), a being-at-a-distance, as Heidegger says of existence. We always understand the accident as that which is to come; we do not know precisely from whence it comes, as that which is imprecise and distant, as the stranger (*L'Etranger*). The accident is always thrown, or always throws itself, from or toward a beyond, but it never exhausts itself in what is present, proceeding instead to constitute itself in the horizon and halo that surrounds things—in that which is out of focus before itself. Stretched out in its projections, the accident is a remainder par excellence, what remains as a surplus; it is excess (*super-esse*). In virtue of another of its dimensions, the accident is what is fragile and fractured, what with equal originality is both in being and not in being. There lies its essential vulnerability or affectivity, the "encountering itself" in the Heideggerian sense, but, at the same time, the not knowing what to depend on, the not adhering in a definite sense, hesitation, or zozobra. In its adhering or inhering, existence is a labor on substance, a taking care in it, an attending it, a working it, a managing it.

2.11. The accident, defined in accordance with the preceding, should serve to explain or make sense to the being of the Mexican [33]. The modes of conduct that our investigators have revealed as being particularly Mexican, a full inventory that has yet to be completed (however, we do not need to wait for its completion in order to begin our ontological analysis), allow us to see the accidental being that serves as their "conditions of possibility." Only when we locate the being of the Mexican in the horizon of the accident can we affirm that we have placed it in its proper context. Before arriving at that context, we were completely at a loss, and it seemed that when we did get close to a shadow or region of the appropriate horizon, we did so only by "intimation" ("*corazonada*"). Now we are in the right place from which the "things themselves" can speak. We will claim possession of the originary phenomenon of accidentality of the Mexican by demonstrating that every one of the fundamental structures revealed until now (inferiority complex, resentment, hypocrisy, cynicism, zozobra, etc.) must be conceived as accidental "in their foundation," that is, in their base. In other words: conducts or behaviors of Mexicans persons are "modes" of accidentalization belonging to an originary accidentality.

Thus, when we say that the ontological origin of the Mexican person is found in the accident, we are not suggesting that in order to grasp the Mexican in his concretion, in "flesh and bone," we would still need to add something (concrete) to the accident. The concrete is the accidental itself. When in our "Essay on an ontology of the Mexican" we asked into the manner in which "inferiority" can "surge" from "insufficiency" (which, as we have seen, is one of the primordial "modalities" of accident), we did not concern ourselves about first positing the problem of history or the evolution of that "inferiority complex" or of the ends that this "choice" of being is supposed to accomplish. What we asked when we sought the *ontological genesis* of inferiority was only this: what are the conditions, or the ontologically necessary conditions, found in the ontological constitution of the accidental being of the Mexican that make it possible that the Mexican may exist in the mode of inferiority? Once we fix ourselves on (*dejado en fraquía*) the accidental being of the Mexican, our task becomes to *repeat* the analysis of those behaviors to which we have alluded earlier from the perspective of the accident [34].

3. The Radical Sense of the Investigation into Mexicanness (*lo mexicano*)

Not everyone understands in what sense we may interpret this interest in *lo mexicano* (in *the being of that which is Mexican*), especially when it originates with philosophers, since, by definition, philosophers should be concerned exclusively with the universal and not with the national, whatever this may be. But, as a matter of fact, the difficulty goes away when we consider that if philosophers worry over that which is Mexican, it does not mean, in the least, that they will remain there indefinitely. It is not about constructing, with the aid of reflection, a perfectly bounded image or outlining a rigid essence that could be used to guard against all confusion or intrusion. *Lo mexicano* must be conceived as a juncture or nexus of multiple paths, and the work of the philosopher resides in clearing up those paths, in highlighting their place on the map, and of articulating their direction. When we speak about the search for the being of the Mexican, what we mean is that we seek to arrive at a system of communicative relations, an ontological crossroads, a means of relating ourselves to the great currents of humanity; it does not refer to constructing a repository wherein we will hold a minuscule portion of humanity, particularized for our exclusive use, aggressively purified and protected against the incursion of any foreign element. If nationalism defines so as to confine, the tendency of our studies into the Mexican is thus an anti-nationalism, since our studies are motivated by a need to clarify how it is that our being represents a space upon which we could raise the figure of the human without prejudice, motivated, moreover, by a generous sense that the most legitimate aspect of humanity, that which is truly general and truly particular about human beings, can be found in an accidental being. The definition of the human as substantial, regardless of how open it may seem, excludes many modes of being human. We do not subscribe to that definition; rather, in offering another definition, we desire not to fall into the error of exclusion. What we seek is to make available more comprehensive commonalities.

There's nothing new about the radical dimension of this anti-nationalist tendency. In truth it is about facing humanity in its nakedness once again and brushing off the sedimentation that history has consecrated as eternal and permanent. Our history speaks about that which is human in a sufficiently clear language to anyone willing to listen, and what motivates us is our commitment not to let that voice be drowned out for any reason, not even for the sake of that familiar and intimate tonality by which many pretend to imprison our mode of being. Our "local color" dangerously covers over "our human color," but anything we can do to prevent that is welcome. The task of revealing that primordial region of being through which man can be defined coincides with the task of bringing us back to the originary source of our own history.

In the project of self-purification, which is coincident with the purification of the human, resides the force of philosophy in our time. Philosophy would have no role to play if the obligation was imposed upon us to return to our origins without the parallel demand to return to the origins of human being itself. The search for authenticity puts us on a specific path that will allow us to simultaneously grasp the horizon of truth within which the human being can be recaptured without deformities. In that horizon, we locate the familiar moral profile of our responsibility, its universal structure; from there we embark on the, apparently pretentious, search for a repetition that serves to teach humanity the means to avoid every sort of alienation. The truly decisive question of our ontology could be posed in the following way: Is the Mexican character capable of allowing itself to be grasped in a perception that captures the ontological foundations of the human being itself?

Many times I've asked myself if my critics, who are many, have *at least* felt the sincerity of *my ontology of the Mexican*. I fear that a particular way to formulate it, which may have been implied and not explicit, may have been the cause of much misunderstanding [36]. I now feel justified to specify in a precise way the problems before which it is incumbent on us to take a stand and to cut off at the roots that entire series of "objections" that persist in the vicinity, if not on the margins, or even the outskirts, of our ontology. I am aided in my intervention by the conviction that our character enjoys a special or exceptional ontic particularity, as Heidegger would say. More fragile, but better clarified than any other aspect of our character, is our way of being an excellent lens through which to look at the way the West has constituted the human being. The goal of my work can thus be reduced to this. It could be said that any other character (besides the Mexican) allows for the same kind of operation, but I have my (Mexican) character proximally at hand and it would be absurd to appeal to something other than myself as a means to find the truth—it would be like cleaning my neighbor's glasses so that I may see better. To those who feel learned in foreign techniques, I give my congratulations. Let them do their work with Greek, German, or French tools. What's important is that at the end of the exploration our results coincide, or else we must go our separate ways. It would be interesting to see a restoration of what it would mean for the human being to be substantial. But I am convinced the being of that kind of being is accidental and not substantial.

In other words, our character, that structure of our being that history has bestowed upon us, has been "executed" from the impressive depths of ontological auscultation. It has been revealed to us as permanently fatalistic, in a dangerous communication with limit situations, and from this unending dialogue with the physiological and foundational aspects of human being, there has emerged a *mode of being* on which finds an original layer of being that has been informed by everything, that absorbs everything—this is its most characteristic symbol. That being from which we have organized our conception of the human authorizes us to question other ways of organizing the human that have been "imposed" on us and that, with arrogant "sufficiency," have proposed and offered as more "radically" human than ours. But the moment of crisis has arrived, the instant for discomfort, in which we feel that the style of being with which we have become accustomed is not appropriate and authentic, and the violent gesture with which we have tried to rid ourselves of it has made us see that, by detaching ourselves from the spurious, we likewise rid man of a mask [37]. The recent history of our autognosis articulates, with an incorruptible accent, the imperative of unmasking, of radically refuting the "impostor" within us. But, after this, the man who underneath still nourishes the dross (*nutre aún las escorias*) is no longer exclusively the Mexican returned to his truth, but is more accurately man—simply man.

It is clear that Mexican humanism is saturated with explosive essences; moreover, as soon as we expose what it is that we mean by humanity, many retreat in fear, not wanting to recognize themselves in what is shown. But the authentic does not have to agree with the comfortable, with what is simple, with any shitty or petite-bourgeoisie manner of a *happy end* (*modalidad ñoña o pequeñoburguesa de happy end*). The opposite is the case. We now see why we have been accused of being pessimists. The imperative of purification is often an imperative to accept a tragic destiny. The Mexican knows this and his history eloquently illustrates it.

This ontological ground, this manner of being which is ours, is what we should promote in all corners of the globe as a promising crossroads upon which the paths of the human take flight and reorient their trajectories. In other words, our being is not a private essence that cuts us off from the rest of humanity and gives us an incomparable profile, but, on the contrary, it is a common "essence" that unites us and brings us closer to that which is human, empowering us to recover it in its fundamental dimension and detaching it from or clearing it of certain regrettable characteristics in which we lose ourselves and, once lost, fail to recognize the uniquely human or different ways of being. The Mexican aspires, in living with his mode of being, to represent a human intonation clearly and more authentic than that of other humanisms, which doesn't mean that it doesn't speak to the enthusiasms of other men, but precisely the contrary, that it can understand them in a more generous way, do them more justice, recognize more fully the voice of their vindications and their rebellions.

Philosophy is simultaneously a rigorous and careful attentiveness to the call of the ground or the origin [38]. The perplexity, the anxious fascination that *lo mexicano* inspires, must not be reduced to a negligible sort of curiosity or extravagance. The discomfort, the uneasiness before a human reality is the clearest sign of a solicitation that comes from what is originary, of a concern that takes one to the source. That which is Mexican (*lo mexicano*) attracts, demands, and posits the riddle of a strange disquiet related to the necessity of clarifying the meaning of the very fascination it evokes. The foreigner will try to explain the fascination with genuine interest. But, the English, in particular, have found only frustration in trying to crack the code of this obsession. The philosopher, however, is faced with the obligation to radicalize the obsession, to grasp it with a fundamentally ontological interrogation because the disquiet is not of a psychological kind, it is not "mental" or "subjective." (All interpretations that take the psychological route will remain irremediably narrow.) Being peeks from profound depths, and its peculiar fascination is the only one that can do justice to that disquieting enigma posed by Mexican existence. Ultimately, it is not that philosophy has become Mexican; on the contrary, that which is Mexican (*lo mexicano*) has decidedly "gelled" ("*cuajado*") in a philosophical dimension.

> From my insomniac eyes
> my death is spying on me,
> it spies on me, yes, it enamors me
> with its sluggish eye.
> Come on, whore of the icy blush,
> come on, let's go to hell!
>
> —"Death without end" (*Muerte sin fin*), José Gorostiza[16]

4. Humanism and the Mexican Person

Without needing the intervention of a theory about the meaning of the mode of being of the Mexican, the Mexican is interpreted pre-theoretically as a particularized representative of a human style of living. Pre-ontologically or preconceptually speaking, the Mexican person refers to himself and his world *as* a human self and a human world, which means that when he looks at his life he sees reflected in that life an *image* of man [39]. Prima facie, it seems trivial to consider the explicit enunciation that the Mexican person conceives himself *as* a man. But, however, in this simple expression we find an affirmation whose justification demanded, in a past period of our history, certain complex theories and conceptual elaborations of a predominantly theological kind whose meaning we are still far from adequately grasping. We refer here to that famous dispute that arose in the 16th century regarding the "humanity" of the Indian, regarding his apparent or obvious "brutality" that was not "humanity," to put it in the words of one of our more prestigious and profound historians.[17] In ways that we still ignore, the Mexican has affirmed himself in the course of his venturesome history as "man," even when he makes a mockery of his humanist dimension by degrading it in "machismo." But Mexican being limits only a certain human way of being, even when we trace a particular nationality to his entrails. In a certain sense, its fights for freedom, such as the reform movement or the revolution, are reflections of a human struggle in which the Mexican finds himself engaged, a struggle lived with such *originality* (*origenariedad*) that from it spring forth other ways of being that are more like legitimate benefits rather than tumors waiting to be excised.

But with equal *originality* the Mexican refuses the human and closes himself up, with indelible vows of ferocity, in his *nationality* and brags about this in affirmative expressions that go beyond the limits of prudence and into the grotesque, the brutal, the disgusting, and even the bloodthirsty. With equal spontaneity the Mexican thus affirms himself *as* Mexican and *as* human, but nationality hardens and reinterprets the former *officially*, transforming it, creating a complicated system of exceptions and privileges that, while well justified along certain lines, are for the most part destructive. The Mexican finds comfort in his nationalism, thus validating an intimate humanism. However, both interpretations (the Mexican and the human) are incompatible, representing a kind of struggle whose tragic hues have colored with an iridescent light all of our activities from independence to revolution.

In the Mexican person, as history presents it, there is an easy mix of humanism and nationalism [40]. We open ourselves up with equal originality to the human and to *lo mexicano*, and in the understanding of this bilateral condition resides the justification of many of our attitudes. As a result of historical motivations that can easily be explained, the Mexican has sought in nationality a refuge, a cover that will keep him safe from the voracious appropriations of alien others. The idea of a prosperous *homeland* has been tied to the idea that there is a legitimate group to whom it belongs. *Mexico for Mexicans* has been the motto for nationalist reclamations. The homeland is not conceived as a continual construction in which Mexicans must participate in a preeminent way, but as a *commodity* (*un haber*) or as a reality at one's disposal or for one's use, something for which one does not have to work, as it is immediately at arm's length, yet well protected from the exploitation of others.

Making (*hacer*) the homeland gets overshadowed by the stubborn arguments for *having* a nationality. Nationalists imagine Mexico as a set of elaborated goods that may be enjoyed without effort and they worry about safeguarding them from those that may, also without effort, steal away our riches. This mercantilist attitude has not disappeared from the popular or official mentality, but has been reinforced in a pathological way by the revolution. Salvation through a *having*, through the hacienda, is a false salvation that sooner or later leads to desperation. Moreover, it is an immoral or unethical solution to the problems of human conduct, a conduct that makes sense of its dignity in the making and not in the having, which is the only way to represent human morality.

But most concerning about nationalism is not its idea of the homeland as a *having*, something that is already in itself concerning and dangerous, but the separation or secession that it operates in the Mexican person, creating a separation from the human and constituting Mexican existence as if in a distinct reality, one that excludes all participation in what others do because doing so does not affect one's lot in life; it is a particular reality that is alienated from the proximal and immediate. This is why it is degrading to be a nationalist when one can simply be a person. For our purposes, it is enough to have identified, in the Mexican, this nationalist interpretation of his own being as a Mexican, and we emphasize that it is not the only interpretation and even less the most spontaneous, despite appearances to the contrary [41].

When Mexicans live life in full forgetfulness of nationality, life itself becomes a way of being that touches upon, in a foundational way, the fountain from which springs all humanism. The "feelings" of abandonment, gratuitousness, fragility, oscillation, sorrow, and so forth, which are familiar to the Mexican as a "matter" of their own being itself, offer a unique base upon which to ground our humanism. At its most extreme, the Mexican conceives himself as "accidental and *zozobrante*," which means that he opens himself up, without defense, to the human condition in a profound way. In a general sense, he intends to flee from those "sorrowful" feelings and to seek, by any means necessary, whether through faith, science, culture, or history, a ground for the human condition, a state in which he may feel safe and "substantial." But the Mexican person does not flee from these "categories" or "existentials" of the being of man, but rather remains there and returns to them, has them present at hand, not in the innocuous sense of theoretical representations, but as contents of his ordinary and extraordinary life—he has them there, he feels them there every day, every night, at all hours.

This peculiar "courage" or "clarity" to open up to the "misfortune" or "abandonment" of the human lot is the originary model for opening oneself to that which is human, to that most subterranean sphere in which has been prepared a sense that must be communicated, through compassion, sympathy, or affinity, to others, to all things that intend to pass themselves off as human. The Mexican understands the human other through a transposition of the sense of his own life. The compassion that he so frequently shows in all facets of his life (the Mexican expresses compassion for animals and even plants; he continually refers to anyone he meets as "poor" [*"pobre"*]) is the visible expression of that continuous operation through which the sense of one's own life is transferred to what is other. This complicated operation demands that the originating term, from which this transference is executed, be a life unobstructed by concealments; that is, that one's own life, which serves as the absolute center of reference from which sense emanates, be effectively familiar, that we carry it within us as we carry ourselves, because at the moment in which communication with the originary is obstructed, all compassion is paralyzed [42]. And, on the flip side, when the Mexican person sees that something that he does not recognize is being passed off as human, something that does not fit with his own original sense of humanity, he immediately rejects it from that realm and treats it as a thing and not as "human." In the same way that he is compassionate, the Mexican can be equally indifferent and brutal, inconsiderate, and can easily gloss over the "evidently" human with cold-blooded neglect. So long as the seemingly human lacks an obvious semblance with that which is Mexican (*lo mexicano*), there is no need for compassion, since the thing is not *seen* as human.

Our life is a familiarity with that which is human, and this because the characteristic we use to describe man in general can also be used to describe the Mexican person in particular. We don't have to run a parallel comparison between the Mexican and the human; there is an originary "pairing" (*en "pareja"*) between that which is Mexican and that which is human. We have seen that the same is true with the concepts of life and death. Previously, we suggested that death is, for the Mexican, a symbol of his own life, since the parameters with which we delineate life are the same parameters that allow us to delineate death.[18] Life and death configure themselves as "pairs" (*en "pareja"*). They are together, but more than that, they summon one another. One invokes the other, and vice versa. Edmund Husserl was the first of our philosophers to call attention to the particularities of our associations as "pairs," as "pairing" (*Verkoppeln*). This specific way in which things go together gives rise to interesting phenomena. When two contents, such as life and death, or Mexicanness and the human, appear as forming a pair, this means that they are "similar" and "different" simultaneously. There is an air of familiarity, of similarity, between life and death, but at the same time certain distinctions between them are made evident. Similarity is not so extreme as to be equality, but the distinction is not so explicit that we may say that there is no difference [43]. The pair maintains itself in the limits of similarity and difference. As such, it allows for the event of a "transmission" or "transference" of characteristics from one reality to another configured as a "pairing." There is a reciprocal borrowing of meaning. One term can be explained by the other and the other by the first. There is an incessant circulation of meaning, a coming and going, a receiving and a giving, an interminable coming and going of significations from one extreme to another through which the unitary meaning of the pair emerges, which is the meaning of the pair and not the meaning of one of its terms in isolation. We comprehend one of the terms as conforming, in conformity, with the sense of the other, to such an extent that we don't believe in the differences that would annul the transposition of sense, nor any equality that would likewise annihilate the transference of meaning.

That which is Mexican and that which is human constitute a pair. What is Mexican is the point of departure for what is human. What is human receives its primary meaning from its similarity to Mexicanness. If this similarity fails to attend to the ground of those relationships between us and others, then no sort of humanism can arise. But similarity is also burdened by a consciousness of a distinction. If the Mexican person is compassionate, demonstrating with that compassion that he feels a universal similarity with all others, he likewise intuits that his fate is not completely shareable, that there is a center on which it is impossible to communicate.

Foreigners of great sensibility have made us aware that Mexicans exhibit a peculiar attitude: an openness to all things human, the mixing and intermingling without fear or scruples, appears to allow for an unlimited communication between Mexicans and others, in which equality shines as a supreme ideal. But, in spite of this undeniable communicative ability, there is a serious obstacle. If the Mexican person can assimilate himself to the foreigner, the foreigner, in turn, cannot fully assimilate himself to the Mexican. There is a remainder that cannot be overcome, that does not avail itself. Hospitality does not prevent the appearance of the insurmountable obstacle. The creation of this difference cancels the pair: *that which is Mexican* and *that which is human*. If this difference is made explicit by the Mexican person herself, it leads almost immediately to nationalism [44]. If it is not made explicit or recognized by Mexicans, it will still be obvious to others. But what constitutes this obstacle? The Mexican will never be able to say. Mexican humanism fails to recognize it and it fails to do so with legitimacy, since in conceiving it as grounded in the formation of a "pair," he has to ignore the barrier a priori.

More than a sense of equality before others, we possess a sense of "pairing" or "bringing together" while the nationalist possesses a sense of "difference" or "prying apart." Not all humanism constitutes itself along these lines. Generally, it is believed that humanism presupposes the affirmation of equality and that, without it, there is no possibility for humanism. But this is a mere prejudice. The same is thought about life and death, namely, that the "difference" between both phenomena is the indispensable premise of all theory about life and death. But we have seen that this is not the case. The Mexican person "pairs" them by stretching their similarity until they achieved "equality." The same thing happens with humanism. That which is human is familiar to the Mexican person because it is with him as that other extreme with which he establishes meaningful communication, a reciprocal borrowing of services and favors, a transference of sense that allows him to explain his own life as human and, similarly, to articulate that which is human as that which is Mexican. The consequences of this structure cannot be further discussed here.

III. History

5. Insufficiency and Inferiority

We can indicate three important contributions made by Mexicans to the field of philosophy in the middle of the 20th century [45]. First, they have contributed to the bankruptcy of positivism and to the pretensions of natural science to establish itself as a guide for human life at the exclusion of art, religion, and philosophy. Second, they have contributed to the elaboration of an aesthetic and sensuous vision of the human being and of the world in which the Mexican is seen more authentically than through a scientific framework; third is a contribution that I consider the most significant of all, a determining of the essence of the Mexican person, that is, of a particular style of life, of a radical project of existing that only belongs to Mexicans and that distinguishes them from Spaniards, North Americans, and Europeans.

At the turn of the 20th century, we find Mexican thought vigorously rejecting positivism, or the idea that man is a natural object that science can exhaust through all of its methods; that is, it begins by rejecting as ridiculous a pretentious "rational and exact conception of the Universe and of Life."[1] There's nothing precise about human life and even less so about Mexican life. Such was the proposal, in essence, in the work of Antonio Caso. After him, José Vasconcelos substitutes a positivist vision of man with an aesthetic conception in which sensibility and passion define the human being while asking for an explicit recognition of emotion as an essential aspect of being human. This phase of Mexican thought corresponds with the great muralist period of José Clemente Orozco and Diego Rivera. We could say, in a figurative sense, that Vasconcelos's synthetic philosophy (*filosofiá plastica*) was more decisive in this direction. Finally, there appears a third contribution.

The Mexican person can no longer satisfy his desires for self-knowledge by seeing himself in paintings [46]; now he wants to grab hold of his own essence in pure reflection, no longer merely figuratively in art, but conceptually in philosophical discourse. Samuel Ramos's reflections initiate this course of thought, one excellently adopted by such literary figures as Rodolfo Usigli and Agustin Yáñez, and later by historians and philosophers such as Leopoldo Zea. In our own time, these pursuits spread to all corners of our culture, nourishing the theories and points of view of philologists, literary critics, historians, poets, novelists, painters, etc. It is dominated by an eagerness to characterize the essence of the Mexican in history as well as in his ordinary and extraordinary life. A *Mexican* philosophy is thus the most important contribution that our scholars have made in one-half a century of reflection and meditation.

The doctrine that most appropriately captures Mexican reality seems to be the philosophy that Mexicans themselves have created in this first half of the 20th century. This is a philosophy that developed from the study of and attention to Mexican reality, and which has emerged from the decisive facing of the problems of Mexicans themselves, a philosophy that has as its best representatives in Caso, Vasconcelos, Ramos, and Zea. Doctrines that deviate from this tradition run the risk of unhinging themselves from Mexican history itself and of creating artificial problems that have their justification in other circumstances, but not in ours. A philosophy that refuses the search for that which is Mexican (*lo mexicano*) as its central theme would just be, for us, and in the best case, an elegant flower in an academic greenhouse.[2]

Our observations regarding the general sense of philosophy in Mexico during the first half of our century have recently received notable corroboration by a number of Mexican philosophers that responded to an inquiry about the results of our philosophical labors. Those who participated in the inquiry included José Vasconcelos, Samuel Ramos, Eduardo García Máynez, José Sánchez Villaseñor, Leopoldo Zea, Agustin Yáñez, and Francisco Larroyo [47]. In what follows, I'd like to briefly analyze some of their responses so as to highlight the correspondence between them and what we have already said regarding this theme.

Agustin Yáñez articulates with a formula of priceless precision the general sense of what seems to us to be the dominant tendency in contemporary Mexican philosophy: "The most important thing in the field of philosophy is that it has focused the solution of the eternal problems of knowledge in Mexican reality, and it has also emphasized amongst those problems those that are more directly related to the human being in general. I don't think this would have been possible if at the start of the century the philosophical task in Mexico had not been able to overcome the limitations of positivist philosophy." He continues: "I, of course, have always sustained that a special kind of reflection on literature would give us a profound understanding of Mexican reality."

Without a doubt, a philosophical anthropology of the Mexican person can only emerge if we reject the pretensions of positivism and of natural science to have the last word on these matters. The critique of positivism opens up a path toward a "new humanism." Those who continue to insist on seeing in science the final sense of all things human have little interest in the contributions of literature or philosophy. When physicists or biologists lord over the culture of a generation, the humanist project suffers an inevitable decline. The Athenium[3] executed in Mexico a masterstroke in liberating us from the shackles of a scientism without human horizons. Its lessons should never be forgotten.

It is clear that our philosophy cannot renounce the task of positing the great universal problems of philosophy. What it has learned in the past half-century is that it must, however, determine the ground or horizon from which such problems must be posited. These problems cannot be understood in an indeterminate generality. Every problem proposed demands a concrete subject that proposes it and that can respond to it. The Mexican person, in this case, is the source from which the answer and the solution to these problems must arise. But of those philosophical problems, those that more directly touch upon the concrete person are exactly those to which our meditation attends [48]. We consider, for instance, the much-debated theme regarding the sense of responsibility of the Mexican person.

Yáñez's appreciations would require a more extended commentary. Briefly, however, not everyone understands that, through literature, one can obtain a more adequate knowledge than, say, through psychology.[4] But it is a fact that so-called psychology only gives us generalities that it cannot justify, while literature gives us the concrete and particular problems of Mexicans and only Mexicans. Personally, we believe that the pair, specific to (Mexican) literature, of "*pelados*"[5] and "decent" ("*decentes*") folks, highlighted by Yáñez in his study, "The Mexican Thinker," is of great promise for an analysis of our own being. The study of literature allows us to create a catalog of concepts for the description of the being of the Mexican, one that may enjoy the great advantage of immediately concurring with the very same object it describes and that, moreover, does not interpose between this object and its corresponding concepts the inevitable distance that brings about generalizations not related to a concrete plane. "Pelados" and "decent" folks are much more immediate categories than those of "resentment" and "complex of inferiority" for the description of the being of the Mexican, and here lies its great value, or the inherent value of all investigations that have taken up "literary experience" as its point of departure. Personally, we have maintained that the poetry of López Velarde, an ontological poetry *par excellence*, has firmly grounded my "Essay on the Ontology of the Mexican." "Zozobra," as the central concept of López Velarde's poetic work, opens our path or serves as a horizon for a reading of the being of the Mexican that is truly genuine.[6]

Leopoldo Zea advances these ideas in his response to the inquiry previously mentioned.

> The preoccupation with this concrete reality (i.e., Mexican reality) tells us that it need not think itself inferior to any other reality [49]; it has given rise to investigations in which a mode of being proper to Mexico and the Mexican person has been made explicit. This mode of being of the Mexican that our philosophers have captured in their reflections

expresses itself in certain behaviors that, in their originality, make obvious forms of behavior belonging to the human being in general but that, up to now, had not been grasped by philosophers in other countries. The investigations carried out so far regarding the history of our ideas and about the being of this concrete entity we call "the Mexican person" represent an important contribution in the field of philosophy in general.

Leopoldo Zea is very aware of the genuine motivations behind our investigations into the "ontology of the Mexican." But what distinguishes his position in this regard is his insistence that an ontology of Mexican being does not stop to consider problems belonging to ontology in general but, rather, puts them aside and considers a concrete entity, in this case, the Mexican person. In the mode of being of the Mexican are expressed, as Zea notes, the modes of being of man in general, but *the originarity of the Mexican's lived experiences allows a repositing, from its own ground, the general sense of humanism.* In other words: *It is worthless to begin with a definition of man in general in order to illuminate with this idea a "particular" human being which is the Mexican, but the inverse is true; moreover, paradoxical as it may seem, it is better to begin with the being of the Mexican in order to illuminate from that being what will be called man in general or the essence of man.* The idea of "man in general" cannot be the starting point for an ontology of Mexican being because in the idea of man in general that would serve as the criteria for ontology, there have been deposited "prejudices" and "presuppositions" that have nothing general about them but that are the result of bad "generalizations" of specific perspectives regarding European man. When one speaks of man in general, in truth what we mean is European man, to whom it seems as a fact of his history that there is no other general idea of man than one that begins from his own European being. Against this entrenched prejudiced we pronounce the ontology of the Mexican being that seeks an exegesis of its own being so as to advance, from that point, "toward a new humanism" [50]. Asking about the "essence of man" comes after, and not before, ontology (*A la ontología sigue, y no precede, preguntar por la "esencia del hombre"*). "*Humanism*" *is the second task of "ontology."* The European does not ask himself the question regarding his own being because he immediately identifies the human and the European. He does not justify himself before humanity because, for him, his own being is the measure of the human.

We, on the other hand, have to justify ourselves. It is a historical fact that endures, one registered on the historical record, that humanity has been denied to us, being men has been denied to us, but it is from this original situation that we must elevate our thinking. Only in the last few years of philosophical reflection in Europe, with the existentialist philosophy of Heidegger and Sartre, have the dominant prejudices of philosophy been recognized; from this recognition, it has engaged in the problem of executing its own ontology so as to advance a new definition of man.

> We had never seen France ... it was so natural to be French, it was the simplest lens, the most economical way to feel oneself universal. There was nothing to explain: the others, the German, the English, the Belgians were the ones who had to explain their bad luck or the sins that kept them from being properly human. Now France is upside-down and for the first time we see it, we see an enormous spoiled machine and we think: that's it. That: an accident in the midfield, an accident of history. We are still French, but we no longer find it so natural. All we needed was an accident to make us understand that we were accidental.[7]

The European, like us, has to justify himself before humanity. We are in the original situation in which an authentic sense of the human being must emerge. From the ontology of the Mexican being, there will emerge a Mexican humanism and, from that original source, a new sense of the human in general and of being in general. "The universality of the concept of Being is not opposed to the 'specificity' of the investigation, that is, in going toward (the universal concept of Being) through the path of a special interpretation of a determinate entity, human existence, in which the horizon for the comprehension and possible interpretation of being must be conquered" [51].[8]

Finally, Samuel Ramos also sees in a philosophy that emerges from our own particular circumstance the actual sense of Mexican philosophy in our own day. "It is obvious that we have to learn and assimilate other philosophies. But when we are capable of thinking for ourselves, that thinking must be determined by our own situation within a particular geographic, cultural, and historical environment. To negate the influence on our thinking of our circumstances is equivalent to taking a concrete human being for an empty and abstract entity." Moreover, "the working hypothesis which is more capable of explaining Mexican reality would include any doctrine that explains in a satisfactory manner the *majority of possible facts*. I have used Adler's psychological theory to interpret *certain aspects* of man and culture in Mexico. I believe that, so far as we can't find any other theory, the application of Adler's theory is still valid."[9]

Ramos's essay, "Profile of man and culture in Mexico," contains a "psychoanalysis of the Mexican person," in which he "rigorously" applies the psychology of Alfred Adler to the "Mexican case." The idea of an inferiority that constitutes the being of the Mexican person is without a doubt an idea that helps explain a great number of facts about Mexican life. Ramos gives us, as proof of his theory, a great number of facts that are explained by it. But, even if we recognize, as we do, in fact, recognize, that its reach is very broad, it seems to us that it unnecessarily delimits itself by holding itself to a determinate psychological theory and, moreover, that it does not make the necessary distinction between "inferiority" and "insufficiency." Let us begin with this latter point.

It is clear that the concepts "inferiority" and "insufficiency" do not overlap, neither in extension nor in comprehension. A situation that is "inferior" is not, necessarily, "insufficient," and inversely, an "insufficiency" is not, necessarily, an "inferiority." A few examples serve to make clear the indispensable limits of these concepts. A "food" or *menu* can be sufficient or insufficient, on the one hand, and superior or inferior, on the other [52]. There are "foods" that are superior in quality but insufficient insofar as they do not satisfy the necessary nutritional requirements of an average individual. There are also "diets" that are sufficient in terms of their nutritional content, but inferior in "quality," and finally, there are foods that are at the same time "insufficient" and "inferior," or "sufficient" and "superior," the latter being the best case scenario among those mentioned.

Sufficiency is understood as the fulfillment of the demands set by a specific level of life. Superiority expresses a higher rank in the scale of levels of life. What is superior is a grade higher in the levels of life; sufficiency is the consummation of a particular *status* that can be superior or inferior. In principle, both criteria function independently, but their mixture or the "contamination" of one with the other brings about situations that are more complicated or harder to clarify. Within its own limits, Mexican culture can fulfill, as an aspect of its cultural production, the demands of a determinate cultural *status*. If it does not fulfill or consummate the demands, it is then an insufficient culture. Sufficiency and insufficiency represents an "immanent" or "intrinsic" value scale. But if we compare Mexican culture with European culture, if we look for an "extrinsic" criterion of valuation, the problem of "superiority" and "inferiority" is automatically introduced. When we cease to look at ourselves from within and instead seek to adopt the perspective of others that is directed at us, there emerges the valorative pairing "inferior–superior." For now, we do not see why we must expose ourselves to the judgment of the other. That our intimacy has *at the same time*, and with the same originality, an external face is not a fact that we can derive from a higher principle, but is rather a pure and simple fact that is there, that imposes itself on us, and before which we cannot avoid assuming a certain intellectual posture.

Sufficient or not, Mexican culture "declares itself" as inferior to the European. But the "recognition" of this situation of inferiority does not correspond, in any way, to evidencing a "complex of inferiority." To recognize a hierarchy of values is not to manifest a "complex of inferiority," and knowing how to "admire" (something that is far from being a symptom of "inferiority") speaks more of a generous and "sufficient" nature in regard to one's moral health [53]. One could also talk about an "indifference" before the fact of a supposed inferiority, making ourselves completely alien to the fact of having to confront other, "superior," forms of life. But indifference is ontologically inconceivable. We are not indifferent to the way we appear to others, whether we want to or not, we are always "interested" in how we are seen "from the outside."

The simple "admiration" of values recognized as superior can lead one to an attitude that we call "resignation." This is a deficient situation. Resignation feeds on the defect of one's "standing still" or being paralyzed before superior values. Resignation kills the will to appropriate superior values. Whoever feels their inferiority and *does not resign* themselves to it tends to a conscious appropriation of the (superior) values, by creating them themselves, living them, enjoying them, or keeping an appropriate attitude before them. But when the appropriation is envisioned, the *impotency* of doing so can occasion the original trauma of a "complex of inferiority." There is no complex of inferiority without this feeling of impotence before foreign values. On the other hand, whoever recognizes themselves as "insufficient" before those (superior) values, but nonetheless has faith in his capacity to realize them, does not suffer an inferiority complex. Impotence carries with it the willingness to negate those values that are not accessible to us; it carries with it devaluation. The recognition of "inferiority" becomes a "complex of inferiority" when the hierarchy of values appears misrepresented by "resentment," "emotionality," or "an imaginary project of life." The "*complex* of inferiority" makes its appearance when one tries to cover over inferiority by negating the superior "status" of that which is admired because it seems to be beyond our reach, or when one imagines oneself superior to it as a result of one's own "impotence," or when one is incapable of being like that which one envies.

In the "complex of inferiority," the recognition of what is superior is replaced by the negation of the (superior) values and the elevation of one's own to the highest level of the hierarchy [54]. What is inferior replaces what is superior. But in this type of behavior there is not only the suspicion that one is acting "maliciously" but also that the impotency that motivates our actions has tricked us, since, once we finally recognize what is superior, it becomes obvious to everyone that an inferior value is at play. The complex of inferiority is dialectical; it entails an incurable *circulus in probando*. Pretending to manifest himself as superior, the individual afflicted with this complex shows himself in his conduct as inferior. It is simpler and easier to recognize superiority outside of ourselves, so long as we do not resign ourselves to it or boast of our indifference regarding it, thus keeping ourselves from claiming that we are superior only to show our inferiority in our conduct.

In addition to "indifference," "resignation," "simple recognition," and the "complex of inferiority," there is another attitude equally deficient. It consists in giving oneself over servilely to the value that is recognized as superior, adopting as infallible the norm that emanates from "superior culture." Here we may speak of "Malinchistas," "indigenists," "pochos," and "Europeanizers." We have touched on this in our "Essay on the Ontology of the Mexican." Inferiority is, in this case, giving oneself without appeal to a foreign value (i.e., the superior value), thus making impossible any attempt at autonomy. It is a servile submission, while the complex of inferiority is a rebellious submission, even if incapable to lift one victoriously against whatever is seen as superior. Just as the complex of inferiority suffers a radical impotence but sanctions and adds legitimacy to this impotence, "giving oneself to a foreign value" exemplifies the perfection of this attitude before inferiority.

In the presence of these differing attitudes, the only one we accept as legitimate is the one that transforms inferiority into insufficiency, and the present work proposes to bring about this insufficiency by insisting on the individual's capacity to give himself the sufficiency that he lacks. We thus take "inferiority" as an opportunity to remove the sense of helplessness that accompanies the complex of inferiority [55]. Thus, we assume "inferiority" so as to bring about the fulfillment of "sufficiency." If we recognize a specific value as superior, the only appropriate conduct toward it is to assume insufficiency upon its recognition, and not by a supposed, deceitful, and even disdainful "superiority" before it. Only in this way can we overcome the complex of inferiority and at the same time the submissive project that has it that others will save us. With this we go from the duality of "superiority–inferiority" to that of "insufficiency–sufficiency." That is why, in my "Essay on the Ontology of the Mexican," I have said that "inferiority is an insufficiency that has renounced its origins, that has lost itself and seeks to cover over the demands that its own decisions impose upon us—rooted as they are in zozobra and accidentality."[10] Inferiority must be brought back to its origins, which is precisely the horizon of insufficiency, and only in this way will one free oneself from the snares of the "inferiority complex."

To apply the thesis of an "inferiority complex" to the *criollos* who toward the end of the 18th century fought for Mexican independence seems "just" and "true." However, it seems to us overly simplistic to explain this as involving *only* an inferiority complex. The criollo felt "sufficient" and even "superior" before the man from the peninsula. The results of their battles for liberation, however, revealed precisely the contrary, that is, their "insufficiency" and their "inferiority." Is this an accurate assessment? As far as the actual facts, there is no doubt. After a period of time in which optimism and confidence in their own capacities were the dominant attitude, there came a period in which "bitterness," pessimism, and "discouragement" characterized the entire era. There then appeared "deliverists" (*"entreguistas"*) and the "foreignizers" (*"extranjerizantes"*) that pretend to see Mexico's salvation in its submission to foreign politics. But this is followed by a new period of confidence and struggle in which Mexico affirms, through its own will, the conquest and the recognition of its independence.

In truth, the criollo did not suffer from an "inferiority complex." His defect actually consisted in drowning out the sense of insufficiency by preoccupying himself with the impressive inventory and catalog of his own riches, of the excellence of his character, and the wealth of his culture [56]. He desired to own it all, as if by merely extending his hand he would make it his and all that would be left to do would be to defend his certain, and permanent, possession of it with another who would challenge him. The notion that he was being robbed by the man from the peninsula (i.e., Spain) blinded him from seeing that he was, in fact, poor. And when he was able to expel the intruder, he found that his possessions (*los haberes*), which were promised for his enjoyment, had disappeared. Bitterness was then inevitable, and so was desperation, which unfortunately did not reach a necessary extreme, since he was still deceived by the fallacious idea that the sense of his life was in the having and not in the doing. Insufficiency was not satisfied with an *hacienda* that is "sufficient," but with the everyday labor that grants sufficiency in the course of work and struggle—something that cannot be ignored, even for a day. As López Velarde wrote in his poem, "Nochebuena," "We don't *have* delights, only necessities."

With the *criollo* we see, for the first time, a fundamental project that, for centuries, appears in the Mexican person as a real curse. The idea of a nation rich and abundant in resources has influenced our character in decisive ways. This richness, considered partly imaginary and partly real, especially when we focus on certain types of resources, for instance, and more recently, oil and mining, has given rise to the formation of a fundamental project so original as that of being saved by others. In a certain sense, property allows independence from others. *Independence is thus, like dependence, an equivocal notion, since dependence itself points to both an autonomy of choice and freedom through labor, while independence means something similar but in terms of having the wealth of ownership. These two ideas of independence (freedom of choice and freedom to own property) operate in the criollo as a project of ownership, as "economic independence."* Salvation is thus conceived as the enjoyment of those natural gifts that are already there, elaborated "naturally," which is the inevitable contradiction of this fundamental project. In a radical sense, what is sought is the *enjoyment* of what one has, which allows us to call this project an "esthetic" project" [57]. Whoever lives in an esthetic state unilaterally accentuates the "given," the natural, the immediate, and places happiness and salvation on that givenness and immediacy. The natural can be a landscape, one's character, or the richness of the world in general. In every case, man is fascinated by the object before him. It is a project of torpidity before things, of dullness, of stupefying perplexity, of spiritual impotence before the imposing exteriority of nature. In that which is natural we see reflected the image of ourselves, which is at the same time what is foreign to us as it appears under the aspect of things. Ownership allows the unification, in an apparently dialectical fashion, of our interiority with what is external, other. One communes with the earth and forms a unity with her in a "wild paradise." Such a project, however, doesn't realize the intended synthesis, but rather, and far from bringing it about, traps one in desperation. The desired communion with the earth is never achieved. Instead, we are wounded either by nature's indifference or by the abandonment of spirit given to its own forces. Poets who sing about the beauty of the landscape are confronted by poets who speak to us about nature's inhospitableness and about the earth's indifference before the anxieties of man, with those who speak to "mother earth" or "stepmother nature" ("*madrastra naturaleza*"). The despair and bitterness of the criollo were tied to the project of independence as the possible enjoyment of resources. But this was not the only notion of independence that motivated the criollo in his rebellion [58].[11]

Before the complex of inferiority, understood as a voluntary choice to be saved by others, and the deliberate, yet frustrating, insistence on saving oneself, there is a pure and simple surrender to someone else's will, one that renounces any voluntary change and holds on to the negation of our freedom, to the "invalidity" of "this side" and the absolute "justification" of "that side." But before the two deficient ways of affirming freedom, one that holds it as external and superficial, while implicating it and denying it in interiority and depth, and the other that uproots it from both the intimate and the external, we have a true autonomy-affirming attitude, the independence movement.

Prior to a being saved by others, there is a saving of others, or an inversion of values. The inversion of values has a family relationship with "resentment," but they differ in a fundamental way, since it is virtue and power and not "impotence" that characterizes the inversion. To devalue is limited to denying the idea that the supposed "superior" values are effectively "superior," but the "inversion" of values goes further and replaces superior values with inferior values. The inversion of values is cynicism, while devaluation is merely a critical and skeptical attitude that definitely brings one to dissolution, detachment, and renunciation. Cynicism is, according to our definition, *the conscious acceptance of an inversion of values*.

The cynic boasts of being a plebian, a "pelado." The cynic places the low over the noble, ruin over splendor. The cynic exhibits vital excess and not bashfulness or timidity [59]. It is an attitude of dignified rebellion before the complex of inferiority, which is itself a submissive rebellion, or, at bottom, the submission of rebels. The cynic is carefree and bold: he challenges a world of "superior" values with the clear purpose of putting it on its head. In cynicism the desire to put "the world upside down" is self-assuredly affirmed, an insistence, according to Hegel, that defines philosophy itself. Cynicism is, then, in its pure form, philosophical work.

The lordship of the cynic comes from his condition as referee, from his unbounded refereeing, from his "doing whatever the hell he wants" ("*real gana*"). In cynicism, man puts himself as the final judge regarding the management of the hierarchy of values; he decides whether they go "upward or downward," or are put "on their head." In cynicism, "inferiority," appropriated as "insufficiency," is presented as "superior" and "sufficient" and held as such by the hand of the lord (*el senor*), by a rude, hard, gross, and brutal hand. As all lords, the cynic is sensible to the compliments of courtesy, to the fine and the gifted, to the polished and polite. In the cynic, there is always a gentleness, as in the soul of any true lord. It is common to oppose hypocrisy to cynicism, as if they were water and oil, impossible to mix. We concede that hypocrisy is the contrary of cynicism, but we agree with Hegel that the concrete is the dialectical unity of contraries and the abstract is separation without continuity. Pure cynicism is pure hypocrisy, and hypocrisy, in turn, is pure cynicism. What is "real" is "contamination" or "shading." There, where we find a cynic, we must look also for his respective entourage of hypocrites, of flatterers and bootlickers, that run behind his lordship so as to deify his judgments and works, and then suddenly to abandon him and take the kingdom for themselves, motivated by an overflowing desire to become the referees and judges of values.

But there also, where the hypocrites congregate, we must look for the cynic, that from the back of the congregation functions as lord. "All cynics have the hypocrites that they deserve," a phrase that recalls the famous saying that all peoples have the government they deserve. There is no cynicism without the dialectical support of a hypocrisy that opposes it. Hypocrisy is discretion, distinguished manners, dissimulation, and concealment of true intentions. *To be a lord or master, one must first have been discrete. Lordship begins its history with courteous and respectful gestures toward superior values* [60]. It cozies up to them and learns their language. The "pelado" coexists with the "decent fellow" in the interior of every Mexican, and out of their constant struggle there emerges the concrete figure of the Mexican character. But discretion is a provisional behavior that awaits its turn to invert values so as to manifest itself then in its true form: lordship. In discretion we accept to be saved by others; in discretion we accept to be seen as passively giving ourselves away, but discretion itself is not an end in itself; it is tacit and tricky and seeks only familiarity, that is, to be trusted before embarking on the adventure of inverting values. *Hypocrisy is, then, in the cynic, a wise and prudent strategy, as it seeks to swoop down on its prey as quietly as possible before attacking it and bringing it down.* The cynic wants to be a lord, but not just a lord, but an effective, victorious, and triumphant lord or master. His is not the conduct of the nonreflective type nor of adventure in the sense of adventure as an improvisation or an unconscious act. Moreover, he is quick to recognize his responsibility whether he wins or loses. Cynicism is clarity; it is always intellectual labor due to its transparency and the cold-bloodedness of its decisions. The force and brutality associated with it is not born, however, from a sense of sufficiency itself, but, rather, from that of insufficiency, although cautiously veiled to the eyes of others. The lord or master appears before those who follow him as a "man of integrity" (*hombre de "una pieza"*), but to those close to him he reveals himself, either in writing or in person, as "broken inside." Only those closest to him have had the suspicion about his interior desperation, his zozobra, his angst and his fear. The intimate life of the lord is always threatened by ruthless spurts of discouragement, of desperation, of disturbances. Insufficiency lives in the cynic in the most authentic way possible; everything is a horizon of accidentality and zozobra. If we were to attend to these aspects of his existence, we would agree that the cynic, more than anyone else, would be justified in fully giving himself to the gaze of the other so that he may be rescued from his interior zozobra by another's decision. But precisely because of his authenticity he does not renounce himself, does not give himself away, but fights and insists on bringing his autonomy to fulfillment, an autonomy he knows is a construct of his own *accidentality* [61].

What we find paradoxical about this form of human existence is the fact that while it is possible for us to be saved by others, it is the cynic who saves us. It is the most in need that will come to the aid of others, who will assign themselves the task of fulfilling others and give them the sufficiency that they lack. But it would be more precise to say, not that the cynic passes from the project of being saved by others to one of saving them, but rather that the cynic's project is one of liberating others, and not one of saving them. Salvation, like liberation, is sufficiency and fulfillment, or consummation, but of a radically different kind. To be saved means that we wait for something that we lack to be *given to us*, that we must be fulfilled with possessing a certain thing, with something that is *given* (*gegeben*), but to be liberated does not depend on waiting for a gift, on being fulfilled by something given, but, and simply, it depends on a *proposal* (*aufgegeben*) as a task, a mission, a destiny to be realized. Liberation is salvation through the finding of a mission, of a sense of life; liberation does not reside in being capable of paying for it ourselves. Cynicism does not promise wealth or riches, but work—from there arises the disillusion and even the shame many will feel toward the "liberator" or the "liberators." Whoever lives in the project of being saved by others will always complain that his own people do not give him with the same riches that others promise as payment for his submission. "Heroes"[12] always have to disillusion the stubborn masses who expect from them not liberation but salvation, something the heroes cannot do, and from this perspective they were thought impotent, which is why they made themselves useful, as they did in the plundering and looting at the start of the War of Independence or with "expropriations" during the revolution. With a people that suffered less from an inferiority complex and more from a *peculiar "esthetic state"* (Kierkegaard), the business of liberation could not find an echo [62].

Whoever expects to be saved by others has no eyes for liberation; whoever expects to be saved by others despairs, and this because the insufficiency that constitutes him, and the project of sufficiency before him (not, however, sufficiency in regard to resources), violently collide with and resist his intimate project of life. Cynicism calls for action, but salvation is expected by a creature who is unwilling, apathetic, and lethargic. The encounter with a radially adverse project marks leaders of tragic temperament. The leader is naïve when he allows himself to be swayed by the illusion that others aspire, like he aspires, to liberation, to autarchy. From there arises his final bitterness and almost always his holocaust (*su holocausto*). He promises liberation and he promises salvation, something that always occasions doubt in the consciousness of his followers. His frustration is almost always proclaimed when it is obvious that he has left his followers worst off then they were before—in misery, rather than in the poverty in which he found them. But many, even if late, do open themselves up to his mission and understand it.

Previously we said, regarding Ramos, that it seemed likely to us that his theory could be fulfilled in two possible ways: first, with a phenomenological analysis that carefully separates "inferiority" from "insufficiency," and, second, retracing his psychological theory to more fundamental and properly ontological dimensions. We have already spoken about the first. As far as the second way, the distinction between *autognosis* and *ontology* of the Mexican person will serve as a connecting thread. Fundamental reasons have driven José Gaos to reject our use of "ontology" to characterize our own efforts in the clarification of the being of the Mexican; rather, Gaos favors employing the term *autognosis* [63].[13]

It is true that an ontology of the Mexican is also autognosis of the Mexican, but the inverse is not the case. There are some very rich modalities of autognosis that are not ontological. Let us mention two prominent examples: the investigation of Ramos and Yañez, but also that of Zea, although with a small caveat. In the first case, one does not feel the radical incompleteness of the exegesis of the being of the Mexican, and in the second case, reflection itself pushes one toward asking decisive ontological questions.[14]

What justification protects us when we speak not of autognosis but of ontology? Right away, we clearly hear in the second part of the question the philosophical nature of the investigation that we are pursuing, while the first part of the question is involved in unavoidable ambiguity. Autognosis can and must be, with equal right, philosophical and nonphilosophical knowledge. In contrast, ontology designates philosophical knowledge *par excellence*. But not only this. Autognosis gives expression to the tendency of a kind of reflection on the Mexican person that comes from afar and which points to a philosophical radicalization [64]. The autognosis of the Mexican that is of most immediate interest to us, those of Ramos and Yañez, the ontological aspect clearly comes through, even if their authors do not recognize it. Autognosis itself demands its own ontology of the Mexican because it finds itself already inserted in a general philosophical direction that has found its culmination in ontological analysis. The psychoanalysis of the Mexican proposed by Ramos is rooted in the psychology of Adler, and the analysis of resentment proposed by Yañez is rooted in the phenomenological psychology of Max Scheler. But both psychoanalysis and phenomenological psychology ground their most profound tendencies in ontology. These investigations are guided, then, by philosophical principles toward ontology, even if such a tendency to guide cannot be clearly discerned "from within," but is rather made visible "from outside" when, in fact, we have already installed ourselves in the perspective of phenomenological ontology.

III. History

Beginning with José Ortega y Gasset, it is common to speak among us of generations and to characterize generations as real effective subjects of historical becoming. The generation points to a goal and finds its meaning in holding itself accountable, with vigor and rigor, to the realization of its objective. A generation rises or falls with its theme—that theme to which it has tied its fate. Now, it is not easy to *arrive at* a generational theme, and that generation can think itself *fortunate* that makes precise its objective with sufficient transparency and certainty. The generational theme of Hyperion is precisely the ontological characterization of the being of the Mexican; it is the radical moment, as far as we are concerned, for the autognosis of the Mexican. For the generations that have preceded us, this is an alien theme. But we are not talking about simple autognosis, but autognosis of the ontological kind, as we have previously shown [65].[15]

The autognosis of the Mexican person reflects the reflective nature of Mexicans themselves. We don't just want to live; we want to *know* and, if possible, simultaneously to know how we live. Reflection is an effort to recuperate that being that unreflective action disperses and divides. Reflection is not the attempt to lend a plan to action, but the effort to throw ourselves into it fully aware of our purposes. What in action seeks its realization as a purpose freely chosen cannot be revoked by reflection, but it can be illuminated and made transparent. Almost from birth we have sought our interiority through reflection, we have been determined to know what we are and where we are going. Within this tradition of autognosis we find inserted our ontology of the Mexican. But as an authentic advancement of philosophical knowledge, ontology is the only course of thought and action that can do justice, by being radical, to the secular tradition underlying the autognosis of the Mexican. The knowledge that Mexicans can have of their own possibilities points, by the very intentions that animate it, to a radicality that only ontology can satisfy [66].

Psychology may be enough to fulfill certain demands, but the suppositions with which it operates are not clarified, and due to the opacity of its grounds, it cannot pinpoint precisely to those things to which it aims. Through psychology, the Mexican person obtains an extremely provisional understanding of himself, but not only this; likewise by seeing himself psychologically, he runs the risk of "objectifying" his own person and absolving himself, through this act, of all responsibility. In employing the expression, "ontology of the Mexican," the task is "to show (*demonstrar*) that the questions posited and the studies made until now regarding the (Mexican), without prejudice in regard to their the results, are ignorant of the *philosophical* problem and that, therefore, while they continue to ignore it, cannot be *capable* of acquiring that which they truly seek."[16]

Critics are quick to deny that there can be an ontology of Mexicanness. Ontology, they insist, can only refer to being in general and, in the case of a fundamental ontology, to the analysis of not a particular type of man, but of "man in general." In spite of repeated attacks against the idea of a "man in general," this objection continues to operate uncritically and is in dire need of clarification. It is true that ontology asks for the sense of being in general, but it is also true that it is always a question asked by man himself; moreover, asking about being seems inconceivable if being is not grounded in man. In this sense, man and being are inextricably linked. But this link between man and being is not made as a link between being and man in general, but is made with concrete modalities of man, one of these modalities being that of the Mexican. The being of man is not a generic being in which diverse types of human beings would appear as subordinate species. Because these "objections" are apparently made from the point of view of Heidegger's philosophy, we will consider his terminology in what follows.

In *Being and Time*, Heidegger tries to rigorously posit the question that asks about the sense of being in general [67].[17] He distinguishes as fundamental for his purposes between Being and Entity, "Being is not something like an Entity."[18] There is a radical difference that Heidegger calls "ontological" between Being and Entity that metaphysics "represents" but does not "think."[19] Man, who Heidegger designates with the term *Dasein*, has a particular manner of being that distinguishes itself from other modes that do not have an existential form or are human.[20] The form of being of Dasein he calls existence.[21] "The word 'existence' is used in *Sein und Zeit* exclusively to designate the being of man."[22] Man has as his "essence" his existence, which is in each case his own, or mine (*je meines*); man does not have a determined material "essence."[23] This "existence" has nothing to do with the traditional concept of *existentia*.[24] (According to Heidegger, Sartre employs the term "existence" in its traditional sense, and for that reason the latter has nothing in common with Heidegger's own thought—he seems to me to be confused on this point.) This "existence" I have to make in each case my own: "I decide for my existence through a radical possibility that is my proper constitution." [25] In Dasein, "there is a preeminence of *existentia* over *esentia*"[26]—a proposition that literally appears in Sartre's work but that has lamentably been misinterpreted by Heidegger.

Existence has, then, *Jemeinigkeit* as a radical "property"; it has, that is, the property of a being that is in each case mine, and not an existence in general (the existence of everyone and no one), a generality that is inconceivable from the Heideggerian perspective. From this perspective, then, it is legitimate to speak about an ontology of the Mexican [68].[27]

In his essay on Kant, Heidegger uses as equivalent the expressions metaphysics of Dasein and ontology of Dasein, assigning to them both the task of "unconcealing the constitution of the being" of Dasein (*Kant und das Problem der Metaphysik*, p. 222). But this unconcealment of the Being of Dasein must be executed in such a way that it makes possible the comprehension of its own being. In other words, in the constitution of the being of Dasein, it must be made visible how this constitution is at the same time a comprehension of the being that constitutes us (*Kant*, p. 222). The ontology of Dasein is not a "philosophy of life" (Dilthey, Bergson, Simmel), in the sense that its constitution could be explained by reverting to the idea of life. The being of man is not illuminated by explaining it as life or becoming (*Kant*, p. 229), but rather the exegesis is conducted by the question that interrogates the sense of Being in general.

In ancient ontology, the horizon or field in which the sense of being in general must be cultivated is left undetermined (*Kant*, p. 229) [69]. However, this has not prevented that ontology from speaking on the sense of being in general, even with the consequent limitations of not being able to properly clarify a genuine horizon. "The Being of the Entity is here obviously understood as *consistency* and *persistence*" (*Kant*, p. 230). "What does it mean for the Entity to be understood as οὐσία, παρουσία, in a meaning in which, fundamentally, 'presence' means 'a having' immediately and always present?" (*Kant*, p. 230). That means saying, "Being signifies the persistence of the present"; "the entity as such is understood as entity with respect to the present; that is, it is conceived as presence (οὐσία)" (*Sein und Zeit*, p. 26).

But if Being is interpreted as presence, betraying in this way, or alluding in this way, to time as the horizon for the meaning of being, ontology falls into an insuperable *circulus en probando* when it interprets time as "the present" (*Kant*, p. 231). It is possible to show that the analysis of time that Aristotle carries out in his *Physics* (217, b29 to 224, a17) is directed by an understanding of Being that understands it as what is actually permanent and, consequently, goes on to define the "Being" of time with the "now" (*nunc*), that is, by that character of time that forms in it, always, a present, what in the ancient sense of Being is considered as Being proper. In other words, if in ancient ontology, Being is interpreted as "substance" (οὐσία) starting, inadvertently, from time, then time is interpreted as Being, that is, as substance. The ancients "substantialized" Being and, at the same time, "substantialized" time as well.

Very well then, we think, no longer with Heidegger but within our own specific ontological perspective, that Being can receive an interpretation that is precisely contrary to that of ancient ontology, that is, to see it and to understand it not as substance but as "accident" precisely because we have placed it in its proper horizon, which is temporality and which we must also interpret, consequently, also as accident. However, it is worth explaining this further [70]. In a certain way are we saying that the being of the Entity that does not possess existence as form (*Ente no existenciforme*) is "accidental," but that, in the context of ancient ontology, is understood as "substantial." However, the sense of Being of the Entity that possesses existence as form (*el Ser del Ente existencioforme*) we understand as "accident." As such, the meaning of Being in "Being in General," which would include the Being of the Entity, which possesses existence as form and the Being of the Entity that does not, would then be "substantial-accidental."

Medieval philosophy speaks of Being as transcendental, which means that it is "superimposed" ("*por encima*") onto both substance and accident. The defect of this ontology resides in conceiving the being of man as substantial and not as accidental. The substantialization of the being of man is common to ancient and medieval ontology, and more generally to all of Western philosophy, in spite of its disenchantment in Christianity, which tended to see in man an accident. Only in America does man appear as accidental, but not only in Spanish America, but also in Anglo-Saxon America, as in pragmatism, and above all in the philosophy of "contingency" of John Dewey.

America, Hegel said, is an accident of Europe. *This proposition must be taken literally.* To be accidental should not involve, for us, an inferior value before the substantiality of Europe, but it should highlight precisely the notion that that which is authentic or genuinely human is nothing consistent and persistent, but something fragile and fractured. This ontological condition is more originary, more primitive than that of man as substantial, which represents a derivative state, one that at bottom represents a deviation from the demands posited by the human condition at its very core. In all of European philosophy there is a transference of meaning from being as substance, not from being in general, but from the being of the entity that does not possess the form of existence, a transference of this meaning to the being that possesses existence as form. Thus, we get Hegel's formula [85]: "It all depends on understanding 'substance' at the same time as 'subject'" (accident). But in truth, things have gone in the opposite direction. Far from "subjectifying" "substance," European philosophy has "substantialized" the "subject." We can see that clearly in Hegel's own philosophy, in which "absolute knowledge" represents the "fullness" or "completion" of the subject with the totality of substance, in such a way that everything else is simply "an understanding of the subject as substance" [71]. These characterizations allow us to define, in a concrete way, what we have in certain occasions called "comparative ontology," that is, the confrontation or dialogue with different manners of being.

Relation between Spaniards and Mexicans is not in any way fixed or definitive, but multifaceted, and consequently, its definition has varied as a result of the passing of time, different epochs, and the cultural and social *status* in which this relationships are made. It is, however, possible to reduce to a common denominator this variation in the state of this relationship that, although empty in its generality, would fulfill the function of orienting us in the task of finding a more adequate characterization. One could say that, for the most part, such relationships are relationships of conflict, struggle, quarrel; in a word, these are relationships of opposition and not of community.

Already from the first generation of criollos, relations of opposition were established, and, since then, history has continued to add new and old conflicts without canceling out the radical and original animosity. The relation that opposes Mexicans and Spaniards is not, however, an adjectival opposition, but substantial and constitutive of the mode of being Mexican; the case is not the same with Spaniards, in whom such opposition, when it is felt, represents nothing more than an adjective in his manner of being. In that relation of opposition, the Mexican wagers his being, while the Spaniard plays only *one* of his ways of appearing.

The case is different with Mexico's relations with the United States or France. With the first, there is conflict, but not opposition, while with the second, there is community. Our conflict with the American mode of being does not constitute our being, and our community with France is also not constitutive. There are, then, negations that do not define us, such as those that the Mexican has with the North American, or affinities that likewise do not determine us, such as our relations with France [72].

If, then, there are oppositions in the soul of the Mexican, not all of them are found at the same level; one of them, in particular, cuts deeper and makes itself definitive and distinguishing of a particular mode of being. *And if to oppose oneself is to determine oneself, as the philosophers say, then the negation of that which is Spanish is in the Mexican person* (del mexicano) *the determination of that which is Mexican* (lo mexicano). Every other opposition is derivative or secondary and always presupposes the originary and radical negation of Spanishness (*lo español*). *The Mexican chooses himself as "accidental" or precisely as the negation of Spanishness, which presents itself as "substantial." This originary election of accidentality before a determined substantiality gives direction to an entire history of that which is Mexican and, of course, to our relations with the world and with Spanish men.* The Mexican negates his past as a Spanish past and conceives it as what *has been* and *should not* be again. That which is Spanish is a past that constitutes the fulcrum of a history that is no longer ours, a fulcrum that must be acknowledged, but one that one would have preferred not to acknowledge. This past is accepted reluctantly as a mode of being that is always found deep in the Mexican character, but that must not be repeated, but that presents itself, however, as an obstacle [73].[28]

The substantiality of (the Spanish) character reveals itself to Mexicans in the most common and trivial behaviors and in certain differences that Mexicans will almost never confess. For instance, one speaks of Spanish "wine" or "bulls" or "character," and we insist that our wine, bulls, and character are "not substantial," that they lack marrow, heart, or "body." But where this aspect of substantiality in the Spanish character does become obvious is in those behaviors in which he shows himself as "resistant" and "tough" before our own "fragility" and "delicateness." *Among themselves, Spaniards shout and speak loudly, the interjections and insults fly without injury; however, among us, we know ourselves as overly "fragmented" and avoid the least provocation, even the most gentle and inoffensive ones, and we avoid also the raising of our voice or the harsh word* [74]. A nature that is substantial also manifests itself in the predictable, clear, and somewhat mechanical way with which the Spanish takes a position before certain limiting situation of human life: love, death, kinship, friendship. In all of these situations, the Spaniard reacts in an always expected way (he knows what to count on), while the Mexican always hesitates and has to extract the appropriate attitude out of his zozobra. The Mexican does not know how to explain his conduct and feelings; he does not objectify himself, but rather lives in indeterminateness and vagueness, and is often depressed. On the other hand, the Spaniard brutally objectifies himself, calls bread "bread," wine "wine"; he grabs hold of himself with certainty and confidence, while we unravel among our indeterminations.

This comparison between the "substantiality" of one project and the "accidentality" of another brings us to posit the problem of the relations between ontology and history. An ontology that understands itself cannot be anything but historical. The clarification of ontology's great themes requires historical inquiry, but that *does not mean* that we should relativize ontology in a negative way or *that we should give ourselves over to the fallacy that the proposed structures are valid only in the historical moment*. But we cannot presume that these structures be definitive and complete, but provisional and incomplete. But if they are to be completed, and if they are to lose their provisional nature, such an accomplishment cannot come from anywhere else but ontology itself and not from non-ontological "disciplines" and, of course, not from history understood as "historical science" [75].

Ontology cannot do without the history of problems that repeat themselves. *Through repetition we understand the immersion of a problem in its essential possibilities.* Maintaining a problem in those originary possibilities and nourishing it in those possibilities is repetition. *Insufficiency, as the central theme of the ontology of the Mexican, requires history; it requires it for the illumination of those "historical moments" in which, in an extreme way, insufficiency is lived authentically or inauthentically; that is, it requires the repetition of those historical periods in which insufficiency is made explicit or is covered over* (se acusa o se sepulta). There are three specific moments in which the theme of insufficiency requires repetition. The first is the epoch of the conquest and the years immediately following that event, in which the criollo appears for the first time as a factor in our mode of being. The second is the epoch that precedes our independence, in which the criollo thinks himself sufficient in the project of appropriation. And the third is the moment of the Mexican Revolution, in which the consciousness of our being emerges as never before. The elaboration of these three "moments" of repetition satisfies, for us, the project of "historicizing" our ontology. We pursue our investigation in this direction.

IV. Poetry

6. The Meaning of the Mexican Revolution [76]

A malicious conviction, sanctioned without end by common sentiment, sees the poet as a creature unexceptionally graced with the gift of thought. To poeticize and to think are opposed just as things that have too little or too much of some quality are opposed. Thought wanders through regions inaccessible to poetry and what the poet reveals is set apart (with almost religious care) from the dominions accessible to thought. Today, we begin to suspect that the tradition has imposed on our minds a separation of (philosophical) thought and poetry that in more originary and more original epochs would not have even been considered. Our logic is so dry and narrow that it is not recognized in poetry; poetry is habitually so clumsy and biased that it cannot be recognized in thought. But our century begins to heal itself of its own myopia and opens itself to a new idea, namely, that poetry and thought communicate with each other via robust connections that due to the narrowness of our vision we think as impalpable and subtle. Poetic thought reveals itself as rigorous as philosophical thought. It may lack exactitude or precision, which are but accidents of the art and of the office, but a capacity to problematize, which is where rigor resides, it has in abundance.

In seeking, on this occasion, to think about the Mexican Revolution, we appeal to a poet who in an essay of great renown abounds in deep and interesting appreciations. We are speaking here of Ramon López Velarde, who in his "El Minutero" talks to us concerning the "novelty of the homeland."[1]

Before the revolution, our homeland (*la patria*) appeared as "pompous, wealthy, honorable in its present and epic in its past." For outsiders, the justification for the homeland was already done. But with the revolution, this varnish of legitimacy has dissolved. It was necessary to live "years of suffering so as to conceive of a less external homeland, a more modest and perhaps more precious homeland" [77].

The revolution is an "inversion of values." What before appears on top of the page is placed as a footnote, written as a mere accessory; to the top of the page ascend an accumulation of "anti-values." In this movement, suffering plays an essential role. In the interiority of suffering, "official" values are displaced; they die with the process of suffering itself. This is why despair without suffering is nothing but revolutionary rhetoric.

That the revolution has brought about a "new homeland" ("*nueva patria*") is something we still do not understand. The years since have again installed in the Mexican soul the pompous, the richness, the honorific, the epic. In its dimension of interiority, the revolution no longer nourishes us. Grandiosity begins to engulf us with the most spectacular exhibitionism. The modesty of the human condition revealed by the revolution is forgotten. And as we approach the halfway mark of the present century, we ask, "What thinker will dare to profile the homeland that was born with the revolution and that López Velarde himself witnessed?" "Is not our philosophy guilty of a radical blindness if it does not translate what poetry has taught us about the revolution?"

With the revolution, López Velarde sees the emergence of a homeland that is "not historic, not political, but intimate." But who will understand what we are asked to think with these words? In a generation that has been both saved and, at the same time, bastardized by historicism, no one understands what Mexico, and that which is Mexican, might mean (aside from the fact that they are products of history). I insist, however, that we are in history more than we are history. And politically, will we be embarrassed to define ourselves through reasons deeper than political reasons? But the revolution signifies more than the historical or the political. It signifies something intimate. But here, we reach our limits. There is no thinker capable of thinking what López Velarde intimately understands. We are far, indeed, from having understood what the revolution has taught us.

The new reality that the revolution has brought about is an everyday reality. "We have discovered this new reality through everyday feelings and reflections" and tirelessly, "as the continuous prayer of St. Silvino" [78]. It is true that we talk about the revolution every day, that we unpack it in our daily conversations. But this is not what allows us to discover it. López Velarde asks us to "reflect," not to talk. Transforming the novelty of the homeland is an everyday affair, and so is tirelessly repeating its possibilities, otherwise forgetfulness will dispel it and confuse it. The task is, then, vigilance and watchfulness so that the essence of what the revolution has produced may be transformed into an everyday reality lived and repeated in ordinary situations.

But what becomes more urgent for us is our attitude before that new possibility. "We see it made for the life of each one of us," that is, individualized. It is given to us as a matter of obligation and responsibility. *Tua res agitur*. It is about something that concerns each one of us, not to an anonymous and social mass. The revolution revives or destroys its possibilities with each Mexican person on an individual basis and confers on each person their unique individuality. This goes unnoticed quite frequently. We are asked to maintain the revolution, to hold it in perpetuity, but what is overlooked is that the uselessness of that demand resides in the vagueness of whom it is demanded; the demand is not demanded of a group without personality, but of isolated and particularized subjectivities.

These reflections remind us that our thought has yet to say anything about the revolution. Glossing over the surface of appearance, it has allowed what is essential to escape. The problem of the revolution is precisely the problem of the reality that it has produced, the problem of the meaning that it has birthed and with which we deal without clarifying or making precise. We live immersed in that meaning, but being immersed in it does not mean that we have appropriated it, but, simply, that without noticing it, we live at its expense. But the task of philosophy consists of coming into conscious possession with that which we already possess (*entrar en posesión consciente de lo que ya tenemos*), of that previous having in whose bosom we find comfort and in whose light we understand everything that happens to us in our everydayness.

Thought must be rigorous for the task of consciously grabbing hold of the meaning of the revolution. It is not ready to hand, requiring only an outstretched arm [79]. The interpretation of the revolution is an arduous undertaking that demands a kind of attention and continuity of which we are not accustomed.

López Velarde knew the difficulty of this enterprise. "A great artist or a great thinker could articulate this new homeland (*esta nueva patria*). The namelessness of its being has not kept us from cultivating it in verses, in paintings, and in music." The words of the thinker and of the poet name being and in naming it raise it to a new life. The life toward which being emerges is the life of possibilities, the dimension of projects and plans. Before this, what is nameless exists in a reality that is incapable of projecting it in its simple possibilities, but that imprisons it and blinds it. But "before" the philosophical interpretation of a certain reality, there is an artistic "cultivation" that already operates in its possibilities, that projects forward, although not as clearly as philosophy, since it nonetheless appeals to "sensible" phenomena as the ground for the possible.

"Evidence" of what López Velarde means is given to us in the form of Mexican painting. Painters are the ones who have better "understood" the revolution, that is, who have with more confidence deployed it in the realm of the possible. Poetry, too, although more in an indirect way, has brought about the "possibilities" of the revolution. But for philosophy, as a right, there has been reserved the task of taking this enterprise to its culmination. Can we affirm that our philosophy has placed itself on the path toward this end?

If philosophy's task is to "define" the new homeland, today we should dedicate ourselves to "observing" it. For the poet, this means that he must "imagine" the homeland, propose its hypothesis, articulate the points of view that will more adequately allow us to grasp it, seize it, and interpret it. But what is a point of view if not a "party" (*un "partido"*)?

The revolution has given birth to parties. In the history of these parties we can perhaps find more than a clue for its comprehension. We cannot dwell on this theme here, but we can perhaps point to it. The names of these parties already contain a lesson, namely, a symbolic lesson. The first party was called the "National Revolutionary Party." Here, the revolution is placed in the service of the nation [80]. It takes advantage of the revolution for the sake of the nation. Let us emphasize this: of a nation, not of a "new homeland." This is a decision in favor of the nation, not in favor of the homeland. The second party is the party of the "Mexican Revolution." To our understanding, it is the deepest and most comprehensive title that could ostensibly be given to a party of the revolution. What is Mexican is defined here by the revolution itself. Mexicanness is that which is revolutionary, the being of the Mexican is a being that has emerged from the revolution. Finally, another "party" that is spoken about is the "Institutional Revolutionary Party." The revolution in this case, as that which creates institutions, has solidified, it has become "official." The revolution is invoked as a guarantee of the institutions.

Our reflection should be directed to the second of these parties, since only in that party do we hear with pristine clarity the sense of the Mexican Revolution without commitments to nation or institutions.

For López Velarde, the definition of a new being of the Mexican must be achieved not so much "in cold blood," but through an "intimation" ("*corazonada*"). More precisely, rather than simply coming to that being, it must surprise us, violently and suddenly (*a manera de rapto*), in such a way that it solicits and takes possession of our thinking. "The alchemy of the Mexican character does not recognize any instrument capable of identifying its components of grace and solemnity, heroism and apathy, carelessness and cleanliness." With that, López Velarde points to apparently contradictory characteristics that anticipate one another. Can we now say that we have at our disposal an "instrument" capable of specifying the elements that make up our being? This is a question deserving of our philosophers.

7. Character and Being of the Mexican in the Poetry of López Velarde

Whenever one speaks of that which is "classic," reflection seems to rest on safe harbor. In contrast, whatever is "romantic" throws us into a sea of confusion in which the most disparate images exaggerate their claim to legitimacy only to show us their incurable homelessness (*su incurable bastardía*). There is a "classic" image of the Mexican character, and there are a slew of "romantic" conceptions of the same, but there is also a prudent middle ground of acceptable proposals [81]. Here, we will once again sketch that classic image of our mode of being, that interpretation or revelation that "corresponds" to our reality with the least possible margin of error. Our confidence in having attained, with that classic image of ourselves, a true gravitational point, the true location of our being within our own reality, has been reinforced. We assumed this to be the case, that is, when we meditated on what remains constant in our history and our nature, but now we are assured, especially after seeing it gracefully unfold from a series of testimonies that are authoritative in their own way.

We invoke here the names of friar Diego Durán, Alfonso Reyes, Xavier Villaurrutia, and Ramón López Velarde, as those who with true clarity have discerned our classic structure; we shall demonstrate that in their unanimity they have provided further proof of objectivity of that classic schema. In a certain sense, we will lend our attention to a reconsideration (*a un repaso*) of evidences or a repetition of convictions. In order to highlight in a convenient manner the peculiarity of that image, we will contrast it with the image proposed by Samuel Ramos and thus arrive once again at the problem as to why, it would appear, we have two images of our modes of being that are prima facie irreconcilable—that project, however, must be left for another time.

Elsewhere, we have called attention to the valuable testimony of friar Diego Durán regarding the character of the Mexican (cf. *Mexican History*, No. 3). We pointed out that the mode of being of the Mexican is oscillatory and pendular, moving from one extreme to the other, making simultaneous two instances while never sacrificing one for the sake of the other. The Mexican character does not install itself *over*—for lack of a better term—two agencies, but *between* (*entre*) them. The Nahuatl term "nepantla" captures this phenomenon perfectly; it means "in between," in the middle, in the center. We thus have before us, in all its purity, the central category of our ontology, autochthonous, one that does not borrow from the Western tradition, satisfying our desire to be originalists. The content within which our being oscillates is, suddenly, indifferent in regard to its matter; there is, for its part, nothing that would invalidate the form that binds it together. In friar Diego Durán's case, which serves as the ground for (phenomenological) ideation, or the process of arriving at an eidos, we are talking about two laws, the Christian and the Indigenous [82]; with Alfonso Reyes, the scheme is filled with hypocrisy and cynicism; and with López Velarde, with religiosity and love, to put it in the words of Xavier Villaurrutia.

We could also try to figure out the pairs "decent"–"*pelado*," brutality–sensitiveness, fragility–toughness, and so on. What must be kept in mind as decisive is not, I insist, the content, but the schema, one that we preliminarily refer to as logical, pendular, oscillating, and zig-zagging. In a word, zozobra.

What we say about the logic of oscillation corresponds to what we may say about zozobra. This peculiar ontological movement that is zozobra does not correspond either to a linear formal logic or to spiral dialectical logic. Contradictory terms exclude themselves in a formal logic, and in order to construct an image of a justifiable character, one must reject one of the terms in order to preserve the other. In a dialectic, both extremes are overcome and are synthesized so as to give birth to a third moment that will absorb the contraries, sublimating them perfectly in a new term.

In contrast, zozobra is a "not knowing what to depend on," or what is the same; it is to simultaneously depend on both extremes, to accumulate, to not let go (*no soltar presa*), to hold on to both ends of the chain. The incessant rocking to and fro, the coming and going, has no end; we could say with López Velarde (who will always have the last word in our ontology) that "our lives are pendulums."

Zozobra refers to the extremes (*Zozobra remite a los extremos*). It refers in its movement and not merely in allusion. But at its most profound, zozobra hides a peculiar sorrow, a private suffering. The inevitable wound that afflicts the type of being revealed by zozobra is incurable. It never heals. It is a deep wound that cannot close, that does not scar, a permanent wound. Our immersion in the originary announces itself in the irrepressible screams that emanate when we touch, with our bare finger, that open wound, our branding by fire, which is permanent and bloody. The movement of zozobra has a resemblance to that of a weaver. It is a sad and gentle activity that weaves our life or, better yet, that life itself allows to weave in a passivity whose definition is hard to articulate [83]. In this pendular movement there is a passive synthesis, a fulfillment of things brought about through the sorrowful chance of heterogeneous encounters. To reunite in a single equation those elements that compose our accidental mode of being is not easy; there is reference, movement, sorrow, open wounds, blood, and synthesis. Only a very fine analysis of the poetry of López Velarde allows us to properly calibrate the fragile essences that are here intermixed. To develop a hierarchy of these essences would no doubt demand an objective account (of the work of López Velarde), an alert intelligence with an almost impalpable emotional refinement. Let us proceed with more precise observations.

> Evening of rain in which worsen
> equally with an intimate sadness
> a meek disdain of things
> and an emotion, fragile and contrite, that prays.
>
> —López Velarde, "La Tejedora"

All the "elements" of our character are present in this stanza. We see that they are all connected, woven in a kind of unification. First, emotions; then, inactivity; and finally, melancholy, which is our manner of rumination, or our second nature.

The depth of character is given by melancholy, adequately represented by the image of an "evening of rain." The grayness and the sadness of its incurable state are there plainly suggested. Unwillingness, as we said in our "Essay on an ontology of the Mexican," is correctly characterized as "a meek disdain of things." The emotions appear as fragility, as delicateness, but are qualified as the contrite and beseeching. We will return to this below. The sorrow of zozobra is represented in the verse above as an "intimate sadness." "Devoted" blood binds, but smoothly and with an almost imperceptible delicateness. To give oneself fully is unconscious, soft, and life escapes through almost imperceptible spaces. The externality of the blood loss is reduced to a minimum. The wound *is* not; the wound is made, incessantly woven, as in a fragile process of a reverse cauterization, of interrupted coagulation [84]. That's what must be understood: character traumatizes itself and forms itself through the zigzagging wound that each instant creates. That which is random is in this way the artifice of our permanent evasion. Images resists the suggestion of intuition; they resist these suggestions because it is about representing a process of synthesis that is not a process of consolidation, but of dismemberment, a synthesis without prior substance that would disintegrate it from within. Everything is, in a certain sense, more external than internal, since there is no nucleus resistant to excavation; rather, from the beginning, there is an opening that invites us to understand the genesis of the wound, but not of its healing.

The "evening of rain" (the exterior or noematic element) pairs itself with our character (the noetic element), interchanging meanings that allow one to understand one through the other, and vice versa. This is a random "encounter" (it would be better to say that the entire verse comes to us as a description of a random situation). The confrontation "aggravates" "simultaneously" inactivity and emotions. Both aspects of our character are activated—they are launched from calm waters into raging currents. The ontological wound, from which the intimate sadness emanates, illuminates, nourishes, and communicates a character felt as more primal than our ordinary character; it is submerged in the originary. Thus, we have a sort of awakening of an ancestral wound on *an evening of rain*. Nothing would be more useless than to think about this as a causal relation (as if everything is casual) and not something motivated or moved by a field of climactic relations that soften a manner of being through its insinuations, bringing it (this manner of being) to feel its proximity to its own irreparable wound.

The taste of guilt or of debt suggested by the contrite is not forgotten. That wound, that fissure, tastes like guilt. That is inevitable. We cannot gloat about our innocence with our existence ravaged. And from guilt surges prayer, pleading, begging, especially when there's no intermediary whatsoever. Prayer is the voice of guilt. Debt merely implores. But if we talk about prayer, we don't mean to point out a determinate religion. Neither do we mean to point out an indeterminate religion, because if religion is an attachment with the divine, a linking, guilt does not, in its origins, point to any sort of attachment [85]. Debt speaks in prayer, but not about an attachment to the divine. This is an addition and a solution to the enigma in which it dwells. That prayer alludes is certain, that it knows to what it alludes is doubtful. One simply prays and does not question if there's someone listening to one's prayer.

> *Weaver: weave into your thread*
> *the inertia of my dream and your confided illusion;*
> *weave in silence; weave the cowardly syllable*
> *that crosses our lips and says nothing;*
> *weave the fluid voice of Angelus*
> *with the creaking of doors:*
> *weave the systole and diastole*
> *of the punished hearts*
> *that are alert in the shadows.*
>
> —López Velarde, "La Tejedora"

The thread of life that in its zig-zagging movement weaves opens the wound. The thread is not spun by a providential hand, or a logical one, but an adventurous and random hand. The weaver is not the omniscient predictor of effects and causes, but is the abandoned inspiration of accidentality. Neither does logic select the type of thread to spin, because in this operation of passive synthesis, which is life, agencies mix together without respect to their kinds—linen's right to neatness does not take priority over the coarseness of agave fibers (*henequen*). Randomness (*el azar*) is, in essence, what is hybrid, the pairing of incompatible kinds, of contradictory kinds. If we were to represent the universe to ourselves as an unlimited series of parallel threads that run tiredly next to each other without ever intersecting, randomness would not have a role to play. As in the Epicurean universe, the vertical fall of atoms has to endure an inflexion so that their encounter comes about; this *clinamen*, this breeze that twists but communicates, is the home of randomness; it is the crooked furrow that in a sudden crisscross brings together the heterogeneous, connecting the specific and particular in a rigid definition. The coming together of heterogeneous series is randomness; zozobra is nothing else but the bare skeleton of that universal to and fro that allows creatures of all kinds to communicate one with the other (it is like an erroneous movement in which the ink has bled in a painting of parallel lines [*cuadro de paralelas*], making it possible that, in that bleeding, lines that are close and lines that are far apart contaminate one another) [86].

López Velarde asks that the inertia of the dream and the confident illusion be woven in one single thread. Notice that these are contrary agencies. If one is present, the other is annulled, but what logic makes impossible, life, in its synthesis of random events, achieves. In a certain sense it puts in the hands of randomness and chance the labor of reconciling the contraries, of mixing diverse kinds. For itself to be realized, a dream would ask for activity, for a doing. But the inertia of dreams conspires in a decisive manner against its own embodiment in the real, depriving or mutilating every ideal of force with which it would model things and transform them into concrete things. But laziness wants to commune with the confident illusion, not put it in question. But leaving the illusion intact, not revealing that it depends on inertia (*inercia*), would come to provoke the most radical disillusion. This impossible synthesis is what our poet leaves as a task for our weaver. He then asks the weaver that the silence of lovers also be woven—silences where there are no words, no dialogues, and, moreover, where there is no active synthesis of expressions, but incommunicable silences that randomness will communicate and form into unities.

We find the same call for help, one asking the cowardly syllables to link themselves with one another, and in a more obvious way, as far as the operation of framing diversities, of forming hybrids, in the verses that follow, in phrases like "the fluid voice of the *Angelus*" and "the creaking of doors"—phrases that while wildly distant demonstrate those contrary moments within which communication takes place. The allusion is clearer when zozobra, oscillation, is made concrete as systole and diastole, movements of the heart that lend a perfect image to the to and fro of zozobra. What is of the heart (lo cordial) symbolizes an oscillation that is more emotive than volitional. The oscillation is not like that occurring between two poles from which the will must choose, but between two "intimations" (*"corazonadas"*), between two affects. The nuances of sadness are evoked a second time when we speak of the "*punished* hearts." We are now at the final verse [87].

We have said that in the movement of zozobra, the core of randomness itself, its ground, there is a groove into which we expect something to fall. This expectation gives rise to prayer, to imploration. To forge our character as zozobra is a call to randomness, to chance; it is an invocation or incitation. It is to gather oneself in an alveolus in an attitude of expectation. The hollow space in which the ground of randomness has been prepared is somewhat somber, cavernous; one cannot say that it is an opening bathed in light. It is chiaroscuro, twilight, "penumbra." But attention shines in the depths of that cave, as does hope, the vigil of the prayerful. We must understand the situation that we are here attempting to describe in its fullness. Hearts that are punished and in zozobra lie in a gloomy hollow, but there they are alert. Here we note the combination of darkness and light. To submerge oneself in originary zozobra seems to be a movement that brings us closer to darkness, toward the annulment of consciousness. But, at the extreme point when we are about to give ourselves over to twilight, our wakefulness shines, a subtle antenna readies to receive the message.

We mentioned also that in that original voice of guilt there is an imploration, but we denied that it was a direct call to God. In truth, the situation clears up if we look at the movement of the weaver, which seeks to bring about the synthesis of different consciousnesses or which seeks to bring about intersubjectivity: the getting out of insular consciousness and arriving at communal consciousness. This is the end of the movement, when randomness no longer captures our attention. This is not the place to give a long philosophical explanation. It suffices to say that we are aware of this movement from the solitary to the popular, from the individual to the collective.[2] According to López Velarde, this power of extroversion and communication is love.

> I wander between dead chimeras and between nascent dreams,
> and I am prone to cry without reason
> I go, with my soul scattered
> In the effusive and misty afternoon,
> contemplating you, Love, through a fog
> of condolence, through an ideal curtain [88]
> of tears, while you weave joy and mourning
> in a sentimental limbo.
>
> —Lopéz Velarde, "La Tejadora"

We thus arrive to a provisional end of our characterological analysis, and we can now, with some confidence, propose a synthesis, a unification of the different layers of meaning that the analysis has uncovered.

In the depths of the sentimental character, in which emotion, unwillingness, and melancholy are bound together, and where is born the primordial language of a guilt that prays and implores, there resides, or to use a metaphor of depth, there we find like a sinking vessel, zozobra, that in an incessant to and fro and oscillation refers to one extreme or another, sews instances that can be contrary to one another or simply different than one another. Sentimentality forms the atmosphere, the horizon, the space in which zozobra executes its incorruptible march and counter-march as the "widowed oscillation of the trapeze" (Velarde, "Memorias del circo," 74). Zozobra finds itself suspended in a sentimental *limbo*, or to put it differently, it does not oscillate inside an obscure and simple space, but rather, the space is colored, or painted, with a sentimental atmosphere.[3] That is why we have said that more than a movement of will, zozobra is an emotive to and fro, it is sentimental. Zozobra and the sentimental character are implied as background and form.

> I have discovered my symbol
> in the lamp in the form of a ship
> that hangs from the Creole domes
> its crystal wise and its prayer faithful.
>
> —Lopéz Velarde, "El Candil"

Another series of considerations are tied to the nature of sadness that is zozobra, to its condition as wound, to its openness to randomness, and to the work of the weaver in which subjectivities are joined so as to model the form of community [89].

Zozobra is, for now, an intimate sadness. The adjective seems to suggest that we are talking about a constitutive and essential sadness, not an accidental one; a sadness that, as a priori sentimental, precedes and conditions all pain big or small that experience brings about, that living brings about. Before the concrete loss of an object or a person makes us sad, we are a radical, conditioning, and incurable loss. The sadness that life puts us through reminds us of that fundamental sadness, that which we are, as things in the world reminded Plato of the world of ideas. We are innately sad, by birth, and that is because we are originally a loss, penury, debt, and lack.

> I am nothing more than the nave of a church in penury,
> a nave in which eternal funerals are celebrated,

because a stubborn rain does not allow
taking the coffin out to the rural streets.

—Lopéz Velarde, "Hoy, como nunca"

This sadness, correlate of the lack that is our being (since loss and sadness both give themselves as two sides of the same coin), qualifies itself precisely as a tear (*desgarradura*), as wound. In all those ways we can describe as involving a lack, a deprivation, a wound, what feeds the tear is what particularizes the pain of zozobra. Being zozobrante is painful, as painful as a wound, as a tear in the living fabric, in the living flesh. There is no other pain that in its indeterminate generality can refer itself to other meanings. Sadness, loss, and wound draw a profile of zozobra, they make it precise.

> My spirit is a cloth of souls, a cloth
> of souls of a church always in need;
> it is a cloth of souls covered in dripped wax,
> trampled and torn by the unfortunate flock. [90]

—Lopéz Velarde, "Hoy, como nunca"

The reasons for sadness, for misery and tearing find their unequivocal expression. Zozobra reveals its being to be "simultaneously" ("*al par*") needful and torn.

Very well, that wound, that lack that produces a sad aching, is a manifestation of a movement, and is therefore not something static, but permanently dynamic, in motion. It is not, rigorously speaking, a wound, but a perpetually being wounded, a constant bleeding. Zozobra operates a small yet intimate hemorrhage, a draining or spilling of blood. It occurred to López Velarde to adjectivize blood and call it "devout." This we can explain. As a being that is wanting, or as privation, zozobra speaks of guilt, of debt, and it prays, it implores. This wound, due to its condition of guilt, wants to tell us something that we cannot but locate in the realm of the "devotee" (a realm that we should, perhaps, differentiate from the realm of "saint" or of the religious). The realm of the "popular," or of the communal, cuts into the realm of the devout and the religious. Religion, which tries to express zozobra, does not have the sense of a communication with God, but with the other, with the other I. To talk about guilt is an imploration, an evocation, and with magical specificity, of community, of togetherness, it solicits or calls for company. This is the role played by the weaver in the poetry of Velarde. We can thus say that López Velarde allows us to witness the formation of intersubjectivity, one that initiates us into the most complex mystery of establishing a communication. To come out of solitude and to integrate oneself into the solitude of another so as to form community is not a movement that is easy to explain. Reliving this trivial event requires a kind of analytical acuity that, in philosophy, perhaps exists only in the work of Husserl. The German philosopher places us as witnesses to this event in his 5th *Cartesian Meditation* [91].

"The weaver" represents that crimping paper in which subjectivities previously isolated put themselves in communion, or communicate themselves. The movement is here obvious, and fully disclosed, and the poet shows it to us in its richly colored network. But in two other poems, which we find to be ontologically interesting, we will find this movement ignored, suspended, or negated. What do we mean?

> We recall a poem that begins:
> Where could the girl be
> that in that place
> during a night of dancing
> spoke to me of her desires
> of travelling, and spoke to me of
> her tedium?
>
> —López Velarde, "Nuestras vidas son pendulos"

The girl forgets that her drama has its correspondence also in me, that she is not a "windowless monad," within which the horrendous sacrifice of her feelings consumes itself without another consciousness that discovers her agony. One already lives *among* and not *within*, but the girl does not know this.

> And the girl forgot
> that in complaining of tedium
> with me, she complained
> to a pendulum.
> —Lopéz Velarde, "Nuestras vidas son pendulos"

The one confided in is a pendulum, a receiver that brings the crude pain of others to his own subjectivity, that brings to himself the tedium of the other. Zozobra is represented as a movement of carrying the suffering of others. And this form of communication and communion is not fleeting, not a type of habit; the moment does not die in apathy, but it drags itself across one's entire life, as if the wound is opened further by understanding that the stranger will burden us again, but in a definitive manner [92].

> *Girl, you who told me*
> *in that hamlet*
> *during a night of dancing*
> *the secrets of your tedium:*
> *wherever you exhale*
> *your discrete longings,*
> *our lives are pendulums.*
> —Lopéz Velarde, "Nuestras vidas son pendulos"

We have here an achieved intersubjectivity that is, simultaneously, ignored. But this is not a serious situation. The problem, the most painful frustration, is found in negation, in the refusal of intersubjectivity. López Velarde lives this in, arguably, one of his most profound poems, one with which he has more accurately captured our constitutive manner of being. That poem begins:

> Prolong your maidenhood
> like the empty intrigue of chess.
> —Lopéz Velarde, "Despilfarras el tiempo"

Already the initial chords illuminate for us the situation in its entirety. Maidenhood is a virginity that is guiltily prolonged. To compare it with an empty and complicated game like chess allows us to see that, if, then, the sense of playfulness is original to our mode of being, we have to understand it in a particular way. The game, for the simple fact that it is a game and involves randomness, is not what one wants. The meaning of life as game is more acceptable, perhaps, to life as duty, but this holds only so long as the game is a game of intersubjectivities and not of solitary beings. Communication with the other is the privileged field of randomness and whoever refuses to play condemns themselves to uselessness, "excommunicated" to the task of playing on their own. The clash, the "dislocation" that inevitably allows us to see solitude and the game together tells us with sufficient reason that the "real game" is not *this* game. On the contrary, we find here a pernicious negation.

> Your balcony blushes from the lamp
> you waste time and emotion.
> I waste, in an absurd waiting,
> fantasy and fire. [93]
>
> —Lopéz Velarde, "Despilfarras el tiempo"

We have already said that the attitude of expectation in which the randomness of communication occurs simultaneously synthesizes what is illuminated and what is hidden. But when light is not the sign of the consciousness of expectation, but of stubbornness and secrecy, when, as is commonly said, "consciousness does not lend itself," then there is no possible givenness, or it is frustrated because the movement of acceptance cannot stand that brazen light of reason with its rays deployed like protective wires. That lamp that lightly caresses the balcony is as deceitful as the color of someone's cheeks that, far from being a sign of health, is frequently a sign of fever, of sickness. Ultimately, there is no communication, intersubjectivity does not form, there is no *among*, but two *interiorities* in which life consumes of itself.

López Velarde feels the interrupted operation of intersubjectivity as a squandering (of being), as decay. Whoever lives through this short circuit of communion, who experiences this frustration, cannot but admit that his being itself escapes, that it slips through his fingers. This, because we cannot keep our being in isolation. Put differently, solitude puts us in the presence of the decay of our within, of our irreparable *un-being* (*deserse*). One of the most criminal disfigurement we can think of is one that invites us to remain in our solitude with the hope of coming into contact with a firm foundation or of coming to possess an imperishable flow. But solitude is not a means for the preservation of being, but, rather, is a way to perdition. Only community "assures"; only community affirms.

> Those who are lavish in their habits
> should come to us to learn
> how all being is wasted.
>
> —Lopéz Velarde, "Despilfarras el tiempo"

The situation is very clear to us. When intersubjectivity is interrupted and two solitudes wall themselves off in the doubtful prestige of their interiority, the process of squandering being is a result of the dizzying pendular movement of zozobra. In this case, zozobra operates as a true bleeding, as a hemorrhage. In solitude the supreme impotence of our being is felt, the impotence or impossibility of being able to handle it, to understand it, to initiate it [94].

The spectacle of the squandering of being is not of a kind capable of bringing about joy and happiness, but on the contrary, it loudly screams sacrilege and impiety. The blood that flows out is no longer devout but, as López Velarde tells us, excommunicated. If communion asks for the region of the devout as its adequate horizon, solitude asks for the atmosphere of the inhospitable and impious.

> *And before the illustrious extravagance*
> *of the treasures treasured*
> *by the site of the souls, something*
> *very deep in me is scandalized and cries.*
>
> —*Despilfarras el tiempo*

We have here the view that intersubjectivity can represent itself as achieved, as forgotten, or as negated and interrupted.

In this quick glance into insights found in the poetry of López Velarde, we have been guided by the task of uncovering the key aspects of our character. Let us pause and summarize our findings.

Our character is of a sentimental type, which means that it is a synthesis of the fragility of emotions, unwillingness, and the melancholic varnish of all its properties. Because of our emotions, we are fragile, overcome with sensibility, everything gets to us and hurts us. Unwillingness makes us see the world with a gentle disdain, and melancholy forces us to mournfully recall what has already been lived. Our character represents a depth over which zozobra, as pendulum, oscillates and zig-zags. In zozobra we find foundational moments in the formation of intersubjectivity, with all of its modalities.

8. Note on the Original and the Originary

We have spoken on several occasions about the character of the Mexican person. In the previous section, we pursued its definition through an analysis of the poetry of López Velarde [95]. As is well known, the most important notion found in his poetry is zozobra. Zozobra refers to a mode of being that incessantly oscillates between two possibilities, between two affects, without knowing which one of those to depend on, which justifies it, indiscriminately dismissing one extreme in favor of the other. In this to and fro the soul suffers, it feels torn and wounded. The pain of zozobra is not obviously identifiable with fear or anxiety; it takes from both in an emotionally ambiguous manner. To find oneself in zozobra is to find oneself solicited by contrary demands that do not support their own exclusion, but that impose, or demand, their simultaneous consummation or fulfillment. Character formed in the style of zozobra constantly looks for contradictory instances of life or of history, and its "decisions" do not reside in suppressing one instance, in quieting the voice of the solicitation so as to continue living, with the exemplary docility, in the silence following deciding on one in favor of the other. In that stalemate in which rights and demands viciously suffocate our character, character bitterly enjoys its unjustified foundation and suffers its gratuity. What is "disgraceful" about our character can be found in its radical grounding (*bisagra*) on which moments "support" themselves so as to operate their game. But this ground is not a fixed and firm foundation, but rather it is unstable quicksand upon which nothing firm can stand. To constantly refer to that region in which possibilities face and confront themselves creates a spiritual state that is nothing close to tranquility. Prima facie, to feel oneself endowed with this (doubtful) capacity for radicalization benefits no one, and many feel that unveiling the structure of this mode of being is to contribute to a "useless truth," to contribute in a negatively way to the project of making ourselves better.

The discomfort produced by the discovery of our character obeys a fallacious reasoning that our evaluative preferences are monopolized by a predetermined ideal. We are hostages to a previous order when the ideal eludes us; we feel "betrayed." But no one promised us that in the process of revealing ourselves we would find the ideal (and borrowed) image.

Our character beautifully mocks the lies and vulgarly places on us the obligation to assume it without excuses [96]. It is then that the task begins, either to close our eyes to that character, that is, deny it, or to discard the a priori ideals and accept without reservation what we intimately are. The pleasure of acceptance has its correspondence in the terror of knowing ourselves. Many want to cover over the opening and refocus their attention away from it and speak of other strange things, no longer insisting on this business of self-knowledge. But all of these efforts of "diversion" are useless. The history of our moment wants us to know ourselves and those who lack the courage to endure the revelations are refuted in advance. There is no shelter whatsoever for cowardice. The subtle objections that the fearful invent are swept away mercilessly, and the analysis of the being of the Mexican continues on its way but with the sterile guidance of the inconvenienced.

"Dogs bark ... the caravan continues."

—Arab proverb

In a gesture of desperation, it is now said that what ultimately matters is not self-knowledge, but transformation, that the task is to change our mode of being and not to illuminate it with reflection. What is desired is blind change—pleasure in darkness. But what blindly changes does not change, but continues being vaguely the same that it was before. Many would like to see themselves transformed without consciously taking any note whatever of their metamorphosis. These are accomplices to a militant and obscure mysticism that rejected the analysis while waiting for others who can say, once the transformation is achieved, that we are no longer the same. They appeal to some strange power that may absolve them and declare them free, finally free, of the old larvae and transform them into butterflies. They don't entertain at home because they must prepare themselves for the visitor to whom they are indebted. They are victims who have given themselves over to foreign ideals yet do not consider themselves worthy of the master's attention. But the task is not to fix oneself into a beautiful figure, it is not to learn a role so as not to be embarrassed before strangers, but to assume without pity what one is. We are witnesses to a poorly articulated struggle between the value of accepting ourselves and the desire to flee. It is poorly articulated because the revolution does not demand that we should flee in shame; it demands, rather, that we recognize ourselves in our misery and identify ourselves with it so as to build upon it. The "indecent man," who does not want to know himself as such, but who fears that his behavior may come to light, did not bring about the (Mexican) revolution [97]; the person who brought about the revolution was he that looked at himself as he was, bravely accepted himself as he was, and from that point on, and not from an ignorance of his own manner of being, pushed forward toward significant transformations. The ideal of the proletariat is to not seem bourgeoisie. If he were to forget his origin at the hour of triumph, he would be imitating bourgeoisie culture.

Beneath this kind of activism an old habit rears its head, that of shame, and unmasking it is almost an obligation. Some do not want to know themselves because our consciousness is ashamed, shaped as it is by ideals about what a Mexican should be.

And it is believed that a solution will come if we loudly demand that we change without knowing what it is that we must change, but only with the hope that once changed, we will be seen as less unworthy of being like the superior models. But, I insist, this is not the time for models. Every archetype that has appeared has expired, and those that still believe in saving themselves by being true to the distorted ideals of the metropolis still have much to learn. The metropolis has ceased to be a model. Today, the metropolis reveals itself in its figure of exploitation, lacking any promise to serve as ideal or to bring about the elevation of men.

In confronting our manner of being, we cannot escape the imperative to assume ourselves as we are. This means, first, that we should not be ashamed of ourselves; second, that we should not allow ourselves to feel marginalized and negated; and third, that we should avoid the blind man's stick that in the darkness seeks to destroy our character and "change" us. The autognosis of the Mexican began as an elegiac mediation about our own melancholic mode of being. The catharsis, the transformation, the demand to see our defects so as to leave them as a serpent sheds its skin was the persistent elegy of the first explorers of our character. More than knowledge, what was demanded was a pedagogy, a technique that would deliver us from the monster revealed by the "psychoanalysis of the Mexican." Our character was thought to be detestable, but we were comforted with the thought that change was easy and that we could easily stop being so deplorable. Then, there was the effort to show that in accepting ourselves as we were signaled a reduction in humanity, that our nets could only hold on to a few drops of a vast sea [98]. There was no sense of the profound, and the profile of our character made visible by the analysis showed its limitations before our very eyes.

Every time there is talk about that which is Mexican no one dares to look behind the curtain, but is quick to complain about the defects once they are found. There is no patience or curiosity to see things from different perspectives, to consider how they can allow us to see many more possibilities of being, which is a richness in itself, and, therefore, there is no thought that one should not prejudice what is seen and allow what is disclosed to speak for itself. Enter the maniacal activists, inheritors of the ashamed, who seek to draw attention to themselves by frantically moving their hands and being as noisy as possible. The activist is a modality of the distraught, and its most extreme limit. So as not to see, he stirs, he agitates himself and with that tries desperately to distract his view.

Every possibility of evasion is cut off. There is no other attitude available but one that assumes our own character. The important thing is to assume it through the execution of a conscious inversion of values. The slave puts his values in place of his master's. Stupid and incomplete would be his labor if, rather than displacing, he would limit his action to revitalizing those values that at some point the master or lord considered worthy and fulfilled. The point is not to certify the lord as incompetent so as to replace him and continue his work with renewed vigor and sincerity. To inherit Europe cannot mean to continue what Europe has done well in the past but today does badly or inauthentically. The Mexican mestizo cannot define himself as the executor of ideals betrayed by the white man. Imitation is not acceptable, not even as work of loyalty to the best moments of the imitated. The copy, in spite of its authenticity, cannot erase its original vice, which resides in its condition of being a copy, and not in its condition of being a good or a bad one. In place of some ideals we must put others, others that in the tradition were considered despicable or shameful. The cynical gesture, always victorious throughout history, consists in highlighting what the old morality considers detestable [99].

In depending on our character, in assuming it, we do not seek to be original. With our character, we do not contribute, as many think, a particularity never before seen, but an originarity never before experienced. What was allowed to be shown in epochs of crisis was silenced in periods of normalcy. But our character contributes a permanent crisis that will never be normal. Our normality is our crisis, not that which is transitory. People from other cultures that contemplate us exhaust themselves in explaining how it is that we have survived all these centuries or, to put it more crudely, how we have "progressed" and how we continue to "progress." We have a lesson to teach; we owe the world a lesson of a vital crisis, one that is virile, that is brave. And on this sense of what is radically human, we must construct our humanism. The image of man that will emerge here will not be original, but it will be originary, which means that in it one will be able to recognize those others that through a thousand accidents of history, of culture or society, have been framed by the catastrophic. But this "morbidity" and this "catastrophism" are only negative if one's focus is squarely on consecrating their contraries as positive. Originality would consist in being incommunicable, in defining only the particular, the irredeemable. Character as zozobra is not an enclosed pool, but an open channel.

> My brothers from all centuries
> recognize in me a similar pause
> their own complaints and their own furies.
>
> —Lopéz Velarde, "El son del corazón"

To appeal to a poet like López Velarde has been, for us, a task imposed by our obligation to return to the origin. When the poet speaks of our character, he does so with a pristine echo that lends dimension to his observations, that does not reduce or obscure them to their simplest meaning, but rather "aggravates" them and casts them once again into the sea of their own possibilities. In contrast, when the professional analyst speaks, those aspects of our character lose their dimension of profundity and remain on hand as "decorations," stamps that allow the third, and vital, dimension [100]. The poet does not allow himself to be deceived by first impressions; everything that is said stands within a horizon of signs and significations that can mean or refer to any possibility.

Our language, which confuses us every day and alienate us, has sought to speak about the character of the Mexican person. Fortunately, our voice has not been the only one. While the investigation into the Mexican got underway, poets kept on their path, they spoke, but their transmissions, their harvest, could not be framed with that of the philosophers because the latter, in their insistence to exclude, did not grant them any rights. Thus, we claim as a uniquely original that we have heeded the voice of the poets. Those complexes and those resentments we mentioned do not emanate from the poetic voice of the Mexican. Freeing the Mexican from speaking in that manner has not been an easy task; today, however, we can speak of that task as realized.

Much has been said lately regarding our eidetic attitude, regarding our "unhealthy" insistence to contemplate the essence of our character. Phenomenology itself has been unjustly reduced to an investigation of essences, and it has been forgotten that it is radically something else, a something else that can be described as an advance toward the nutritive and originary roots of our character and not toward fixing a limiting and particular structure. This level of depth has been our principal preoccupation and our earliest writing on these themes testifies to this commitment. That is, without it being necessary to make it explicit, we were already attending to the poets. Thus, when our philosophical efforts are studied calmly and without violence, the truth of our claims will become obvious. (Let this important clarification remain here simply as a footnote.)

Notes

1. Prolegomena to *Analysis of Mexican Being*

1 José Gaos, "Epistolario y Papeles Privados," in *Obras Completas XIX*, ed. Alfonso Rangel Guerra (México: Universidad Nacional Autonoma de México, 1999), 240–3. Emphasis in original.
2 By "reading," I mean both an interpretation and a critical analysis of the text. This term is preferred because the intent of Part One is to be an aid or a guide for an inclusive reading of Uranga's text rather than a critical introduction, which may be more argumentative and exclusive.
3 For excellent histories, commentaries, and arguments on or about Aztec "philosophy," see Miguel León-Portilla, *Aztec Thought and Culture: A Study of the Ancient Nahuatl Mind* (Norman: University of Oklahoma Press, 1967); more recently, James Maffie, *Aztec Philosophy: Understanding a World in Motion* (Boulder: University of Colorado Press, 2014).
4 See, for instance, Mauricio Beuchot, *The History of Philosophy in Colonial Mexico* (Washington, DC: Catholic University of America Press, 1994).
5 Insightful analyses can be found in Gregory Gilson and Irving Levinson, eds., *Latin American Positivism: New Historical and Philosophical Essays* (Lanham: Lexington Books, 2013).
6 See Carlos Alberto Sánchez and Robert E. Sanchez, eds., *Mexican Philosophy in the 20th Century: Essential Readings* (Oxford: Oxford University Press, 2017). Refer especially to "Editors' Introduction."
7 Samuel Ramos, *El perfil del hombre y la cultura en Mexico* (México: Espasa-Calpe Mexicana, [1934] 1952). Translated as *Profile of Man and Culture in Mexico*, by Peter G. Earle (McAllen: Texas Pan-American Press, 1962).
8 The term "autognosis" means "self-knowledge" or "knowledge of one's self," from the Greek *auto* (self)-*gnōsis* (knowledge). Uranga uses the term as both a verb and a noun—as a process and as what is achieved in the process.
9 A more thorough appreciation of the Hyperion group can be found in Guillermo Hurtado, *El Hiperión* (México: Universidad Nacional

Autónoma de Mexico, 2006); in English, see Carlos Alberto Sánchez, *Contingency and Commitment: Mexican Existentialism and the Place of Philosophy* (Albany: State University of New York Press, 2016).

10 Readers are directed to Aurelia Valero Pie's excellent biography, *José Gaos en México: Una biografía intelectual* (México: El Colegio de México, 2013).

11 The group consisted of Emilio Uranga, Jorge Portilla (1918–1963), Luis Villoro (1922–2007), Ricardo Guerra (1927–2007), Joaquín Sánchez McGregor (1925–2008), Salvador Reyes Nevarez (1922–1993), and Fausto Vega (1922–2015). See Hurtado, *El Hiperión*, for a collection of shorter works written by members of Hyperion.

12 Leopoldo Zea, *El positivismo en México* (México: El Colegio de México, 1943).

13 According to recollections from fellow Hyperion Ricardo Guerra, "The group preoccupied itself mainly with contemporary philosophy; with philosophizing rigorously and technically as much as possible. … [Our main task] was the problem of the Mexican or the problem of knowing that which was Mexican [*lo mexicano*]." Ricardo Guerra, "Una historia del Hiperion," *Los Universitarios*, no. 18 (1984): 15–17.

14 As Leopoldo Zea put it, the task, at the time, was "to demonstrate the Mexican person, together with his possibilities, as *similar to all mankind*." In Leopoldo Zea, *Conciencia y posibilidad del Mexicano* (México: Editorial Porrúa, [1952] 1974), 42. This sentiment was an echo to Octavio Paz, who in his celebrated *The Labyrinth of Solitude* had proclaimed Mexican "solitude" as an "opening" that would make community possible, writing, "Transcendence is waiting: the outstretched arms of solitary beings. For the first time in our history we are contemporaries of all mankind." In Octavio Paz, *The Labyrinth of Solitude* (New York: Grove Press, [1951] 1985), 194.

15 For a detailed exposition of the different ways in which Hyperion sought such inclusivity, see Sánchez, *Contingency and Commitment*.

16 An essay that I will not discuss here is "Merleau-Ponty: fenomenología y existencialismo," which begins Uranga's ontological trajectory. I do not treat it here simply because it is not directly focused on "ontology" as Uranga understands it. For more on this essay and its value, see Sánchez, *Contingency and Commitment*, chapter 1.

17 Alfred Adler (1870–1937) was an Austrian psychoanalyst who first recognized, what he called, the "inferiority complex." Adler theorized that a feeling of being less than first manifested itself in childhood as one felt inferior when in the presence of competent adults. Afflicted with a "complex of inferiority," one then spend one's life overcompensating for this feeling. Ramos takes this theory and applies it to an entire people.
18 Samuel Ramos, *Perfil del hombre y cultura en Mexico* (México: Espasa Calpe Mexicana, [1934] 1982), 112–13.
19 Ibid.
20 Ibid., 51.
21 Ibid., 52. Italics in original.
22 Ibid.
23 Emilio Uranga, "Essay on an ontology of the Mexican," translated by Carlos Alberto Sanchez, in *Mexican Philosophy in the 20th Century: Essential Readings*, ed. Carlos Alberto Sanchez and Robert Ely Sanchez (New York: Oxford University Press, 2017), 165–77.
24 Ibid., 167.
25 Ibid., 166.
26 Ibid., 167.
27 Ibid., 172.
28 Ibid., 173.
29 Ibid.
30 Ibid., 176.
31 Ibid., 177.
32 Ibid.
33 Emilio Uranga, "Notas para un estudio del mexicano," *Cuadernos Americanos* 10, no. 3 (1951): 114–28.
34 Ibid., 114.
35 Ibid.
36 The reductions are: the "phenomenological reduction," in which judgments regarding the existence or nonexistence of the world are suspended; the "transcendental reduction," which is a reduction to "pure" consciousness and to the meaning of things *as existing*; and, finally, the "eidetic reduction," whereby observed entities or things are grasped in their "whatness."
37 See Edmund Husserl, *Experience and Judgement*, translated by James S. Churchill and Karl Ameriks (Evanston: Northwestern University Press,

1973), 357ff. Husserl, speaking of performing this variation on colors, writes: "Starting from an arbitrary red and continuing in a series of variations, we obtain the *eidos* red" (357).
38 Uranga, "Notas," 114.
39 Ibid.
40 Ibid., 116.
41 See Sánchez, *Contingency and Commitment*, chapter 4.
42 Uranga, "Notas," 114–15.
43 Ibid., 116.
44 Ibid., 115.
45 Emilio Uranga, "Merleau-Ponty: fenomenologia y existencialismo," *Filosofia y Letras* 15, no. 30 (1948): 240.
46 Uranga, "Notas," 115–16.
47 See José Ortega y Gasset, *Meditations on Quixote*, translated by Evelyn Rugg and Diego Marín (Chicago: University of Illinois Press, 2000), esp. 40–8.
48 Martin Heidegger, *Being and Time*, translated by John Mcquarrie and Edward Robinson (London: SCM Press, 1962), 94–5.
49 Uranga, "Notas," 127.
50 Ibid., 123.
51 Ibid., 118.
52 Ibid.
53 Ibid., 119.
54 Ibid., 124.

2. *Analysis of Mexican Being*: A Reading

1 Of course, we know that Hume's book is titled *Treatise on Human Nature*, thus avoiding the provincialism that may turn readers away from Uranga.
2 Octavio Paz, *The Labyrinth of Solitude*, translated by Lysander Kemp (New York: Grove Press, 1985).
3 See Diego Durán, *History of the Indies of New Spain*, translated by Doris Heyden (Norman: University of Oklahoma Press, 1994).
4 Here, we can likewise translate "estamos nepantla" as "we are *being* nepantla," thereby highlighting its ontological aspect, an aspect that will prove increasingly significant below.

5 Page numbers in brackets refer to the pagination in the original, 1952, publication of *Analysis*, which has been translated here for the first time—see Part II.
6 A consummation of the task first envisioned by the *Ateneo de la juventud* (Athenium of the Youth) and articulated by the Mexican literary giant Alfonso Reyes: "We shall [finally] have a clear view of [the Mexican person] only when we reconcile him to his existence." See Alfonso Reyes, "La X en la frente," translated by Roberto Cantú, in *Mexican Philosophy in the 20th Century: Essential Readings* (New York: Oxford University Press, 2017), 234.
7 This sort of criticism of Uranga is common and is perfectly articulated in Guillermo Hurtado, "Paths of ontology," *APA Newsletter on Hispanic/Latino Issues in Philosophy* 10, no. 2 (2011): 17–21.
8 According to fellow Hyperion Luis Villoro's excellent introduction to the 1990 re-edition of *Analysis*: "The truth is that [we] did not have a precise methodology for our project. As such, the term 'ontology' did not have a metaphysical reach, it was understood as Husserl understood 'regional ontologies,' which designated a description of invariant characteristics ('essences') of a region of objects." See Luis Villoro, "Emilio Uranga: La accidentalidad como fundamento de la cultura Mexicana," in *Emilio Uranga, Analysis del ser del mexicano* (Guanajuato: Govierno del estado de Guanajuato, 1990), 12.
9 Auguste Comte (1798–1857) was a French philosopher and founder of positivism, a doctrine that promised social evolution (progress) through a rigid faith in science and scientific knowledge. Herbert Spencer (1820–1903) was an English philosopher and social theorist,who he synthesized Comte's positivism with Darwinian theories of evolution.
10 Members of this group included luminaries like Alfonso Reyes, José Vasconcelos, Antonio Caso, and Pedro Henriquez Ureña. The group formed in 1906 and disbanded in 1911. In the meantime, it held conferences and published its own journal, *Savia moderna*. An excellent history is found in Susana Quintanilla, *Nosotros: La juventud del Ateneo de Mexico* (Barcelona: Tusquets Editores, 2008).
11 Speaking about the poet Philip Larkin, Rorty writes: "I think Larkin's poem owes its interest and its strength to this reminder of the quarrel between

poetry and philosophy, the tension between an effort to achieve self-creation by the recognition of contingency and an effort to achieve universality by the transcendence of contingency" (25). See Richard Rorty, *Contingency, Irony, and Solidarity* (Cambridge: Cambridge University Press, 1989).

12 See Richard Rorty, *Philosophy as Poetry* (Charlottesville: University of Virginia Press, 2016).

13 See Soren Kierkegaard, *Fear and Trembling/The Sickness unto Death*, translated by Walter Lowrie (New York: Doubleday Anchor, 1954), 44. In the relevant passage, while lamenting his inability to assume Abraham's dread on being commanded by God to sacrifice Isaac, Kierkegaard says that we can, however, assume the heroism of other heroes because their exploits concern us, "jam tua res agitur," a reference to Horace's *Epistles*, where Horace writes, ""For it is your own concern, when the adjoining wall is on fire: and flames neglected are wont to gain strength" (Book I, Epistle 18, 199). In Horace, *The Works of Horace*, translated by T. A. Buckley (New York: Translation Publishing Company, 1920).

14 For a more detailed interpretation of this "lesson," see Carlos Alberto Sánchez, "The gift of Mexican historicism," *Continental Philosophical Review* 51, no. 3 (2018): 438–57.

3. Key Concepts

1 Here, I borrow the distinction made by the German phenomenologist Eugen Fink, who distinguishes between "thematic" and "operative" concepts. Thematic concepts are made thematic, defined, interpreted in the philosophy, for example, in Uranga's *Analysis*, while operative concepts are those that operate in the background, so to speak. See Eugen Fink, "Operative concepts in Husserl's phenomenology," in *Apriori and World: European Contributions to Husserlian Phenomenology*, ed. William McKenna, Robert M. Harlan, and Laurence E. Winters (The Hague: Martinus Nijhoff, 1981), 56–70.

2 Gottfried Leibniz, "*Monadology* and associated texts," in *Modern Philosophy: An Anthology of Primary Readings*, ed. Roger Ariew and Eric Watkins (New York: Hackett Publishing, 2009), 238.

3 Recently, Manuel Vargas has identified Uranga's notion of "accidentality" with zozobra and nepantla, namely, that all three refer to a being ungrounded (see Manuel Vargas, "The philosophy of accidentality," *Journal of the American Philosophical Association* (2019): 1–19) (italics in original). Vargas writes: "I characterize as accidentality ... a sense of profound unease or ungroundedness of a special sort" (2). This seems to follow Uranga's reading, who writes that "*every modality of being grounded on accident is characterized by a lack of ground*, grounded on a shifting and fractured base" (17). However, Vargas's interpretation of accidentality seems to make a psychologistic commitment that is not necessary to being accidental. That is, the *fact* of our accidentality does not translate to a *feeling* of unease or groundlessness. In Uranga, being accidental does not mean that one feels so; the feeling of "profound unease" comes with zozobra.

Vargas goes on, however, and lends an interpretation of accidentality that is much more useful and novel (and, I'll suggest, more fitting to Uranga's philosophical ambitions). Rather than "grounds" or "foundations," Vargas talks about "normative packages"—these are "packages of social meanings, values, and practical norms that, in the ordinary sense, tend to be relied upon to address various challenges in a form of life" (2). A being as substance (or an "agent" who may be thought of as substantial) will "experience themselves as having a relatively stable and unified package (or packages) of commitments about norms, values, and meanings." A being as accident (or "agents who are not substances") does "not experience themselves in this way" (4). In other words, "accidentality is about the absence of a stable, taken-for-granted relationship to normative culture" (5). This second reading helps us make sense of that on which the accident depends, before which it is insufficient, and in relation to which it may be ungrounded.

4 Ibid., 2.
5 Mariano Velázquez de la Cadena, *The New Velázquez Spanish and English Dictionary* (El Monte, CA: Academic Learning Company, 2005), 298.
6 In this, Uranga is right. Intuition can be associated with "the mind's eye" (René Descartes), with perception itself (John Locke), or with some *feeling* of truth (Henry Bergson).

7 Quoted in Ramón Troncoso Pérez, "Nepantla, una aproximación al término," in *Tierras prometidas. De la colonia a la independencia*, ed. Bernat Castany Prado. (Barcelona: Centro para la Edición de los Clásicos Españoles-UAB, 2011), 375–98.
8 Ibid., 378.
9 See James Maffie, *Aztec Philosophy: Understanding a World in Motion* (Boulder: University of Colorado Press, 2015), 523. Maffie also offers an in-depth etymology of the term on page 355.
10 Gloria Anzaldua, *The Gloria Anzaldua Reader*, ed. AnaLouise Keating (Durham: Duke University Press, 2009), 310.
11 Leibniz, "*Monadology* and Associated Texts," 228.
12 Jean Wahl sponsored Uranga's stay in France in 1956, so they were both aware of each other and Uranga was certainly aware of Wahl's work. See Javier Weimer, "La muerte de un filosofo," *Revista de la Universidad de México*, no. 17 (2005), 28.
13 Jean Wahl, *The Philosopher's Way* (New York: Oxford University Press, 1948), 16–23.
14 Ibid., 23.
15 Wahl writes: "If ... we had to choose between the acceptance and the rejection of the idea of substance, we should even have to go so far as to reject it; it has brought so much mischief to philosophy" (ibid., 27).
16 Translator's note: the term Uranga uses in the original 1952 edition of *Analysis* is "aseidad," meaning "being from itself"; in Guillermo Hurtado's 2013 edition of *Analysis*, however, the word was changed to "haceidad," meaning "haecceity," as it was argued that this was Uranga's original intention. I've followed Hurtado's rendering here. See Emilio Uranga, *Análisis del ser del mexicano y otros escritos sobre la filosofía de lo mexicano (1949–1952)*, ed. Guillermo Hurtado (México: Bonilla Artigas Editores, 2013).
17 Velázquez, *The New Velázquez Spanish and English Dictionary*, 932
18 Emilio Uranga, "Essay on an Ontology of the Mexican," translated by Carlos Alberto Sanchez. In *Mexican Philosophy in the 20th Century: Essential Readings*, edited by Carlos Alberto Sanchez and Robert Ely Sanchez (New York: Oxford University Press, 2017), 173.
19 Søren Kierkegaard, *The Essential Kierkegaard*, ed. Howard V. Hong and Edna H. Hong (Princeton, NJ: Princeton University Press, 2000), 138.
20 Ibid., 139.

21 Gabriel Marcel, *The Mystery of Being: Reflection & Mystery* (Chicago: Henry Regnery, 1950), 9.

I. Introduction

1 Page numbers in brackets refer to the original printing of *Analysis del ser del mexicano*, published as Emilio Uranga, *Análisis del ser del mexicano* (Mexico City: Porrúa, 1952).
2 Translator's note: Throughout, Uranga uses terms common in his time and central to the philosophical movement of which he was a part. These terms refer to persons or to the being of those persons. Thus, "lo mexicano" refers to *the state of being of that which is Mexican* or *the meaning of the being of the Mexican*; "del mexicano" refers to *of the Mexican person, of Mexican being,* and likewise to *that which is Mexican*; "el mexicano" to *the Mexican person or persons*. Because "lo mexicano" seeks to refer to a state of being, I have left it untranslated when readability demands it and in order to keep faithful to Uranga's existential-phenomenological, or ontological, intentions; otherwise I translate the term as either "that which is Mexican" or "what it means to be Mexican"; likewise, I have translated "del mexicano" as "the Mexican," or "the Mexican person/being," or "that which is Mexican," and "el mexicano" as "the Mexican person" or "Mexicans" whenever readability and context require it—in certain cases, and because these Spanish terms are not gender neutral, I have been forced (by the text itself) to appeal to "man" and "men" when translating sentences in which "del mexicano" or "el mexicano" are the subjects of those sentence.
3 Translator's note: *el grupo "Hiperión"* was a philosophical and literary group formed in the fall of 1947 and led by Leopoldo Zea. Its members included Uranga, Jorge Portilla, Luis Villoro, Salvador Reyes Nevarez, Ricardo Guerra, and Jorge MacGregor. The group lasted until 1952, when it was dissolved. The first decades of the 21st century have witnessed a growing literature on the group, especially in Mexico; for the United States, see Carlos Alberto Sánchez, *Contingency and Commitment: Mexican Existentialism and the Place of Philosophy* (Albany: State University of New York Press, 2016) and Carlos Alberto

Sánchez and Robert Eli Sanchez, eds., *Mexican Philosophy in the 20th Century: Essential Readings* (Oxford: Oxford University Press, 2017).
4. Translator's note: This would be in 1948. Uranga is referencing those criticisms that follow the series of lectures presented by the Hyperion group at Instituto Frances de America Latina (IFAL) on French existentialism. See Sánchez, *Contingency and Commitment.*
5. Whenever possible, I've translated "el hombre" as "human being" or "person." However, for the sake of readability, I've allowed the context to dictate when "el hombre" is best left as "man."
6. The term "autognosis" means "self-knowledge" or "knowledge of one's self," from the Greek *auto* (self)-*gnōsis* (knowledge). Uranga uses the term as both a verb and n noun—as a process and as what is achieved in the process. See Key Concepts, Chapter 3.
7. Translator's note: If our language does not reflect the material givenness of things as they are given, then what is said about those things reflects only the conceptual prejudices of the investigator, remaining in the "realm of appearances."
8. Translator's Note: text in brackets is translator's added text. Text in parentheses in original.
9. Translator's note: This an important operative concept in *Analysis*. I have translated it as "intimation" so as to avoid "the confusing concept of intuition." See the "Key Concepts" section of the Part One for a more in-depth explanation and analysis.

II. Philosophy

1. Translator's note: See Emilio Uranga, "Essay on the ontology of the Mexican," translated by Carlos Alberto Sánchez, in *Mexican Philosophy in the 20th Century: Essential Readings* (New York: Oxford University Press, 2017).
2. See, "Essay on the ontology of the Mexican."
3. Translator's note: The term Uranga uses in the original 1952 edition of *Analysis* is "aseidad," meaning "being from itself"; in Guillermo Hurtado's 2013 edition of *Analysis*, however, the word was changed to "haceidad," meaning "haecceity," as it was argued that this was Uragna's original intention. I've followed Hurtado's rendering here.

4 It didn't occur to the tradition to talk of being as accidental in virtue of eminence.
5 The Western tradition unifies two senses of man. With the first, it conceives as substance and, as such, as a complete reality; with the second, as a free and autonomous "making himself" and, as a consequence, as an "open" reality.
6 Martin Heidegger, *Sein und Zeit* (Hale: Max Niemeyer, 1929), 42. Translator's note: Uranga does not indicate which edition of this text he is referencing. I've chosen the second German edition and included the publisher and year for reference.
7 Translator's note: see Uranga, "Essay on the Ontology of the Mexican" *The Philosophy of Mexicanness,* translation and introduction by Carlos Alberto Sánchez and Robert Eli Sanchez. Aeon. https://aeon.co/classics/to-be-accidental-is-to-be-human-on-the-philosophy-of-mexicanness.
8 For the distinction between a relation as accident and a relation as the transcendental affectations of being, see Thomas Aquinas, *De Veritate*.
9 Heidegger, *Sein und Zeit,* 102. Translator's note: Uranga does not add page numbers to Heidegger's *Sein und Zeit* in the citations to follow.
10 Translator's note: Here, Uranga has in mind the clarifications of "existence" made in the French and German existentialist movement, in the work of Heidegger, J. P. Sartre, Maurice Merleau-Ponty, and others.
11 Translator's note: Emile Meyerson (1859–1933) was a Polish-born French epistemologist, chemist, and philosopher of science, best known for his *Identitée et réalité,* published in 1908.
12 Heidegger, *Sein und Zeit,* 35.
13 Heidegger, *Sein und Zeit,* 193.
14 Translator's note: The Spanish term "écabe" can be translated as either "to fit" or "close to." Given the context, we have translated the term as indicating proximity, thus the use of the term "proximal."
15 Heidegger, *Sein und Zeit,* 121. Translator's note: Uranga's reference to Sartre's notion of "viscosity" comes from *Being and Nothingness*. See Jean-Paul Sartre, *Being and Nothingness,* translated by Hazel Barnes (London: Routledge, 2003), especially Part IV.
16 Translator's note: Translations of poetry fragments throughout are my own.

17 Translator's note: The reference here is to the famous Villadolid debates between the Dominican friar Bartalomé de las Casas and the humanist scholar Juan Ginés de Sepúlveda held in Villadolid Spain in 1550 and 1551. De las Casas argued that the Indigenous peoples possessed the basic characteristics of humanity despite their brutal cultural and religious practices; Sepúlveda, on the other hand, argued that those same practices meant that the Indigenous peoples were barbarians and inhuman, and thus undeserving of sympathy, freedom, or baptism. While there was no clear winner, Sepúlveda's position was held by many who saw economic and religious opportunities in the enslavement, repression, and destruction of America's Indigenous peoples.
18 Translator's note: Uranga articulated this theory of the Mexican idea of death in several places, but most significantly in Emilio Uranga, "Dos teorias de la muerte: Sartre y Heidegger," *Filosofía y Letras* 27, no. 33 (1949): 55–71.

III. History

1 Translator's note: This quote is likely from Johannes Hessen, *Teoría del conocimiento*, first published in Spanish in 1938. See Johannes Hessen, *Teoria del conocimiento*, translated by José Gaos (México: Losada, 1938).
2 See the survey conducted by Rosa Castro in the magazine *Hoy* regarding the question "Has Mexico produced its own philosophy in the last 50 years?" July 1, 1950, no. 697.
3 Translator's note: *El Ateneo de la Juventud* was a philosophical and literary collective formed in Mexico City at the turn of the 20th century.
4 Translator's note: In footnote 3 of the original, Uranga asks us to "see, in this respect, my *Outline of the Ontology of the Mexican*." We believe he intended, rather, "Notes on an Ontology of the Mexican." See Part One of this book.
5 Translator's note: "Pelado" cannot be directly translated, so I have decided to keep it in its original. It can refer to a "common person" as well as to a "noble bum" or even a "working-class person." But it is closer to what today we would call a "poser." John Ochoa describes Yáñez's use of the term in more detail, situating the *pelado* within Yáñez's hierarchy of

Mexican characters: first, "the *lépero*, (who is) incapable of useful activity, the *lépero* is the worst kind of lowlife. Slightly better is the *pícaro*, the familiar figure from Spanish literature, who is cunning but villainous, low, and cowardly. The highest spot is assigned to a novel Mexican character, the *pelado*. ... This figure seems to be a kind of morally superior *pícaro*. The pelado is a rake who is grounded by an attachment to his native place. ... To his credit, the *pelado* often is a failure as a huckster. Like a *pícaro*, he may try to dissemble, but he is not very successful at this either, since he cannot easily disguise himself: shoes, clothes, and language not his own fit him poorly." See John A. Ochoa, The Uses of Failure in Mexican Literature and Identity (Austin: University of Texas Press, 2004), 204–5.
6 See the essay, "Ensayo de una ontologia del mexicano," in *Cuadernos Americanos*, March–April 1949, 135–48, especially 145.
7 Jean Paul Sartre, *La Mort dans L'ame*, 77th ed., 46.
8 Martin Heidegger, *Sein und Zeit*, 6th ed., 39.
9 Translator's note: See, Samuel Ramos, *Profile of Man and Culture in Mexico*, translated by Peter G. Earl (Austin: University of Texas Press, 2014), especially chapter 3, "Psychoanalysis of the Mexican."
10 Translator's note: See "Essay on the ontology of the Mexican," 177.
11 See Luis González y González, "El optimismo nacionalista como factor de la independencia de Mexico," in *Estudios de Historiografia Americana* (Mexico: El Colegio de Mexico, 1948). In this magnificent study, one finds an abundance of materials regarding the criollo attitude on the eve of independence that proved very useful for our efforts to elaborate our own theory regarding the criollo attitude. We agree, in general, with the conclusions of this author. In the concluding paragraph, to which we appeal, there are various other issues that must be attended to. A reality on its own cannot nourish optimism. Only because there already was an idea about the capacities of the criollo did his own *Umwelt* appear to him as nourishing optimism, but not the other way around. It would be a matter of asking our young historiographer a clarification regarding his "problematic conscience."
12 Recall, as an illustration, that Gracián paired the "hero" with the "discrete man," a duality that corresponds to our own pair, "lordship" and "discretion," "cynicism and hypocrisy," or to Yañez's "pelados" and "decent folks."

13 See José Gaos, "Los 'transterrados' españoles de la filosofía en México," in *Filosofía y Letras* 18, no. 36 (Oct.–Dec. 1949): 224. In a private conversation with Gaos at the start of 1949, in the occasion of our then projected and now published "Essay on the ontology of the Mexican," the professor presented us with a double opposition: first, regarding the methodological principles of the essay, and second, regarding its content. An ontology of the Mexican would be, in his eyes, impossible, since the only thing we could truly speak about would be an *ontic* of the Mexican. So far as the affirmations contained in the essay, he thought them far too pessimistic, even if valid at certain times in the history of Mexico. Regarding the first critique, we will take a position in what follows. Regarding the second, we have already addressed that concern, albeit implicitly, in our critique of the 18th-century criollo. That moment of apparent sufficiency and superiority allows us to see if we can analyze a ground of insufficiency. Also, insufficiency has nothing to do with pessimism. In those days, Gaos liked to refer to our efforts with the title "Meontology."

14 See my essay, "El mexicano y su Conocimiento," in which I explain in detail the non-ontological efforts to elaborate on an autognosis of the Mexican person. As reflection, knowledge of oneself is not a simple fact, but it lends itself to a disarticulation that separates its elements. Reflection on the Mexican is, on the one hand, "impure and complicit reflection," and, on the other, "skeptical reflection." Reflections on the Mexican person regarding his human condition are complicit and impure when they end by justifying his situation without making him responsible for his world or his history. It is about an exonerating reflection or one that frees us from all responsibility. To that we oppose pure reflection. With regard to this kind of reflection, we are talking about a reflection commonly referred to as "ahistorical." No one knows from which negated term reality itself emerged; the sense of continuity and dialectic loses itself so as to face the past as if it its questions were contemporaneous. Ramos and Yañez reveal in the Mexican a reflection of the first kind; Zea makes obvious the second.

15 Luis Villoro adopts a similar definition of the "generational" theme and in a recent article (*Filosofia y Letras*, no. 36) talks about the intentions of the group in the following terms: "What animates the Hyperion group is a conscious project of *self knowledge* (*autoconocimiento*) that will give

us the basis for future self-transformations. We no longer ask about the character of the circumstance, but for the principles that condition it and give it its reason. From a psychological and historical investigation we move to the *ontological inquisition* (*inquisición ontológical*) that gives sense to the element of our psychology and history, tracing these elements to the *ontical characteristics* that ground them. Existential philosophy, which directs itself to being and no longer merely to becoming, gives us the adequate instruments that validate our task. Over the conscious project of revealing being itself, we place its free transformation in a sense both individual as well as social. Hence, here too the existential doctrines that center the being of man in his free becoming will be the most adequate to facilitate the expression of the new project. The transit from historicism and vitalism to existentialism corresponds, then, to an eagerness to refer reality itself to the project of grounding it in reflection. Before it was about revealing the particular characteristics of psychology and historical evolution; now, we inquire into the *ontic characteristics* that make possible that psychology and for those *categories of the spirit* that give reason to that historical evolution; all of this with the immediate goal of making possible a future transformation. To that mindset corresponds historicism, to this one existentialism" (242). Villoro's terminology is confusing. It is not clear if he's talking about ontology, ontics, or autognosis; moreover, he leaves us with several enigmatic categories of the spirit that only add to the confusion.

16 Heidegger, *Sein und Zeit*, 45.
17 Heidegger, *Sein und Zeit*, 1.
18 Heidegger, *Sein und Zeit*, 4.
19 Heidegger, *Vom Wesen des Grundes* (Frankfurt: Vittorio Klostterman, 1929), Prologue to the 3rd edition, 5 (1949); and *Brief über den Humanismus* (Frankfurt: Vittorio Klostterman, 1946), 65.
20 These are *Zuhandenheit, Vorhandenheit,* and *Realität*. See Heidegger, *Sein und Zeit*, 230.
21 Heidegger, *Sein und Zeit*, 12.
22 Heidegger, *Wat Is Metaphysik?* (Frankfurt: Vittorio Klostterman, 1929), 14
23 Heidegger, *Sein und Zeit*, 12, 42.
24 Heidegger, *Brief über den Humanismus*, 70.

25 Heidegger, *Sein und Zeit*, 12.
26 Heidegger, *Sein und Zeit*, 43.
27 Alphonse de Waehlens treats this problem in a footnote in his book *La filosofía de Martin Heidegger* (Madrid: Consejo Superior de Investigaciones Científicas, 1952). "When Heidegger says that *Dasein* (human existence) is characterized by *Jemeinigkeit* (*Sein und Zeit*, 42, 53), one is inclined to believe that this prohibits any affirmation not relative to the *Dasein* that speaks. It must be stressed, however, that Heidegger's whole thinking is an effort to extend to *Dasein in general* the theses obtained from a Dasein understood as irreducible and fundamentally mine (*je meines*). If Dasein in itself truly has the character of *Jemeinigkeit*, this would forbid us to think of a *Dasein as such* (*Dasein als solches*), an expression utterly devoid of meaning" (13–14). We don't see in this an insuperable difficulty; even less do we conclude with Sternberger, cited by de Waehlens, "if those two contradictory significations are distinctly separated, the entire edifice crumbles." To the initiated in these extreme views, I offer these words by Husserl that have served me (in a paper still to be published) as a conducting thread for proposing and "resolving" the difficulty: "We must notice that in going from the ego to the ego in general in my work, I neither presuppose the reality nor the possibility of a movement toward a world integrated by others. The breath of *eidos ego* is here determined by the self-variation of my ego. What I do is pretend to myself as if I were someone else, but I don't pretend others. (I modify in imaginations, I represent as different than I am, I do not imagine an 'other')." *Meditaciones Cartesianas*, No. 34, pp. 129–30 in José Gaos's translation, and p. 61 in the French version. In my transcription I have made an effort to recover all the nuances of Husserl's thought that both translations, *together*, have attempted to convey.
28 In a paper presented at the Ateneo Español de México, in November 1949, which I titled "Spaniards and Mexicans of My Generation," I have elaborated on the theme of the relations between the Spanish and Mexican "character." The comparison with the Spanish project of existing, *for us and not in itself*, is particularly clarifying of our own mode of being. It appears to us that, in general, we characterize ourselves as "antipodes" of the Spanish mode of being. In this mode of being we find an oscillation between "fanaticism" and "disillusion" that finds

much in common with the duality we mentioned above, namely, that of "cynicism" and "hypocrisy." *Fanaticism depends on absolute values, which are those values that can make a "gentleman" out of a fanatic. In "dissolution" those absolute values are missing. Here, the conviction of an incurable relativism reaches both the world and the man that exists in the world.* And this because the conviction of substantiality is as obvious in the Spaniard "insubstantiality" or *insubstantiality* as it is obvious in us, as Unamuno would prefer to *hear it*. In spite of the richness of Spanish literature, I do not find an essay truly decisive that deals with giving precision to the Spanish character. Much less can we ask for an ontological treatment of that being. The Madrid School did not go beyond talking about "styles of life" in the work of García Morente, and, in spite of the goodwill it has demonstrated before German philosophy, it has not initiated an existential analysis of the Spaniard, nor are there signs that this will happen. From this point of view, our *autognosis of the being of the Mexican already goes beyond any studies that have been made of the being of the Spaniard by Spaniards*. This autognosis, which, as I have said, comes from afar, allows us to initiate a "comparative ontology." The conflict between the Mexican and the Spaniard is born in a definitive way from the fact that the character of the Mexican is a negation of the Spanish manner of being; what is virtue in the Spaniard is a defect in the Mexican, and vice versa. The Spanish character that we know is fantastic and understands man ontologically as substance. Concrete modalities of the Spanish project of life are greatness, thrownness (*el arrojo*), arrogance, pride, inconsiderateness, and honor. Illustrations of the American character are scarce in Spanish literature and much less of the Mexican character. There is one notable exception. In a work of Unamuno, *Nothing More Than a Man*, the third of his "Exemplary Novels," we are given *a true and in-depth characterization of what we have called the cynicism of the Mexican*. In that novel, Unamuno relates the adventures of Alejandro Gómez, a rich Indian who having amassed a fortune in Mexico takes his riches from New to Old Spain, including our mode of being. Alejandro Gómez is a "pelado" whose interior being is carelessly and unscrupulously affirmed before the superiority of the decent and "aristocratic" society in which we find him. Gómez refuses honor, gentlemanliness, courtesy, in short, all those values that sustain the community. Before all of this, he flaunts his "manliness" and only his "manliness," or, in words we understand, his "machismo." However, Alejandro Gómez is not a "one dimensional" man; inside he is wounded and his woes exhaust themselves in hiding his "sentimentality" for lack of "manliness." His radical insufficiency is finally revealed and made obvious before his death. Let's ignore the sources of this story and simply posit this problem for whomever decides to solve it. For us, the novel figures as a *truly exceptional document*. I believe, finally, that regarding the substantiality of the Spaniard, it is not about a choice made from eternity, but that it was produced in a particular historical moment. The Spain of Juan Ruiz, the archbishop (of Hita (1283–1350)), was not, of course, nothing substantial. Something happened to the project along the way because ever since then we have that substantiality that today we see in the Spanish character. This "conversion" makes for another interesting theme. Medieval Spain, in its "cynicism," is closer to us than the great "fanatical" and "substantial" Spain.

IV. Poetry

1 Translator's note: "El Minutero" is a collection of poetry, which appeared in 1923 in Mexico City, published by Imprenta de Murguia.
2 Or, philosophically speaking, we see the movement between the fourth and the fifth of Husserl's *Cartesian Meditations*.
3 It's worth insisting that oscillation as sentimental and oscillation as solitary are equivalent. This is why when López Velarde writes, "I am hanged," he is not excluding the sentimental aspect, but simply wants to emphasize loneliness.

Annotated Bibliography

Bartra, Roger. *The Cage of Melancholy: Identity and Metamorphosis in the Mexican Character*. Translated by Christopher J. Hill. New Brunswick, NJ: Rutgers University Press, 1992.
A major work in late-20th-century Mexican intellectual history. In it, Bartra rigorously critiques what he calls the *ideology* of "lo mexicano," which, he argues, was promoted by the intellectuals of the Mexican ruling class for the purposes of maintaining the Mexican status quo. Bartra specifically criticizes the work of *el Hiperión* (and, particularly, Uranga) as a nationalistic mechanism of colonial oppression constructed to reproduce myth; it was not what *los hiperiones* claimed, namely, a rational reconstruction of a real way of life.

Cuéllar Moreno, José Manuel. *La revolución inconclusa: La filosofía de Emilio Uranga, artifice oculto del PRI*. México: Ariel, 2018.
An important examination of Emilio Uranga's political involvement and the manner in which his political activities were influenced (or not influenced) by his philosophical views. It argues against the notion that Uranga was an ideologue of the Mexican government during and after the events of 1968.

Durán, Diego. *History of the Indies of New Spain*. Translated by Doris Heyden. Norman: University of Oklahoma Press, 1994.
A monumental tome in the history of the conquest of Mexico. It is here that Durán recounts his encounters with peoples that existed according to neither a European nor an indigenous religion/ontology, but in between, in *nepantla*.

Gaos, José. *Epistolario y Papeles Privados*. In *Obras Completas XIX*, edited by Alfonso Rangel Guerra. México: Universidad Nacional Autonoma de México, 1999.
Indispensable for anyone interested in mid-20th-century Mexican philosophy. Gaos, through his lectures and translations, motivated Mexican existentialism and the philosophy of Mexicanness. In these "personal papers," we are invited to directly witness his involvement in the life and times of Mexican philosophy. His influence on Uranga and his impact on Mexican philosophy are clarified in journal entries and letters to friends and others.

Guerra, Ricardo. "Una historia del Hiperion." *Los Universitarios* no. 18 (1984).

A firsthand autobiographical account that discusses the actual activities and internal politics of the Hiperion group. Guerra was one of its founding members.

Hurtado, Guillermo (ed.). *El Hiperión*. México: Universidad Nacional Autónoma de México, 2006.

The first anthology of key texts from *el grupo Hiperión*. The "Introduction" by Hurtado gives a panoramic view of Hiperion's origns, activies, and legacy. It is an indespensible text for anyone interested in the overall significance of this important philosophical group.

Hurtado, Guillermo. *El búho y la serpiente*. México: Coordinacion de Humanidades, 2008.

A collection of essays on contemporary Mexican philosophy by Mexico's premier authority on its history. In a key and often-cited essay, Hurtado distinguishes between two models of philosophy: the model of modernization and the model of authenticity, arguing that 20th-century philosophy falls into one of these two modes. In general, the collection highlights the problematics of taking Mexico as theme in philosophical investigation, offering both a critique and an invitation for those who would chose to do so.

León-Portilla, Miguel. *Aztec Thought and Culture: A Study of the Ancient Nahuatl Mind*. Norman: University of Oklahoma Press, 1967.

The first authoritative text on the philosophy of the ancient Nahuatl. Of significance is León-Portilla's recalibration of the Eurocentric notion of philosophy, offering one that is inclusive of other knowledges and other ways of life, specifically Aztec thought and metaphysics.

Maffie, James. *Aztec Philosophy: Understanding a World in Motion*. Boulder: University of Colorado Press, 2015.

Maffie settles the debate regarding the existence and nature of an Aztec "philosophy" with a profound and scholarly account and analysis of Aztec metaphysics. His discussions of nepantla are of particular interest as they will help the reader better situate and understand Uranga's use of this important term.

Ortega y Gasset, José. *Meditations on Quixote*. Translated by Evelyn Rugg and Diego Marín. Chicago: University of Illinois Press, 2000.

Published in 1914, the significance of this text to Latin American philosophy cannot be overstated. It is here that Ortega introduces the circumstantialist principle "I am myself and my circumstances." With this principle in hand, Mexican philosophers found justification for their situated philosophizing and motivation to construct "la filosofía de lo mexicano."

Paz, Octavio. *The Labyrinth of Solitude*. New York: Grove Press, [1951] 1985.
Paz's famous study of the Mexican character. Highly influenced by contemporary discussions on Mexicanness, Paz seeks to lend his study a sociological base. Emilio Uranga dedicates his *Analysis* to Paz in an effort to philosophically mirror it and, perhaps, overcome it.

Pereda, Carlos. *La filosofia en Mexico en el siglo XX: Apuntes de un participante*. Mexico: Direccion General de Publicaciones, 2013.
Pereda weaves autobiographical detail with philosophical analysis and critique in this memoir of 20th-century Mexican philosophy. He recounts his encounters and associations with Mexico's most significant thinkers.

Ramos, Samuel. *El perfil del hombre y la cultura en Mexico*. México: Espasa-Calpe Mexicana, [1934] 1952.
Translated as *Profile of Man and Culture in Mexico*, by Peter G. Earle (McAllen: Texas Pan-American Press, 1962). Perhaps the most important work in 20th-century Mexican philosophy, Ramos's *Profile* proposes "inferiority" as the defining characteristic of the Mexican character. Historically informing this Alderean psychoanalytic concept, the *Profile* continues to arouse discussion. It is the *Profile*'s main arguments against which Uranga reacts in his *Analysis*.

Romanell, Patrick. *Making of the Mexican Mind: A Study in Recent Mexican Thought*. Lincoln: University of Nebraska Press, 1952.
The first authoratative history of Mexican philosophy in English. It paints a picture of an authochtonous movement of philosophy up until the year of publication—1952. Although it says very little about the Hiperion group, the narrative it presents beautifully sets up the event of Hiperion.

Sánchez, Carlos Alberto. "Heidegger in Mexico: On Emilio Uranga's ontological hermeneutics." *Continental Philosophy Review* 41, no. 4 (2008): 441–61.
A first foray into Emilio Uranga's Heideggerian influences in English. The paper seeks to position Uranga's appropriation as faithful to the existential hermeneutic while also as going beyond it.

Sánchez, Carlos Alberto. *The Suspension of Seriousness: On the Phenomenology of Jorge Portilla*. Albany: SUNY Press, 2012.
An introduction and analysis to Jorge Portilla's *Fenomenología del relajo* (1963), published with a translation. A critical reading of Jorge Portilla's famous text. It situates Portilla as a philosopher of values and culture. It also introduces *el grupo Hiperión* as an important philosophical group to an English-speaking philosophical audience for the first time.

Sánchez, Carlos Alberto. *Contingency and Commitment: Mexican Existentialism and the Place of Philosophy*. Albany: SUNY Press, 2016.
A critical appraisal of mid-20th-century Mexican existentialism, specifically "la filosofía de lo mexicano" of *el grupo Hiperión* (Jorge Portilla, Leopoldo Zea, Luis Villoro, and Emilio Uranga). The principal claim here is that Mexican existentialism in particular and Mexican philosophy in general lend privilege to place and circumstance at the expense of abstract universalism.

Sánchez, Carlos Alberto and Robert Eli Sanchez (eds.). *Mexican Philosophy in the 20th Century: Essential Readings*. New York: Oxford University Press, 2017.
The first comprehensive anthology of 20th-century Mexican philosophy in translation. The anthology contains articles on Mexican philosophy from 1910 to 1960.

Sánchez, Carlos Alberto. "The gift of Mexican historicism," *Continental Philosophical Review* 51, no. 3 (2018): 438–57.
This paper focuses on Emilio Uranga's historicism. It argues for the significance and value of historicism for philosophy, but especially for the philosophizing of marginalized groups.

Sánchez, Carlos Alberto and Francisco Gallegos. *The Disintegration of Community: On the Social and Political Philosophy of Jorge Portilla*. Albany: SUNY Press, 2020.
This volume includes previously untranslated minor essays of Portilla together with six critical reflections by the authors. While the focus is on a political reading of Portilla's "other essays," the critical reflections also touch upon Portilla's phenomenology and social philosophy.

Sanchez, Robert Eli (ed.). *Latin American and Latinx Philosophy: A Collaborative Introduction*. New York: Routledge, 2020.
A collection of essays on Latin American and Latinx philosophy, which includes a number of essays on Mexican philosophy of culture. It is a great

resource for those wanting to situate themselves in the contemporary debates surrounding this tradition and its various offshoots.

Santos Ruiz, Ana. *Los hijos de los dioses: El Grupo filosófico Hiperión y la filosofía de lo mexicano*. México: Bonilla Artigas Editores, 2015.
This is a highly researched and immensely informative commentary on the political significance of the philosophy of Mexicanness. It makes several controversial claims about Uranga's role in the 1968 student massacre of Tlatelolco, namely, suggesting Uranga's complicity as an ideologue of the Mexican state.

Troncoso Pérez, Ramón. "Nepantla, una aproximación al término." In *Tierras prometidas. De la colonia a la independencia*, edited by Bernat Castany. Barcelona: Centro para la Edición de los Clásicos Españoles-UAB, 2011: 375–98.
Troncoso Pérez delves deep into the textual origins of "nepantla." Looking at Spanish chronicles of the Conquest of New Spain, Troncoso's analysis helps us understand the evolution and appropriation of this important philosphical concept, one to which Uranga gave special ontological privilege.

Uranga, Emilio. "Dialogo con Maurice Merleau-Ponty," *Mexico en la cultura*, March 13, 1949: 3.
This article reports a conversation with Merleau-Ponty that took place early in the spring of 1949 in Mexico City. On the invitation of *los Hiperiónes*, Merleau-Ponty visited Mexico City and gave a series of lectures on existentialism and phenomenology, much to the delight and enthusiasm of the young existential upstarts.

Uranga, Emilio. "Essay on an ontology of the Mexican." Translated by Carlos Alberto Sanchez. In *Mexican Philosophy in the 20th Century: Essential Readings*, edited by Carlos Alberto Sanchez and Robert Eli Sanchez. New York: Oxford University Press, 2017: 165–77.
This is the precursor to *Analysis*. Written a few years prior, it focuses on the notions of insufficiency and accidentality that would come to play a central role in Uranga's philosophy. The essay is required reading for anyone interested in the development of Uranga's thought in *Analysis*.

Uranga, Emilio. "Notas para un estudio del mexicano." *Cuadernos Americanos* 10, no. 3 (1951): 114–28.
Uranga's "notes" for a method suitable for the study of Mexican being. It is a prelude to the work that will come about in *Analysis*, focusing on the existential phenomenological approach required for such a task.

Uranga, Emilio. "Merleau-Ponty: fenomenología y existencialismo." *Filosofía y Letras* 15, no. 30 (1948): 219-41.
Uranga's introductory analysis of Merleau-Ponty's existential phenomenology. In it, Uranga aims to paint Merleau-Ponty as a philosopher of the circumstance, validating in this way his own long-term scholarly project.

Uranga, Emilio. *Análisis del ser del mexicano y otros escritos sobre la filosofía de lo mexicano (1949–1952)*, edited by Guillermo Hurtado. México: Bonilla Artigas Editores, 2013.
This is the latest edition of Uranga's *Analysis*. It comes with a larger selection of minor works, journalistic pieces, and letters.

Uranga, Emilio. "The philosophy of Mexicanness." Translation and introduction by Carlos Alberto Sánchez and Robert Eli Sanchez. *Aeon*. https://aeon.co/classics/to-be-accidental-is-to-be-human-on-the-philosophy-of-mexicanness.
This publication includes an annotated version of Uranga's "Essay on the Ontology of the Mexican" as well as an introduction to that essay by the Carlos Alberto Sánchez and Robert Eli Sanchez.

Uranga, Emilio. "Dos teorias de la muerte: Sartre y Heidegger." *Filosofía y Letras* 27, no. 33 (1949): 55–71.
As well as discussing Sartre's and Heidegger's views on death, Uranga sheds light on the Mexican idea of death, which he contrasts with the "Western" or European idea of death.

Vargas, Manuel. "The philosophy of accidentality." *Journal of the American Philosophical Association* (2019): 1–19. doi: https://doi.org/10.1017/apa.2019.15
Vargas appeals to Uranga's notion of accidentality to offer his own interpretation of the concept, one that is richer and capable of broader applications. Vargas's analytical rigor makes sense of Uranga's philosophy for a new Anglo-American audience.

Villegas, Abelardo. *La filosofía de lo mexicano*. México: Universidad Nacional Autónoma de México, 1979.
The definitive guide to the "philosophy of Mexicanness." It is a comprehensive analysis of "Mexican" philosophy beginning in the 20th century. More than a historical overview, it is also critical. It finds and highlights the philosophical pitfalls with the movement and with the philosophical results.

Villoro, Luis. "Emilio Uranga: La accidentalidad como fundamento de la cultura Mexicana." In Emilio Uranga, *Analysis del ser del mexicano*. Guanajuato: Gobierno del Estado de Guanajuato, 1990.
An indispensable introduction to *Analysis* by one of Uranga's most celebrated contemporaries and one of Mexico's most important philosophers. This essay is included in the 1990 edition of Uranga's *Analysis*; it historically and thematically contextualizes the work around the concept of "accidentality." Villoro's analyses are original and valuable.

Wimer, Javier. "La muerte de un filsofó." *Revista de la Universidad de Mexico*, no. 17 (2005): 27–33.
Written almost two decades after Uranga's death, this article vibrantly portrays Uranga's last days, connecting the fall of the great philosopher to key moments in his philosophical life.

Zea, Leopoldo. *Positivism in Mexico*. Translated by Josephine H. Schulte. Austin: University of Texas Press, 2004.
Zea's first book takes a critical look at Mexican positivism. First published in 1943, it is Zea's critical introduction to the positivistic ideology that dominated Mexico during the second half of the 19th century. Adopted as the state ideology, it sought to maintain colonial forms of exploitation under the guise of a national "order of progress." A deeply influential book in the history of Mexican ideas.

Zirión Quijano, Antonio. *Historia de la fenomenología en México*. Morelia, Michoacán, México: Jitanjáfora Morelia Editorial, 2003.
A concise history of phenomenology in Mexico, starting with early adopters of the Husserlian method, taking the reader through the height of phenomenological activity in Mexico during the 1940s and 1950s, and into contemporary times. Zirión Quijano's emphasis is on phenomenological work, rather than existential or analytic, so it is a great resource for students of this tradition.

Index

accidentality 11, 14, 30–3, 37, 38, 41, 43, 48, 50, 51, 53, 55, 62, 63, 64, 68, 70, 71–5, 78, 81, 82, 105, 106, 118, 119, 143, 148, 157, 158, 171, 193 n.3, 211
angst 11, 87, 89, 148
anxiety 11, 59, 60, 61, 85–8, 180
appropriation 14, 74, 126, 159
  philosophical 15, 16, 38, 39, 52, 56, 68, 74, 141, 207, 209
Ateneo de la Juventud (Atheneum of Youth) 44, 191, 198, 202 n.28
auscultation 17, 75, 76, 84, 122

Bartra, Roger 205
Being and Time 17, 34–5, 107, 113, 152

care 115, 119
Caso, Antonio 133, 134, 191 n.10
colonialism 13, 24, 40
community 7, 62, 63, 81, 89, 98, 156, 174, 176, 179, 204 n.28
  and love 64–6
complex of inferiority 4, 6–12, 30, 35, 46–9, 61, 65, 72, 78, 79, 84, 103, 119, 120, 133–60, 207
consciousness 31, 55, 63, 64, 65, 86, 94, 129, 149, 159, 173, 176, 178, 183
  annulment of 64, 172
  Mexican 31
  pure 189 n.36
corazonadas 11, 28–30, 35, 37, 56, 66, 69, 76–8, 100, 119, 165, 172
criticism 8, 14, 15, 39, 51, 196 n.4
culture 6, 8, 18, 19, 21, 26, 41, 46, 47, 61, 67, 68, 72, 78, 85, 94, 108, 127, 134, 135, 139, 142, 143, 182, 185, 193 n.3, 208
  Mexican 9, 15, 17, 46, 84, 93, 134, 140
cynicism 47–8, 119, 146–9, 167, 199 n.12, 202 n.28

death 42, 56, 64, 82, 85, 106, 110, 114, 124, 128, 129, 130, 157, 198 n.18, 204 n.28, 210, 211
Dewey, John 155
dialectic 60, 61, 142, 145, 146, 147, 167, 200
dignity 31, 36, 109, 126
Duran, Diego 22, 23, 30, 31, 80, 81, 82, 92, 103, 166, 167, 205

epistemology 76
Eurocentrism 41, 43, 45, 74, 84, 206
  arrogance 33–4, 69
  and logic 60
  and reason 71
existentialism 5, 26, 93, 94, 112, 196 n.4, 20 n.15, 205, 208, 209

fear 7, 19, 59, 76, 82, 87, 88, 123, 130, 148, 180, 181, 182
fragility 9, 11, 30, 42, 73, 86, 116, 127, 157, 167, 169, 180
freedom 11, 49, 86, 110, 125, 144, 145, 198 n.17

Gaos, José 3, 4, 14, 34, 75, 149, 150, 187 n.1, 200 n.13, 205

Hegel, G. W. F. 103, 104, 113, 146, 155
Heidegger, Martin 13, 15–18, 28, 34, 35, 52–4, 105, 106–7, 110,

112–15, 118, 122, 138, 152–4,
202 n.27, 207, 210
historicism 25, 26, 29, 39, 94, 97, 98,
162, 192, 192, 201 n.15, 208
Hurtado, Guillermo 187 n.9, 191 n.7,
194 n.16, 196 n.3, 206

identity 11, 50, 51, 80, 113, 117
  historical 50
  Mexican 55
  mixed 51
  substantial 42
ideology 43, 44, 46, 211
"imperial passion," 14, 15, 16, 18, 33
insufficiency 8–11, 14, 30–3, 35, 41,
  45–8, 50, 51, 53, 55, 56, 64, 68,
  70, 71, 78–83, 103, 104, 106,
  119, 133–59, 200 n.13, 204
  n.28, 209
intentionality 117
interpretation 11, 13, 18, 35, 36, 37,
  52, 72, 73, 83, 106–9. 124, 126,
  127, 138, 154, 164, 166, 187 n.2,
  192 n.14, 193 n.3, 210
intersubjectivity 61, 63–5, 89,
  173, 176–80
intuition 28–9, 30, 51, 77, 101, 169,
  193 n.6, 196 n.9

Kierkegaard, Soren 57, 86–8, 112,
  149, 192 n.13

Latin American Philosophy 206
Latinx identity 82, 208
liberation 10, 11, 49, 110, 143,
  148, 149
"lo mexicano" 3, 4, 24, 25, 27, 36,
  39–40, 42, 50, 93–101, 109,
  120–4, 126, 128, 134, 157, 188
  n.13, 95 n.2, 205
  philosophy of 3, 4, 5, 15, 45, 51,
  207, 208, 209, 210

machismo 125, 204 n.28
melancholy 9, 10, 11, 59, 60, 61, 88,
  110, 168–9, 173, 180, 205

mestizaje 71, 72
metaphysics 83, 152, 153, 206
Mexican Revolution 22, 24, 55–6,
  125, 126, 149, 159, 161–5, 182
Mexico City 5, 198 n.3, 209
mourning 173
myth 3, 205

Nahuatl 57, 58, 80, 167, 187 n.3, 206
negation 51, 61, 141, 145, 156,
  177, 178
  of Europe 31, 50
  of the Spanish 49, 50, 157, 203
  and zozobra 61
nepantla 23, 31, 57–9, 64, 65, 66,
  68, 70, 75, 78, 79–83, 92, 167,
  190 n.4, 193 n.3, 194 n.7, 205,
  206, 209

ontology 4, 5, 12, 17, 18, 19, 27–30,
  35, 28, 40, 44, 45, 46, 50–3, 58,
  61, 66, 69, 71, 75, 76, 80, 85,
  87, 99, 100, 103, 104, 106, 107,
  108, 119, 122, 136, 137, 138,
  142, 143, 149–59, 167, 168, 169,
  188 n.16, 191 n.8, 200 n.13, 201
  n.15, 203 n.28, 205, 209, 210
Orozco, José Clemente 45, 133
Ortega y Gasset, José 16, 17, 95,
  151, 206
oscillation 11, 38, 57, 59, 60, 61, 65,
  73, 86, 87, 116, 127, 167, 72, 173,
  194, 204 n.3

Paz, Octavio 22, 92, 100, 188
  n.14, 207
phenomenology 5, 6, 12, 14, 16, 18,
  20, 25, 29, 68, 69, 70, 113, 186,
  192 n.1, 208, 209, 210, 211
poetry 9, 29, 53–7, 61, 68, 69, 77, 86,
  100, 136, 161, 162, 164, 167,
  168, 176, 180, 192 n.11
politics 28, 46, 143, 206
Portilla, Jorge 188 n.11, 195 n.3, 208
positivism 4, 44–5, 133, 135, 191
  n.9, 211

power 7, 10, 13, 40, 49, 51, 55, 64, 113, 145, 173, 182
powerlessness 7, 8, 30, 48, 78, 110
pragmatism 155
Profile of Man and Culture in Mexico 4, 6, 30, 139
proximity 17, 18, 109, 110, 117, 118, 170, 197 n.14

Ramos, Samuel 4, 6–8, 9, 24, 27, 30, 35, 47, 78, 103, 134, 139, 149, 150, 166, 189 n.17, 200 n.14, 207
religion 42, 44, 133, 170, 176, 205
repetition 57, 86, 87, 88, 112, 149, 192 n.13
resignation 48, 59, 141, 142
resistance 59, 74, 81
Rivera, Diego 45, 133
Rorty, Richard 53, 54, 191 n.11

Sartre, Jean-Paul 15, 112, 118, 138, 153, 197 n.15 198 n.18, 210
Scheler, Max 15, 108, 150
shame 66, 148, 182, 183, 184
silence 170, 172, 181, 185
Siquieros, David Alfaro 45
Spain 7, 12, 23, 49, 144, 198 n.17, 203 n.28, 209
subjectivity 10, 13, 15, 16, 34, 64, 177
substantiality 33, 34, 36, 77, 50, 65, 73–4, 83, 106, 107, 109, 155, 157, 158, 202 n.28

temporality 51, 52, 59, 65, 75, 84

Tlateloco massacre 209
transcendence 53, 65, 188 n.14, 192 n.11
truth 11, 14, 16, 26, 27, 37, 41, 45, 68, 69, 79, 83, 95, 106, 121, 122, 123, 137, 186
   epistemic 11, 29, 53, 76, 78, 193 n.6
   existential 50, 66, 70
   ontological 9, 10, 32, 34, 41, 44, 48, 50, 51, 5, 73, 106
   "useless truth" 181

United States 82, 156, 195 n.3

value 10, 15, 16, 18, 19, 25, 31, 39, 45–8, 52, 53, 68, 71, 94, 100, 136, 140–7, 155, 182, 188 n.16, 193 n.3, 203 n.28, 208
   inversion of 46–9, 146, 162, 184
Vasconcelos, José 133, 134, 191 n.10
Velarde, Ramón López 22, 23, 29, 54–8, 61, 64, 65, 86, 87, 92, 136, 144, 161–80, 185, 204 n.3
Villoro, Luis 188 n.11, 191 n.8, 196 n.3, 200 n.15, 208, 211

Zea, Leopoldo 4, 14, 15, 134, 136, 137, 150, 188 n.14, 195 n.3, 200 n.14, 208, 211
zozobra 11, 57–70, 75, 78, 81, 82, 85–90, 119, 127, 136, 143, 148, 158, 167–80, 185, 193 n.3

www.ingramcontent.com/pod-product-compliance
Lightning Source LLC
Chambersburg PA
CBHW051642230426
43669CB00013B/2411